Palgrave Studies in Priso

Series editors
Ben Crewe
Institute of Criminology
University of Cambridge
Cambridge, UK

Yvonne Jewkes
School of Applied Social Science
University of Brighton
Brighton, UK

Thomas Ugelvik
Criminology and Sociology of Law
Faculty of Law, University of Oslo
Oslo, Norway

This is a unique and innovative series, the first of its kind dedicated entirely to prison scholarship. At a historical point in which the prison population has reached an all-time high, the series seeks to analyse the form, nature and consequences of incarceration and related forms of punishment. Palgrave Studies in Prisons and Penology provides an important forum for burgeoning prison research across the world. Series Advisory Board: Anna Eriksson (Monash University), Andrew M. Jefferson (DIGNITY - Danish Institute Against Torture), Shadd Maruna (Rutgers University), Jonathon Simon (Berkeley Law, University of California) and Michael Welch (Rutgers University).

More information about this series at
http://www.palgrave.com/gp/series/14596

Matthew Maycock • Kate Hunt
Editors

New Perspectives on Prison Masculinities

palgrave
macmillan

Editors
Matthew Maycock
The Scottish Prison Service
Edinburgh, UK

Kate Hunt
University of Glasgow
Glasgow, UK and
University of Stirling
Stirling, UK

Palgrave Studies in Prisons and Penology
ISBN 978-3-030-09745-5   ISBN 978-3-319-65654-0 (eBook)
https://doi.org/10.1007/978-3-319-65654-0

© The Editor(s) (if applicable) and The Author(s) 2018
Softcover re-print of the Hardcover 1st edition 2018
This work is subject to copyright. All rights are solely and exclusively licensed by the Publisher, whether the whole or part of the material is concerned, specifically the rights of translation, reprinting, reuse of illustrations, recitation, broadcasting, reproduction on microfilms or in any other physical way, and transmission or information storage and retrieval, electronic adaptation, computer software, or by similar or dissimilar methodology now known or hereafter developed.
The use of general descriptive names, registered names, trademarks, service marks, etc. in this publication does not imply, even in the absence of a specific statement, that such names are exempt from the relevant protective laws and regulations and therefore free for general use.
The publisher, the authors and the editors are safe to assume that the advice and information in this book are believed to be true and accurate at the date of publication. Neither the publisher nor the authors or the editors give a warranty, express or implied, with respect to the material contained herein or for any errors or omissions that may have been made. The publisher remains neutral with regard to jurisdictional claims in published maps and institutional affiliations.

Cover illustration: GettyImages-494837527
Cover Design: Fatima Jamadar

Printed on acid-free paper

This Palgrave Macmillan imprint is published by Springer Nature
The registered company is Springer International Publishing AG
The registered company address is: Gewerbestrasse 11, 6330 Cham, Switzerland

Acknowledgements

In the first instance, Kate Hunt and Matthew Maycock would like to thank all the contributors to this edited collection who have cumulatively contributed a rich and diverse range of chapters. The editors would like to acknowledge support from the UK Medical Research Council (MRC) and Scotland's Chief Scientist Office (CSO) for funding which has supported their research in prisons and on men, masculinities and health, through grant funding to support work on the 'Understanding and Improving Health in Settings and Organisations' programme (MC_UU_12017/12; SPHSU12') and the 'Gender and Health' programme at the MRC/CSO Social and Public Health Sciences Unit at Glasgow University, and a grant from CSO to help develop the Fit for LIFE programme (CZH/4/886). They would also like to express their thanks to colleagues at Glasgow University (in particular Dr. Cindy Gray and Dr. Alice MacLean) and the Scottish Prison Service and Serco (and especially Craig Mailer and Keith Mason). They would also like to thank the many participants in their research who have contributed to their understandings of masculinity over many years.

Contents

1   Introduction: New Perspectives on Prison Masculinities   1
Matthew Maycock

2   Work, Intimacy and Prisoner Masculinities   17
Martha Morey and Ben Crewe

3   Being Inside: Masculine Imaginaries, Prison Interiors   43
Rod Earle

4   "They're All Up in the Gym and All That, Tops Off, Fake Tan." Embodied Masculinities, Bodywork and Resistance Within Two British Prisons   65
Matthew Maycock

5   "Don't Mess with Me!" Enacting Masculinities Under a Compulsory Prison Regime   91
Nick de Viggiani

6	Saying the Unsayable: Foregrounding Men in the Prison System *Jennifer Sloan*	123
7	Hear Our Voices: We're More than the Hyper-Masculine Label—Reasonings of Black Men Participating in a Faith-Based Prison Programme *Geraldine Brown and Paul Grant*	145
8	A Framework Model of Black Masculinities and Desistance *Martin Glynn*	169
9	Sporting Masculinities in Prison *Hannah Baumer and Rosie Meek*	197
10	Inhabiting the Australian Prison: Masculinities, Violence and Identity Work *Katie Seymour*	223
11	Exploring Masculinity Construction, Subject Positioning and the Relationship with Dad *Tony Evans*	247
12	Inside the Prison Parenting Classroom: Caring, Sharing and the Softer Side of Masculinity *Katie Buston*	277
13	Paternity and the Paradigms of Possibility: Comparing Two Fatherhood Programs in American Prisons *Anna Curtis*	307

Index 331

List of Figures

Fig. 8.1 A framework model of black masculinities and desistance (Glynn 2017) — 175
Fig. 11.1 Evans masculinity spectrum — 261

List of Tables

Table 13.1　Differences between fatherhood groups　315
Table 13.2　An overview of parenting styles mentioned in NCI handouts　324

1

Introduction: New Perspectives on Prison Masculinities

Matthew Maycock

According to the 11th *World Prison Brief*, more than 9 in 10 (93%) of the world's prisoners are male (Warmsley 2016). While over recent years there has been a small but significant increase in the proportion of female prisoners globally, male prisoners still constitute the vast majority of prisoners in all 223 prison systems in independent countries and dependent territories considered in the *World Prison Brief*. Globally, among those countries where data are available, the highest proportion of male prisoners is found in African countries, in which 97% of the prison population is male, while in the Americas, this figure is at its lowest, at 90% of the prison population in the USA and 92% in the remainder of the Americas (Warmsley 2016). Thus, for all of the jurisdictions which feature within the chapters of this book, this picture of male predominance within penal systems is consistently reflected.

M. Maycock (✉)
The Scottish Prison Service, Edinburgh, UK

Formerly, MRC/CSO Social and Public Health Sciences Unit, The University of Glasgow, Glasgow, UK

While these figures somewhat crudely illustrate the importance of gender *per se* within criminal justice systems globally, they conceal the fact that the highly gendered nature of the prison world is often taken-for-granted, and rarely fore-fronted or explicitly acknowledged. The central aim of this book is to illustrate and analyse the complexity of the consequences principally within prison systems, of the incarceration of such a high proportion of men and particularly to question what an analysis of the various performances of masculinity that occur within prisons can contribute to our understandings of them as gendered spaces.

The authors of the chapters in this book draw on recent advances in theories of masculinities to explore and analyse the ways in which prisons shape performances of gender within (male) prison settings, and in some cases following men's release from prison. The book includes contributions based on original data collected from prison settings in England, Australia, Scotland and the USA, as well as contributions which take a broader methodological and conceptual approach to understanding masculinity. Most of the chapters focus on adult male prison populations, although one considers young men within a young offender institution. Cumulatively, the chapters in this collection illustrate the importance of developing a nuanced and theoretically informed understanding of masculinity within prison research.

This edited collection considers the gendered experiences of imprisonment for men, through a diverse examination of prison masculinities. Performances of masculinity play a significant role both in linking gender and crime *prior* to prison (Collier 1998; Messerschmidt 1993) and, subsequently, in shaping the experience for male prisoners serving a range of sentences (Sabo et al. 2001). While previous work on prison masculinities (cf. Sabo et al. 2001) has illuminated aspects of the gendered nature of male imprisonment, this has largely focused on aggressive, hierarchical, emotionally detached and violent elements of the performance of masculinity within prisons. While these aspects of masculine performances remain widely evident in prisons (as is reflected in many of the chapters that follow), previous literature has tended to overlook some of the more subtle, nurturing and emotionally engaged performances of masculinity in prison. This book will consider the ways in which recent advances in masculinity studies can more fully illuminate these aspects of the performance of prison masculinities, adding greater nuance to our understanding of prison masculinities.

Origins of This Collection

In March 2015, the Stoney Brook University, New York Centre for the Study of Men and Masculinities, hosted the International Conference on Masculinities: *Engaging Men and Boys for Gender Equality*, in New York. At this conference, a panel session organised by one of the editors of this book (Matthew Maycock) was composed of six presentations responding to the panel theme, namely new perspectives on prison masculinities. The panel aimed to give an overview of the field of prison masculinities research, reflecting on recent developments in masculinities theory generally, and in research on masculinities in prisons more specifically. Several of the presentations at this panel session in New York (those by Matthew Maycock, Anna Curtis and Tony Evans) were subsequently developed as chapters for this book. Initial conversations at this conference highlighted the need for a book that reflected, and reflected on, recent developments in masculinity studies within the context of penology.

What Can the Study of Masculinity Contribute to Penology?

Through the conversations initiated at the New York conference, it became clear that the recent development of the field of masculinity studies was beginning to influence contemporary prison-based research. Replicating a wider 'malestream' within the social sciences (Gilligan 1982; Morris 1987), studies of prisons have largely focused on male prisoners, reflecting the fact that the majority of prisoners are men (as noted above). However, historically these studies tended not to explicitly consider and problematise the *gendered* experience of men of prison (Morgan 1986). Newton (1994) explored some of these issues and made an early contribution to strengthening the case for explicitly examining masculinities within penology:

> Aspects of masculinities are clearly found in, and help to explain, aspects of the sociology of prisons for men: in, for instance, the hierarchies of domination that are formed in prisons, in codes of solidarity, in expressions of sexuality. (Newton 1994, 194)

Subsequently, a wide range of research has explored aspects of prison masculinities, in some ways in parallel with the development of the field of men and masculinity studies more broadly. Principal among these is the book on *Prison Masculinities* edited by Sabo et al. (2001). This made a significant and continuing contribution to the field of prison masculinities. In their introduction to this collection, Sabo, Kupers and London stated that the importance of masculinity within prisons had tended to be overlooked within criminology and by prison staff, highlighting the ways in which masculinity influences the behaviour of prisoners. However, the book tended to focus on 'ultramasculine' aspects of prison masculinities:

> Prison is an ultramasculine world where nobody talks about masculinity. (Sabo et al. 2001, 3)

Thus certain masculinities were foregrounded, particularly those linked to violence and a wider range of negative associations and behaviours (including the continuation of crime). According to Sabo, Kupers and London, this overtly negative interpretation of prison masculinities is formed through a range of factors and actors within and around the prison context, resulting in the predominance of certain patterns of (negative and harmful) performances of masculinity within prisons. This results in:

> …collusion of prisoners, police, corrections officers, corporations, and legislators in supporting certain patterns of masculinity. (Sabo et al. 2001, 3)

Throughout this earlier collection, hegemonic masculinity is consistently used as the principal theory to guide the analysis of prison masculinities, reflecting the predominance of this theory at that time within the field of men and masculinities. Sabo, Kupers and London suggested that hegemonic masculinity:

…reflects and actively cultivates gender inequalities, but also allows elite males to extend their influence and control over lesser-status males within intermale dominance hierarchies. (Sabo et al. 2001, 6)

While this provided an important context for the area of prison masculinities, Sabo, Kupers and London's valuable collection is now over 15 years old. In the intervening time, there have been important developments in theories of masculinities (such as 'inclusive' masculinity, as considered below) and substantial critiques of hegemonic masculinity in conjunction with a significant expansion in empirical prisons research. These changes, and the continued incarceration of over 9 million men internationally (Warmsley 2016), warrant a new, updated source on prison masculinities that reflects these developments. Furthermore, the Sabo, Kupers and London collection is largely US focused, while the chapters in the current collection have a wider geographical reach, which we hope will enable an analysis of, and reflection on, the implications of penal jurisdictions for performances of masculinity in a wider range of countries.

Certain commonly held positions emerge from the prison masculinities literature outlined above. Principal among these commonalities is the notion that prison masculinities are multiple and complex. Furthermore, existing literature in this area illustrates that specific performances of masculinities are shaped by the prison context. So, despite prison masculinities being connected to performances of masculinity that are *not* shaped by prison contexts (reflecting, in part, the increasingly porous nature of contemporary penal systems (Baumer et al. 2009; Crewe 2009; Moran 2013)), there is something specific about these spaces that results in the distinct constellation of 'prison masculinities', with multiple permutations of this across various locations. This raises the question of the extent to which prisons shape masculinities specific to the prison context, resonant with the wider debate relating to how prison culture evolves, either shaped through external factors (Mathiesen 1965) or evolving indigenously (Sykes 1958).

The prison masculinity research outlined above consistently utilises Raewyn Connell's theory of hegemonic masculinity (1987, 1995). That one theory has been so consistently drawn on within penology raises a number of questions examined below, relating to the nature of the connection between theories of masculinity developed in *non-prison contexts* and performances of masculinity *within prison contexts*. Furthermore, that the theory of hegemonic masculinity has been utilised in penology often quite uncritically, and that this theory of masculinity has been critiqued from a range of perspectives, raises further questions as to why more recent advances in the field of men and masculinities have not found resonance within penology.

Which Theories of Masculinity Can Illuminate Contemporary Studies of Prison Masculinities?

The explicit and substantial study of masculinity began to take shape in the early 1990s, with the development of the field of masculinity studies, orientated around the recognition that masculinities are socially constructed. During the earlier stages of the development of the field, to an extent 'masculinity' was constructed as a constellation of behaviours associated with men, within a binary framework, with the 'masculine' contrasted to the 'feminine' (Kimmel 1994). The field has grown substantially since its inception, due to a large extent to the influential body of work by Connell (1995, 2005), and specifically the development of her theory of hegemonic masculinity. Many aspects of this theory have been widely accepted, particularly those orientated around the idea that masculinities are multiple; indeed, this theory is generally considered to be the preeminent theory of masculinity (Lusher and Robins 2009).

Connell's theory, as originally expounded, outlines four types, or modes, of masculinity—namely, hegemonic, subordinated, marginalised and complicit (Connell 1995, 76–81)—which are organised hierarchically, with the hegemonic form 'culturally exalted above all others' (1995, 77). Therefore, hegemonic masculinity theory (borrowing on Gramsci) implies a compliance by the three non-hegemonic forms of masculinity, with the hegemonic form. Connell's theory of hegemonic masculinity has found resonance in prison studies in a range of research (cf. Evans and Wallace 2007; Jewkes 2005; Karpa 2010; Newton 1994; Sim 1994; Toch 1975). However, there have not been any substantial critiques of this theory within penology or criminology more broadly. This is surprising

1 Introduction: New Perspectives on Prison Masculinities

given that hegemonic masculinity has been critiqued from a range of perspectives within the broader field of men and masculinity studies (Howson 2006; Demetriou 2001; Hearn 2004); for example, it has been argued that this theory is not able to fully account for the nuance and complexity of contemporary masculinities (Beasley 2008). Among a number of critiques, one has led to the development of theories that can be broadly understood as 'inclusive' masculinity (cf. Anderson 2009; McCormack 2012). Inclusive masculinity is in some senses an evolution in the development of men and masculinity studies, one which entails a rejection in particular of aspects of hegemonic masculinity that relate to hierarchy and the importance of homophobia for the performance of masculinity. According to Anderson, men (and University-attending men in particular):

> …. are rapidly running from the hegemonic type of masculinity that scholars have been describing for the past 25 years. (Anderson 2009, 4)

Inclusive masculinity theory, like the theory of hegemonic masculinity, accepts that masculinities are *multiple*, but places an emphasis on a *lack* of hierarchy and rather a more horizontal structuring of masculinities, in which homophobia is far less, and decreasingly, important. Inclusive masculinity theory, as framed by Anderson (2009) and McCormack (2012), also includes a greater focus on emotional and physical openness by men, and fundamentally, Anderson argues, this has a positive underpinning in relation to the ways in which certain men perform their masculinities.

Despite there being some momentum around inclusive masculinity theory, critiques of the theory have also emerged. de Boise (2014) in particular examines the theory through a number of connected arguments. In part these critiques of inclusive masculinity theory relate to a view that the criticisms of hegemonic masculinity have perhaps gone too far, recognising the continuing utility of Connell's theory. de Boise questions the extent to which inclusive masculinity theory can account for contemporary masculinities, in particular raising questions about the decline of homophobia and issues of the measurement of homophobia (2015, 328).

The chapters in this book draw on a range of theory from the field of men and masculinities to help shape the analysis of the wide range of empirical work contained within this collection. It is hoped that this book will facilitate new discourses around prison masculinities, which will find resonance not only within penology but also within a broader body of work on men and masculinities.

An Overview of the Chapters

The book is composed of 13 chapters, each making an original contribution to the prison masculinities literature. Chapters 2, 3, 4, 5 and 6 explore various theoretical dimensions of prison masculinities. In Chap. 2, Ben Crewe and Martha Morey (University of Cambridge) focus on aspects of work and intimacy as important factors shaping prison masculinities. Drawing on the examples of prison work and prisoner friendships, Chap. 2 questions the value of the concept of 'hypermasculinity' in prisons. Its central argument is that orthodox descriptions of male prisoners' masculinities do not do justice to the diversity and complexity of their identities as workers or to the nature of the relationships that prisoners form within prison. Variations in employment histories and professional ambitions, they argue, contribute to distinct modes of prison masculinity, while the relational intimacies and homosocial bonds between male prisoners call into question the idea that men's prisons are places of complete emotional suppression.

In Chap. 3, Rod Earle (the Open University) uses personal experiences of imprisonment and ethnographic research in two men's prisons in south east England to explore some of the predicaments of imprisonment that may be peculiar to men. Earle draws from ongoing work within Convict Criminology in the UK that encourages academic reflexivity among those who combine experience of imprisonment and careers in criminology. The auto-ethnographic approach seeks to examine the ways in which men's experience of imprisonment corresponds with wider masculine projects in society and the way men engage with each other. Earle tries to combine these approaches with postcolonial perspectives that situate contemporary penality within colonial histories.

In Chap. 4, Matthew Maycock (The Scottish Prison Service, formerly of the MRC/CSO Social and Public Health Sciences Unit, the University of Glasgow) examines aspects of the ways in which prison masculinities are embodied. He argues that prison masculinities are evolving in a plurality of ways that have profound implications for embodied masculinities within prison. Using data collected from two high-security men's prisons in Britain, this chapter initially examines accounts of the sorts of bodies that prisoners desire, and aspire to achieve. Subsequently, the chapter goes on to consider the ways in which the prison context shapes both the 'looking' and the 'doing' of male prisoners' bodies. The chapter also examines the ways in which specific manifestations of 'bodywork' and associated performances of certain embodied masculinities constitute resistance to the prison regime. 'Bodywork' and experiences of male prisoners who are trying (and sometimes failing) to achieve the sorts of body/bodies that are seen as desirable within these prisons are also examined. Finally, Maycock examines the ways in which context-specific constructs of 'looking good' constitute an expression of agency and potentially a form of resistance to prison regimes.

In Chap. 5, Nick de Viggiani (University of the West of England) considers the ways in which masculinities are enacted under a compulsory prison regime. Male prisons typify any social situation where individuals interact with others, learn to cope and survive, and contend with normative conventions and expectations. Prison can be an intense social experience that challenges emotional, psychological and social health and wellbeing, exacerbating individuals' efforts to acquire social legitimacy and status. Social survival, de Viggiani argues, is paramount, even if this compromises health, wellbeing and longer term rehabilitation, as prisoners and prison staff engage in self-censorship, self-subjectification and objectification. Deference to the hegemonic masculine institutional culture is played out via prison masculinities that reflect normative social and institutional values evident in attitudes, behaviours and regime processes. De Viggiani's chapter draws upon ethnographic research conducted with male prisoners to illustrate how masculinities are enacted, sanctioned and condoned at individual and institutional levels, consistent with historical conventions of gender, power and discipline.

In Chap. 6, Jennifer Sloan (Sheffield Hallam University) also foregrounds men in the Prison System but argues that, while men comprise 95% of the prison population in England and Wales (MoJ 2017), and dominate the prison and criminal justice systems across the world, they do not dominate the academic and policy discourse surrounding punishment and penal reform. Instead, certain groups such as women, young people, ethnic minorities, religious groups or the mentally ill tend to be given specific (and heightened) attention. This chapter thus questions why it is that men tend to be relatively hidden from view in discussions of prisons and penal policy and research, and the implications of this both for men and for women within (and beyond) the prison system. In particular, by drawing on research with prisoners undertaken as part of an ethnographic doctoral research in 2009 (Sloan 2011), the chapter discusses how, ultimately, there are serious implications for feminist thinking in the process of not considering the men at the heart of the prison system.

Chapters 7 and 8 examine the ways in which race and ethnicity intersect with prison masculinities in formative ways (cf. Alexander 2012; Phillips 2012). In Chap. 7, Geraldine Brown (Coventry University) examines aspects of race and prison masculinities, and unpacks the often negative hypermasculine assumptions associated with black men when imprisoned and following release. Black masculinity, she argues, is governed by a narrow set of negative stereotypes allowing little opportunity for black men to construct their own identity. A reoccurring theme is that black masculinity designates an epitome of masculinity that is feared and revered in equal measure (Clennon 2013). Drawing on data from a study examining the views and experiences of black male prisoners participating in a faith-based prison intervention, her chapter draws on interview and observational data to illuminate how factors such as 'race' ethnicity, gender and religious beliefs intersect and are implicated in how this group of black men construct their masculine identity. This chapter highlights a positive outcome from a faith-based prison intervention, the creation of a humanising space within prison for 'high risk' black men to engage in critical reflection, self-healing, spiritual, emotional and physical wellbeing, and self-awareness and to consider the valuable contributions they could make to others (family, friends, community). She aims to illustrate how this process facilitated men to narrate and perform what it means, for them, to be men, informed by their roles as father, sons and brothers, carers, workers and partners, and to openly speak about their aspirations, hopes and emotions. The intervention facilitated a representation of black masculinity that is ignored or rendered invisible as it allowed scope for black men to move beyond the stereotypes and supports freedom to construct their own identity. Chapter 8, by Martin Glynn (Birmingham City University), outlines a theoretical model of black masculinities and desistance which is informed by the results and findings of his doctoral study (Glynn 2013), combined with ongoing field work in relation to incarcerated black men. Desistance is conceptualised as a theoretical construct used to explain how offenders orient themselves away from committing crimes. Glynn argues that, although previous studies suggest that successful desistance can be attributed to one or a number of factors, the inclusion of race, ethnicity and culture when theorising about desistance is troublingly absent. He argues that 'race and the racialization' of the criminal justice system can significantly impede the desistance aspirations of black offenders. He asserts that successful desistance for black men is bound up in making successful 'transitions' through various stages of masculinity within the context of 'race and the racialization of the criminal justice system' with specific attention paid to the impact of incarceration. The paucity of research information and data when theorising black masculinities in prison, he suggests, exposes a lack of accountability for racialised criminological implicit biases coming from so-called 'mainstream criminology' when looking at masculinities in relation to crime as a whole.

It is well recognised that involvement in sport can be an important aspect of prison life, and this forms the focus of Chap. 9 by Rosie Meek and Hannah Baumer (Royal Holloway, University of London). Their chapter considers academic research and literature which explore the role of sporting masculinities in prisons globally, as well as drawing upon observations and discussions with prisoners and staff across a number of prisons and young offender institutions in England and Wales. It considers the various forms through which masculinity in relation to sport and exercise is constructed by prisoners, the psychological impact these have and how they differ across different socio-environmental contexts.

A discussion of sporting activities in prisons looks at the ability of approaches to questioning masculine ideals, characterised by maladaptive coping mechanisms such as acting stoically and violence. This chapter focuses on the potential for sporting activities in prisons to provide a context in which positive masculinities based on teamwork and social integration can be constructed. The chapter concludes with a consideration of how expressions of hegemonic masculinity in prison gyms can be challenged and reconstructed to become a positive ideal, developing innovative approaches which seek to promote inclusion in physical activity from prisoners who may otherwise feel subordinated in sporting contexts.

In Chap. 10, Kate Seymore (Flinders University) explores various aspects of prison masculinities, focusing on violence and identity work in an Australian prison. Her chapter considers the continuum of normative masculinity practices that are valued, embodied and performed 'inside' and 'outside' of the prison. Drawing on public records generated by official inquiries, she explores the ways in which hierarchies of difference and dominance shape relations within prisons and mirror broader society. Constructs of identity and difference, she argues, intersect in ways that transcend the actions of individuals—including the use of, and talk about, violence. Within a societal context marked by hierarchical power relations and the normalised positioning of certain others as different and lesser, she argues that there is nothing fundamentally different about prison culture; (so-called) prison masculinity(ies) reflect ordinary, everyday masculinity(ies).

The final three chapters of the book explore aspects of fatherhood in prison. In Chap. 11, Tony Evans (University of Roehampton) explores masculinity construction, subject positioning and the relationships with 'dad'. The chapter explores the masculinity narratives of UK male prisoners and identifies three key groups: men accepting and internalising normative codes of hegemonic masculinity; men growing up within these codes but transforming them into something 'softer and gentler'; and men defining their sense of self outside of hegemonic norms. Implications for working with hypermasculinity in prisons are discussed. Evans then draws on follow-up research which explores men's experiences of constructing and performing the masculine self as influenced by the father–son relationship and its subsequent effect on adopting masculinity subject positions and beliefs. He proposes a 'spectrum' of masculinity, representing a range of adopted male subject positions (e.g. thug, dominator position; laddish bravado position; traditional provider emotionally detached position; good provider emotionally holding position; effeminate male weakling position).

In Chap. 12, Katie Buston (University of Glasgow) explores the experience of a group of young male offenders taking part in a parenting intervention. Her chapter draws on ethnographic work with young fathers attending a prison parenting programme in a Young Offender Institution in Scotland. She illustrates how the programme facilitators encouraged sharing and caring, creating a space in the classroom where the men could feel comfortable showing their softer side. By talking about their present and past lives in relation to parenthood, and reflecting on this together, it is theorised that the men will (further) realise how important their fatherhood role is, and hence be motivated to change their parenting practices in positive ways. The chapter explores how hypermasculine discourses and performances contrasted, and intertwined, with much softer discourses and performances of masculinity. The wider implications for prison-based group interventions which theorise behavioural change, around sharing of experiences and developing caring relationships with peers and facilitators are discussed.

Finally, Chap. 13 by Anna Curtis (State University of New York (SUNY) at Cortland) considers the experiences of male prisoners taking part in two parenting programmes in prisons in the USA, which entails examining notions of paternity and the paradigms of possibility. This chapter draws on two-and-a-half years of participation observation of the delivery of these fatherhood programmes inside prison—one at a youth facility and one at an adult facility—as well as content analysis of the programmes' materials. She suggests that group facilitators sometimes struggled to manage and blend contradictory expectations around masculinity and fatherhood within prison. Part of this struggle reflected divisions in expectations for fathers outside of prison; other parts of this struggle hinged on the kinds of masculine performances that prison life demands. Indeed, she argues, the structure of prison demands masculine practices that confirm incarcerated men's parental unfitness. Group facilitators sought to carve out space for incarcerated men to nurture their children emotionally, though they did so by relying on more traditional understandings of masculinity (such as emotional self-control and the importance of fathers protecting their children from harm).

Cumulatively, these chapters represent the beginning of a new discourse around contemporary prison masculinities. The importance of gender within prison contexts has been established for some time now; however, this book develops the analysis of prison masculinities across multiple jurisdictions, utilising multiple theories of masculinity and focusing on diverse aspects of prison life. The 13 chapters each illuminate aspects of performances of masculinity that are largely hidden, but that have significance well beyond the prison walls.

References

Alexander, M. (2012). *The new Jim Crow: Mass incarceration in the age of colorblindness*. New York: The New Press.

Anderson, E. (2009). *Inclusive masculinity: The changing nature of masculinities*. London: Routledge.

Baumer, E. P., et al. (2009). The porous prison. *The Prison Journal, 89*(1), 119–126.

Beasley, C. (2008). Rethinking hegemonic masculinity in a globalizing world. *Men and Masculinities, 11*(1), 86–103.

Clennon, O. D. (2013, November 18). What's the problem with Black masculinities? *Media Diversified*.

Collier, R. (1998). *Masculinities, crime, and criminology: Men, heterosexuality, and the criminal(ised) other*. London: Sage.

Connell, R. W (1987). *Gender and power: Society, the person and sexual politics*. Berkeley: University of California Press.

Connell, R. W (1995). *Masculinities*. Berkeley: University of California Press.

Connell, R. W., & Messerschmidt, J. W. (2005). Hegemonic masculinity. *Gender & Society, 19*(6), 829–859.

Crewe, B. (2009). *The prisoner society: Power, adaptation, and social life in an English prison*. Oxford: Oxford University Press.

de Boise, S. (2014). I'm not homophobic, "I've got gay friends". *Men and Masculinities, 18*(3), 318–339.

Demetriou, D. (2001). Connell's concept of hegemonic masculinity: A critique. *Theory and society, 30*(3), 337–361.

Evans, T., & Wallace, P. (2007). A prison within a prison? *Men and Masculinities, 10*(4), 484–507.

Gilligan, C. (1982). *In a deferent voice.* Cambridge, MA: Harvard University Press.

Glynn, M. (2013). *The racialisation of crime/criminal justice systems and it's impacts on the desistance process* (Doctoral thesis). Birmingham City University, Birmingham.

Hearn, J. (2004). *From hegemonic masculinity to the hegemony of men. Feminist theory.* London: Sage.

Howson, R. (2006). *Challenging hegemonic masculinity.* London: Routledge.

Jewkes, J. (2005). Men behind bars. *Men and Masculinities, 8*(1), 44–63.

Karpa, D. R. (2010). Unlocking men, unmasking masculinities: Doing men's work in prison. *The Journal of Men's Studies, 18*(1), 63–83.

Kimmel, M. (1994). *Manhood in America.* New York: Free Press.

Lusher, D., & Robins, G. (2009). Hegemonic and other masculinities in local social contexts. *Men and Masculinities, 11*(4), 387–423.

Mathiesen, T. (1965). *The defences of the weak.* London: Tavistock.

McCormack, M. (2012). *The declining significance of homophobia: How teenage boys are redefining masculinity and heterosexuality.* Oxford: Oxford University Press.

Messerschmidt, J. W. (1993). *Masculinities and crime.* Lanham: Rowman & Littlefield Publishers.

Ministry of Justice. (2017). https://www.gov.uk/government/statistics/prison-population-figures-2017

Moran, D. (2013). Between outside and inside? Prison visiting rooms as liminal carceral spaces. *GeoJournal, 78*(2), 339–351.

Morgan, D. H. J. (1986). Gender. In R. Burgess (Ed.), *Key variables in social investigation.* London: Routledge and Kegan Paul.

Morris, A. (1987). *Women, crime and criminal justice.* Oxford: Basil Blackwell.

Newton, C. (1994). Gender theory and prison sociology: Using theories of masculinities to interpret the sociology of prisons for men. *The Howard Journal, 33*(3), 193–101.

Phillips, C. (2012). *The multicultural prison. Ethnicity, masculinity, and social relations among prisoners.* Oxford: Oxford University Press.

Sabo, D., Kupers, T., & London, W. (Eds.). (2001). *Prison masculinities.* Philadelphia: Temple University Press.

Sim, J. (1994). Tougher than the rest? Men in prison. In T. Newburn & E. A. Stanko (Eds.), *Just boys doing business? Men, masculinities and crime* (pp. 100–117). London: Routledge.

Sloan, J. (2011). *Men inside: Masculinity and the adult male prison experience.* Unpublished PhD thesis, The University of Sheffield.

Sykes, G. M. (1958, 1971 ed.). *The society of captives.* Princeton: Princeton University Press.

Toch, H. (1975). *Men in crisis.* Chicago: Aldine.

Warmsley, R. (2015). *World female imprisonment list* (3rd ed.). London: The Institute for Criminal Policy Research (ICPR).

Warmsley, R. (2016). *World prison population list* (11th ed.). London: The Institute for Criminal Policy Research (ICPR).

2

Work, Intimacy and Prisoner Masculinities

Martha Morey and Ben Crewe

Introduction

Given the boom in studies interrogating prisoner masculinities in the last two decades or so, it can no longer be said that prisoners' gender identities have been neglected in academic research or, specifically, that the 'maleness' of male prisoners is hidden, invisible or unquestioned. Yet the tendency noted by Joe Sim, writing during the first wave of research on prison masculinities, for themes of domination to be 'emphasised at the expense of contradiction, challenge and change' (1994: 111) has endured. The focus of much research into prisoner masculinities has been troublingly narrow, concentrating on their most spectacular and stereotypical manifestations. The result is that most portrayals of men in prison present a relatively reductive picture of aggression, emotional coldness and machismo (see, e.g., Sabo et al. 2001). Whether or not such accounts were accurate in the closing decades of the previous century, subsequent changes in the broader socio-economic climate, in the nature of

---

M. Morey (✉) • B. Crewe
University of Cambridge, Cambridge, UK

© The Author(s) 2018
M. Maycock, K. Hunt (eds.), *New Perspectives on Prison Masculinities*,
Palgrave Studies in Prisons and Penology, https://doi.org/10.1007/978-3-319-65654-0_2

imprisonment and, therefore, in cultures and practices of masculinity mean that the continuing use of a terminology of 'hypermasculinity' is increasingly questionable. Drawing on two separate pieces of primary prison research, this chapter seeks to explore prison masculinities as they apply to the spheres of work and intimacy, in ways that highlight the complexity and diversity of male prisoners' identities.

Prisoner (Hyper)Masculinities: Compensation and Importation

The prison masculinities literature is well populated with what we term the 'hypermasculinity hypothesis': the suggestion—sometimes explicit, sometimes implicit—that men in prison exhibit an exaggerated form of masculinity and are culturally rewarded for doing so. Hypermasculine traits are described relatively consistently as involving toughness, aggression and violence (Sykes 1958; Newton 1994; Toch 1998; de Viggiani 2012; Ricciardelli 2015), as well as homophobia and hatred of anything that appears weak, effeminate or associated with femininity (Newton 1994; Irwin and Owen 2005; Jewkes 2005). In essence, hypermasculine characteristics in prison represent 'extreme' (Jewkes 2005), 'exaggerated' (Ricciardelli 2015) or 'exacerbated' (Sabo et al. 2001) versions of a stereotypical, primitive and simplistic version of maleness from the community (Sykes 1958; de Viggiani 2012), notwithstanding the frequent argument that unbridled aggression tends not to be accorded respect within prisons specifically (Sykes 1958; Bowker 1983; Toch 1998).

The 'hypermasculinity hypothesis' is broadly based on two theories that map directly onto the deprivation and importation models of 'inmate culture'. Explanations drawing on the *deprivation* perspective contend that prisoner hypermasculinity is a *compensatory response* to the emasculating experience of imprisonment, in a context in which there are limited resources for 'achieving' masculinity through other means (Bandyopadhyay 2006). Here, then, the prison is understood as an institution that deprives the male prisoner of many of the essential qualities of manhood (Sykes 1958), reducing him to 'a state of infantilised dependency' (Jewkes 2002: 55) and denying him many of the conventional markers of masculine esteem. Thus, for example, the deprivation of heterosexual relations and the absence of a female audience reconfigure the prisoner's identity (Jewkes 2005), while deficits in safety, honour and material goods push male prisoners to seek to recoup masculine power and status through forms of behaviour in which they exploit others (Toch 1998; Newton 1994; Jewkes 2002, 2005). In brief, then, from this perspective, the conditions of prison life mean that prisoner masculinities are 'besieged from every side' (Newton 1994: 197), leading to 'prison-induced distortions' of masculinity and identity (Irwin and Owen 2005: 104).

Explanations which are consistent with *importation* theories of prison life point to the congruence between the masculinities of men in the community and their behaviours once in prison. Here, 'masculinity' is often associated with the very acts that have led men—particularly those who have committed violent offences—to be incarcerated (Jewkes 2002, 2005; Ricciardelli 2015), and imprisonment is deemed to exaggerate inclinations that pre-date the sentence (Messerschmidt 2001; Jewkes 2002, 2005). More recently, Messerschmidt has theorised the interrelation of crime and hypermasculinities, stating that 'when other masculine resources are unavailable, specific types of crime can provide an alternative resource for accomplishing gender' (2001: 68). This argument, that crime serves as a means of 'achieving' masculinity when other resources are unavailable, is reminiscent of the almost hydraulic logic of the deprivation-compensation thesis, above.

Looking beyond criminal behaviours, other academics have explained the importation of hypermasculinity to prisons in terms of the population from which prisoners are drawn. Prisoners are assumed to be men from deprived socio-economic backgrounds, in which 'legitimate' masculine resources are largely inaccessible. The idea, then, is that men *outside prison* resort to hypermasculine behaviours even before they enter an institution that compounds their status deprivation (Newton 1994; Jewkes 2005; Bengtsson 2015; Ricciardelli 2015). Ricciardelli, for example, argues that male prisoners frequently import 'street traits' from outside which contribute to prison masculinities that simply 'exaggerate traditional concepts of masculinity evident in larger society' (2015: 170). Just as the broader deprivation and importation theses are not mutually exclusive, it is widely accepted that the analogous perspectives on prison masculinities can also be combined. As Jewkes explains, 'criminal perspectives learned earlier in life combine with the pains of imprisonment to give rise to an enhanced or exaggerated form of masculinity' (2005: 61) that is resultantly 'simultaneously a reflection of wider social norms and a response to the specific, unique properties of imprisonment' (2002: 58). Ricciardelli echoes this sentiment, arguing that the most desirable traits in prison are hypermasculine and that status inside is the result of 'the importation of street "credibility"...combined with deprivation inherent to the prison environment' (2015: 185).

As a general statement about prison masculinities, this integrated position seems indisputable, but at the same time rather limited. Yet research that offers more nuanced or alternative readings of prisoner masculinity has tended to consider these different versions to be 'subordinate' to the hegemonic ideal: that is, identity positions that are 'settled for' when the prisoner is unable to achieve the exemplary form of hypermasculinity (Sykes 1958; Newton 1994; Sabo et al. 2001). Bandyopadhyay (2006) challenges this reading—which derives from Connell's notion of hegemonic and subordinated masculinities—instead identifying competing masculinities 'which challenge the homogenous idea of hegemonic masculinity' (2006: 186). Likewise, Bosworth and Carrabine (2001) question orthodox presentations of hypermasculinity and lament the lack of research analysing 'normal' men in prison, explaining how accounts of violence frequently occlude the less extreme versions of masculinity found in prison. More recently, a number of prison studies have ignored the framework of 'hegemonic masculinity' that is itself so hegemonic within the wider masculinities literature, describing a range of male identities within prisons as they relate to factors such as race and ethnicity (Phillips 2012; Earle 2011), penal power (Crewe 2009) and relationships with female staff (Crewe 2006). Wilson (2004) describes how young black male prisoners choose 'keeping quiet' over 'going nuts' in adapting to life in prison, while Crewe (2009) highlights a range of orientations to female prison officers, from sentimentality and chivalry to more conventional forms of machismo. Meanwhile, Crewe et al. (2013) have argued that prison institutions are spatially differentiated, such that emotional expression among male prisoners is enabled and suppressed in different zones of the prison. Such studies seem more empirically nuanced than much of what has preceded them precisely because they set out to *describe* masculinities rather than *theorise* them; but the corollary of this is that they are largely unanchored from a growing literature on masculinities beyond the prison that might animate their findings.

Contemporary Masculinities

The narrow focus of prison masculinities research is at odds with the increasing diversity of masculinities research more generally. Studies investigating contemporary changes in economy, society and culture have proposed various ways in which these transformations are impacting on the construction of masculinities. With regard to changes in the economy and labour market, the growth and intensification of corporate, free-market capitalism in Britain over recent decades has realigned the focus from producer to consumer needs, transforming the nature and experience of work (Sennett 1998; Haywood and Mac an Ghaill 2003; McDowell 2003, 2009). Given the centrality of work in structuring masculinities, changes of this kind are likely to have significant repercussions for contemporary men's identities (Tolson 1977; Nayak 2006). For example, the decline in labouring jobs, and concurrent growth in service sector employment, has required various adjustments in the masculinities of many men. McDowell (2002, 2003, 2004, 2009) argues that entering the contemporary labour market, built around a service economy, is more confusing and time-consuming than in the past, particularly for the modern equivalents of Willis' (1977) 'lads', as 'counter-school culture' and oppositional attitudes to authority have become serious barriers to entry rather than tacit cultural requirements for labour market entry (McDowell 2003). Furthermore, the 'soft' skills that employees are required to employ in service jobs, including emotional labour, deference and other traditionally 'feminine' behaviours, may preclude men from achieving certain kinds of masculinities (McDowell 2003).

Innovations in culture and the economy also produce their own, new masculine forms. Masculinities can be achieved *with* the body (through work, sports or violence, for example) and *on* the body (through diet, exercise or fashion) (Connell 2000; Haywood and Mac an Ghaill 2003).

The latter has been shown to be increasingly significant, particularly in the ways that branded clothing and 'makeovers' can be used by disadvantaged men who are otherwise unable to access resources to help them achieve their desired masculinities (Haywood and Mac an Ghaill 2003; Hakim 2015). As conspicuous consumption and wealth become significant markers of status in neoliberal market-based economies, masculinities take shape around not only the consumption of certain products and clothing, but also leisure-experiences such as drinking alcohol, clubbing or going to the gym (Hayward 2004; Nayak 2006; Hall et al. 2008; Hamilton 2012; Hakim 2015). Another strand of contemporary masculinities research considers 'inclusive' (Anderson 2008, 2012) or 'softened' (Roberts 2012) masculinities that are responding to cultural and economic transformations by becoming more emotionally expressive and less misogynistic and homophobic (Anderson 2008, 2012; Roberts 2012),

Despite the findings of this broader masculinities literature, there has so far been little attempt by prison sociology to consider how prison masculinities might be changing and moving away from the hypermasculine characterisation. In the remainder of the chapter, we present findings from two separate studies which bring into question the claims and value of this perspective.

Work and Prison Masculinities

The first of these studies, undertaken by the chapter's first author, took place in HMP The Mount, a medium-security men's training prison which drew most of its prisoners from Greater London and a more provincial area just outside it. The aim of the research was to examine experiences of and attitudes towards different forms of work, both in prison and the outside community. The study was exploratory, involving interviews with 34 men from a single 'enhanced' wing who undertook different types of work in the prison.[1] Interviews consisted of four sections: life before prison, which covered childhood experiences and opinions of work (what parents and people locally did) as well as school and previous work experiences of their own (licit and illicit); attitudes towards and experiences of work while in prison; aspirations for employment on release; and more general opinions (about work, masculinity and relationships with women, for example). A typology of prisoner masculinities emerged during analysis, with over two-thirds of the sample representing two distinct masculine identities—*entrepreneurs* and *tradesmen*.

Tradesmen generally experienced traditional working-class or lower-middle-class upbringings in provincial towns outside London. Typically, they had grown up with both parents, often with a father who had a manual trade and a mother who was either a housewife or undertook stereotypically feminine service work, although a minority of the *tradesmen's* parents ran small family businesses. The educational histories of the *tradesmen* varied from having degrees to not finishing school, but their employment histories were similar, in that all had careers in specific trades such as scaffolding or car mechanics, in more general manual work (e.g., as couriers or in warehouses), or in physical professions such as the army or boxing. As a function of the *tradesmen's* age—they were on average older (and a greater proportion were white) than the sample as a whole—some had moved into non-manual work in car sales or small family businesses later in their lives. Also consistent among the *tradesmen* was their plan to return to their previous work once released, with the majority discussing specific job offers from family and friends.

These common experiences prior to imprisonment structured a distinct form of masculinity, in three main ways. First, the forms of work undertaken by the *tradesmen* shaped their masculinities through the relationships they forged with their bodies. *Tradesmen* rarely discussed their bodies explicitly, appearing relatively indifferent to fashion and grooming. Instead, they talked about their bodies as tools for manual work ('blokes are suited to building … lifting 30 [kilos] for ten hours a day ain't for the weak hearted' (Cameron)). For *tradesmen,* masculinity was embodied in physical work and dedication to a trade. The interrelation of physical strength and masculinity was invoked both explicitly (as above) and implicitly during discussion of the (few) women whom *tradesmen* worked with. Those tradesmen who had moved away from manual labour during their careers to white-collar positions used the language of continuing a 'trade' to maintain this aspect of masculinity.

In addition to the largely physical nature of their work, *tradesmen* were employed in overwhelmingly male workplaces, providing context for the second factor that structured their masculinity (see Willis 1977; McDowell 2003; Nayak 2006 on shop floor masculinity). In describing their work experiences, they frequently referenced homosocial bonding with colleagues as one of the highlights of their job, demonstrating the continued significance of work environments that were predominantly male:

> What I enjoyed more [than the work itself] was just like the restroom banter. It was all guys, there were sometimes like 50 or 60 of us in the restroom and it was always a good laugh…you get some good mates there […] Where I worked it was all male except for one time when we had a female work with us…but she was just one of the lads, and that's got a lot more to do with the fact why women don't venture into so-called male environments, because of the banter that goes on and all that sort of stuff. (Theo)

Finally, the *tradesmen's* masculinities were also shaped by contemporary socio-economic changes, in ways that differentiated them from Willis' (1977) 'lads' and other traditional forms of masculinity. They were often keen to demonstrate a 'softer' masculinity, expressing a fondness for cooking or wearing pink, for example:

> No such thing as a proper man anymore. So like my granddad, he's 90, fought in a war and all that crap, and he's a manly man. Do you know what I mean? Aftershave that stinks, my Nan stays at home, does the washing, he goes out to work, comes back all dirty, dinner is on the table, don't take crap from anyone…won't wear pink, won't wear things that have got any type of flowers…[but] I wear pink, pink's a brilliant colour. (Cameron)

Attitudes among *tradesmen* towards gender equality were more variable. A few voiced concerns about women working and the effect it could have on men, especially the breadwinner role, although this was usually coupled with recognition that men often could not afford to be a family's sole earner:

> I think it's been hard for men to accept that women can work as well, that's been a hard thing

Why do you think that?
Men have always been the providers, so if a woman comes along and says that 'I'm going to work as well', and the next thing they're earning more money than their husband, that can become a problem. But the good thing about it now, as life's going on people have got bills that are so much higher now, mortgages and stuff, [women] *have* to work. So most of the time you accept it all. (Wayne)

However, the majority of *tradesmen* expressed full support for gender equality ('Listen, woman and man are equal. You've got [female] body builders too, some women can pick up more weight than men! They're equal, women and men are equal' (Bilal)).

The *tradesmen's* masculinities were also affected by contemporary labour market changes and concurrent socio-cultural shifts. Thus while all of the *tradesmen* were proud of their employment histories and trades, many simultaneously referred to a decline in the value and status afforded to them and their work by wider society. For example:

I was a white van man. Twenty years ago maybe, that was ok, but now you are kind of looked down upon … I'm not sure why that is, but there is kind of a shift in society towards that kind of thinking. A hard day's work is not what it used to be if that makes sense. Yeah, if you worked on a building site 20 years ago, you were kind of respected, like 'He's a real hard grafter, a real hard worker', and kind of respected by your peers. Now it's like 'Is that all you are?!', do you know what I mean? You haven't done very well in life if you're working on a building site is kind of like the impression now… I think unless you're working in an office or a big company or something like that you're kind of looked at as not successful. (Aidan)

This led to a mixture of defensiveness and humility among the *tradesmen,* and sometimes resignation for those who did not envisage promotion in their future:

I'm not one of these people who's going to be 'successful'… I'm just going to be another person that's earning the money to pay the rent and everything, do you know what I mean?… I'm just going to be a driver, that's all I'll be. I'm not going to be like a 'successful', like, I don't know…I'm just going to be normal... I'll do my job the way it's got to be done, I'll do it properly, but I'm not going to make anything, bring anything great out of it. (William)

While most of the *tradesmen* were more positive than William about their futures, their aspirations were typically for respectability and an unexceptional, modest lifestyle. When asked about their plans for work after release, all of the *tradesmen* discussed returning to previous occupations via opportunities offered by friends or family. Theo, for example, had undertaken cash-in-hand grounds-keeping with a friend on his days off before coming to prison and intended to pursue this type of work full-time on release. Cameron, on the other hand, planned to return to scaffolding:

[Going back to scaffolding on release] will be easy as anything. I've got a job waiting for me. I've had people ringing my missus while I've been in prison saying 'where's Cameron? Is he available to come to work?'. (Cameron)

This intended continuity between their pre- and post-prison professional careers contributed to their rejection of a 'criminal' label and meant that trade remained their primary identification.

The second mode of masculinity represented in the sample was that of *entrepreneurs*. *Entrepreneurs* were on average younger than *tradesmen*, more ethnically diverse, from large cities (predominantly London) and were more likely than the rest of the sample to have been raised in a single-parent household. Their employment histories followed a relatively consistent pattern. Typically, *entrepreneurs* began making money illicitly at a young age (around 12 years old, mostly by selling drugs), before finding licit employment as teenagers. Mostly this entailed sporadic catering, retail or other service sector jobs, often found through agencies. Some entrepreneurs had engaged in manual work procured through male relatives. All of these opportunities were relatively poorly paid. As such, alongside their formal employment, the majority of entrepreneurs continued to engage in more profitable, illicit activities. The consistency of the entrepreneurs' illicit activity, beginning during childhood and continuing until imprisonment (generally because of the illicit activity), is in contrast to the experiences of the tradesmen whose consistent income was from licit, trade work. While some of the older entrepreneurs described having already set up successful legitimate businesses, all of these participants had entrepreneurial ambitions for after their release. The entrepreneur masculinity type was thus structured by both licit and illicit work experiences as well as cultural factors, including the rise of conspicuous consumption as a means to status, the 'American dream' narrative of 'making it' and a particular construct of 'men as providers', as discussed below.

In discussing their experiences of licit work before coming to prison, it was evident that the rise of service sector employment provides the context for *entrepreneurs'* attitudes towards work: business and service work were preferential; 'soft skills' and emotional labour were prized; and creativity, innovation and business were central to their identities and positive self-perceptions. While some efforts were made to re-frame service work as physical and traditionally masculine, in many instances, *entrepreneurs* were keen to emphasise their preference for this form of employment because of the interpersonal skills it required ('I used to be a, what did they call, it a customer service, like I was good with customers and that, I was always really polite to them' (Nathanael)). However, while *entrepreneurs* generally perceived licit service work favourably, most had been employed on zero-hour or temporary contracts procured through agencies, leading to insecurity and wages which were viewed as problematic. For example:

> … agency work was just money to pay the bills, and plus I was studying at the time. So juggling the two was difficult because you could never get enough work and when they're calling you for work you're at college. So it was kind of hard to balance the two and I couldn't pay my bills. I was struggling and I was young, I think I was about 17 or 18 at the time, and yeah I took the easy route out of just selling drugs. (Marcus)

The *entrepreneurs'* masculinity was also situated in a socio-cultural context within which wealth and conspicuous consumption are increasingly important signifiers of status, value and success, and the *entrepreneurs* found their formal employment opportunities insufficient on their own to fulfil their broader masculine ideal. As a result of this perceived insufficiency, *entrepreneurs* also engaged in illicit work, chiefly drug dealing. The primary motivation for this work was financial, and the income generated from illicit activities facilitated conspicuous consumption of goods and experiences that offered *entrepreneurs* access to the status markers they desired:

> I could get things that I wanted or needed when I wanted or needed it instead of having to save…if it was someone's birthday I knew I had the money to pay for something that they wanted and get a present for them… It just gave me that bit of independence, that I knew I didn't have to rely on anyone but I knew people could rely on me…
> **You said you could get things you wanted, what kind of things did you want?**
> Clothes, jewellery basically anything that I saw that I wanted I knew that I have the money that I could get it if I really wanted it… I was comfortable enough that if I needed something or wanted to go somewhere or go on holiday, I knew I could just go without having to save. (Connor)

While the *entrepreneurs* accept the potentiality of imprisonment as well as the downsides of the work itself ('you don't never enjoy it…you get stressed out, it's not the sort of people you want to be meeting all the time when you're selling drugs' (Jake)), most also enjoyed the practical and intellectual challenges it presented. Furthermore, many of the *entrepreneurs* were keen to highlight the parallels between drug dealing and business/entrepreneurship more generally:

> I think of things like a 24-hour newsagents, selling alcohol and wine and all that kind of stuff. That to me is quite similar to what I was doing before. Wholesale retail: you buy in bulk and you sell small. That to me, it doesn't take a lot of thinking. I could jump into that, get a shop, rent a shop, go to wholesalers, buy all the stuff and sit there and make it sell. As long as I do the right market research and set the shop up in the right area it's kind of transferable skills to do with what I was doing before. (Zach)

Illicit work was therefore central to the *entrepreneur* identity in terms of not only its financial benefits and the lifestyle it facilitated but also the business skills it required and the status attached to entrepreneurialism. The centrality of entrepreneurialism to masculinity manifested itself in a commitment to an 'American Dream' narrative of coming from nothing and becoming (extremely) wealthy. This is distinct from *tradesmen,* for example, who aspired to more modest and 'normal' lifestyles.

Finally, *entrepreneurs* held a particular attitude towards gender relations. In terms of attitudes towards work, they were generally incredulous at the suggestion that there could be 'men's work' and 'women's work', feeling that this was a 'trick question' ('as in sexism? [...] I think it's very Victorian!' (Harry)). These relatively progressive views on gender equality, at least with regard to employment, related to a number of factors. First, the majority of participants in this type were raised by working, single-mothers who were praised by their sons for their work ethic and ability to provide for their families emotionally and financially. As such, *entrepreneurs* did not grow up seeing work as an exclusively male activity. Second, the *entrepreneurs'* belief that anyone could achieve their dream if they worked hard enough was gender-blind:

> If you put your mind to it… everyone can do anything. It's been proven now hasn't it? After all these years of men doing this and women doing that, I think it's been proven hasn't it?… I think everyone can do everything, there's nothing you can't do is there? The human? (Harry)

Alongside open-minded attitudes towards women working, however, the *entrepreneurs'* masculinity was also still associated with a belief in men as 'providers'. While seemingly incongruous with their otherwise progressive social attitudes, the interviews demonstrated an important nuance between the *entrepreneurs'* narrative of men as providers, and patriarchal beliefs in male breadwinning. While the latter is associated with men providing *at the expense of and in contrast to* women, the *entrepreneurs'* provider ideal was derived from personal experiences of men failing to work or support their families *at all.* As a result, for *entrepreneurs,* 'providing' was the alternative to 'depending' ('I would like to be able to fully support my wife and my kids…without relying on my missus…she's brought your kids into the world! Surely you should be man enough to provide for them…without relying on her' (Nathanael)).

Entrepreneurs thus represented a relatively progressive masculinity that was derived from men working rather than from women *not* working.

The origin of this attitude also related to the absence of fathers. For example:

> … girls now, they always cussing their baby daddy, saying that they're workless, they don't provide for their kids… From what I'm hearing… [men are] not really living up to their responsibilities… I always tell [girls] I'll be working hard when I come out. I'll be working, working, working. I doubt I'll even have time to see friends, and they say 'why's that?' and I say I'm trying to provide, I'm trying to save money up for the future family I don't have yet… that work ethic and those principles should be with every man… a lot of guys are not serious. (Marcus)

The *entrepreneur* masculinity was thus defined by experience of and preference for highly profitable non-manual, service sector, business employment but generally achieved through simultaneous licit *and illicit work* that together facilitated the accrual of wealth as well as the exhibition of 'soft skills', intellect, creativity and entrepreneurialism. The purpose of *entrepreneurs'* work, whether licit or illicit, was to engage in conspicuous consumption in order to demonstrate wealth, status and a successful masculinity. Money was also constructed as a means to independence and the opportunity to provide for one's family within a narrative that was consistent with *entrepreneurs'* generally liberal social attitudes.

Tradesmen and *Entrepreneurs* in Prison Settings

Tradesmen and *entrepreneurs* thus represented distinct prison masculinities, associated with specific kinds of behaviours and attitudes within the prison. For example, *tradesmen* were extremely compliant and willing to undertake most forms of work, as illustrated in their attitudes towards doing the least popular job in the prison's warehouse. While initially expressing negative opinions about the warehouse, a number of *tradesmen* had happily worked there for long periods of time. For these men, the warehouse was seen as relatively similar to outside work environments, and they enjoyed the opportunity to work with civilians with whom they could exchange 'banter'. Furthermore, the warehouse offered a number of high-trust positions (involving handling tobacco and other luxury products) which served to underline their self-conceptions as hard-working and diligent employees.

Tradesmen's attitudes towards prison work were also influenced by their intentions to return to careers they were already qualified to do, which meant they did not feel in need of rehabilitation or 'up-skilling' while in prison. This contributed to two important attitudes towards prison work that were typical of the *tradesmen*. First, they were often dismissive of the qualifications on offer and did not generally evaluate opportunities for work and education within the prison in terms of how they might impact on their life after release:

> It don't matter where you work [whilst in prison]… you just want to do something [to pass the time], and you want to go home. Do you know what I mean? It's not something for the future when you get out. There's nothing they can teach me here that's going to benefit me on the outside. I know how to work, I've worked most of my life. (William)

Instead, *tradesmen's* decisions about prison work were very much focused on its immediate and short-term benefits: how it could make their sentence more survivable, through direct and indirect perks such as extra gym access, more food or simply a way to pass time ['The reason I do servery or cleaning is you get good gym sessions, so it's a means to an end. [I] don't like cleaning, don't like server, but it's a means to an end' (Barney)].

The second way in which *tradesmen's* skilled occupational backgrounds shaped their engagement with the prison regime was in their aspirations to be able to pass on their crafts to other prisoners. While the desire to partake in generative work was by no means exclusive to these prisoners, their motivations were based in a love of their trade, and belief in the prospects it offered, rather than a longing to teach or use interpersonal skills:

> I'm a trained scaffolder, I can train people to scaffold. All the jail needs to do is provide an area, equipment, and [an examiner]… I put a scaffold on,

you put it up, take it back down, show me how you do it. As soon as they start learning you show them how to do things, and assessors come out and test them. So my idea was to try and get people into the scaffolding industry because…there's millions of scaffolders wanted out there but no one gets into it any more. (Cameron)

In contrast, *entrepreneurs* strategically chose courses and jobs within the prison that they perceived as helping them maximise the professional benefits of their sentence:

The only reason I do this job is because I thought, you know, what if I can get some sort of qualification out of it? Maybe give me a better chance of doing something in the future…So yeah I've chosen my jobs very carefully. (Ali)

The willingness to comply with the prison was not, however, a simple form of obedience. Rather, it represented a specific form of compliance with aspects of the institution that were perceived as beneficial in terms of masculine identity and work aspirations for while in the prison, and on release. Recognising that other prisoners had different motivations to engage in prison work (such as financial survival, coping with the pains of imprisonment, preparation for manual work), *entrepreneurs* like Marcus explained that their logic was longer-term personal development:

I don't want to be working for the prison…I wouldn't work on the servery serving prisoners, I wouldn't work in the workshop doing bicycle tires. Like, I find that insulting to me. I'm not doing it. It's slave labour yeah, and the prison makes a heck of a lot of money for doing it, private contracts, while they pay prisoners peanuts. So why am I putting myself through all of that? How am I benefiting from doing their work? No, I don't think so. I'd rather do…a course…I try to look at things in the bigger picture, and what would be beneficial to me, and not for the short-term. Always think long term. (Marcus)

As also suggested here, *entrepreneurs* were more likely than other prisoners to reject workshop work and question the legitimacy of prison labour and its associated wages. Such work was denigrated in part because of the perception that the prison (or an outside contractor) profited unfairly from their labour, but also because manual labour was at odds with their entrepreneurial identities and aspirations: 'everyone's just got…different plans for their future. Mine's *not* bricklaying [laughing]' (Jake); '[workshop work is] exactly what I've been trying to avoid my whole life, the monotony of it…it's the most boring, most monotonous, most soul-destroying thing I've ever done' (Harvey).

Resentment at working for prison-wages and producing a product perceived to be sold for profit was by no means unique to the *entrepreneurs*. However, the aversion to workshop work was striking and unusual, with the *entrepreneurs* all expressing preferences for 'service work', education and generative opportunities. Many described a need for intellectually challenging work ('I feel like I need something more stimulating for my mind' (Marcus); 'anything that lets me use my brain' (Harvey)). For some, this led to resentment that the prison was less accommodating of those who aspired to 'success' and were not interested in manual work:

> The jobs that they give you kind of put you in a mindset that that's all you're going to be good for. In the sense they've got, like, bricklaying, plastering, [warehouse], bike shop, and they're all like…stereotypical to a man…there are people that can draw and can do other things. (Connor)

Meanwhile, in their descriptions of peer mentoring, doing drug or education assessments for prisoners and teaching prisoners to read, *entrepreneurs* revealed their comfort and enjoyment in using 'soft skills':

> I sit in classes…and help out people, give them maybe a bit of confidence… when it goes to an awkward silence I might just throw something out there, start talking to make them feel a bit more comfortable. I talk and let people know that we're here to help. I don't know how much I really care about them…I suppose with doing the role you kind of see people struggling… these people need help, and you <u>can</u> kind of care for them in that way. (Ali)

In this section, then, we have sought to account for two different orientations towards work and identity among male prisoners, neither of which seems consistent with conventional depictions of prison masculinities. In the following section, we move on to discuss a different aspect of this matter, that of friendship, intimacy and emotional expression.

Masculinity, Intimacy and Friendship

Nicole Rafter (2006: 172) has argued that 'prison film friendships gain strength from their single-sex settings' and that, despite their 'unrelenting masculinism' (p. 176), they typically harbour a 'homoerotic subtext in which the buddy gets both a perfect friend and lover' (p. 172). Yet research on friendships among male prisoners is strikingly deficient, and where it exists, it tends to emphasise mistrust, wariness and instrumentalism over trust and intimacy (see Clemmer 1940; Morris and Morris 1963; Sykes 1958; although see Crewe 2009). In a recent study of prisoners serving very long prison sentences from an early age (see Hulley et al. 2016), the tropes used by many prisoners to discuss their peer relationships were highly familiar. In interviews with 125 male prisoners in 16 different establishments, friendships were often described as 'very limited and distant', because of 'the trust factor'; distinctions were often drawn between 'real friends', typically people known prior to imprisonment, and the kinds of 'associates' or 'acquaintances' that were formed within prison. For many prisoners, loyalties and relationships were represented in terms of the willingness of each party to support the other in the event of conflict (see Crewe 2009):

> If they're having a fight, I'll go and defend them. […] I think that's a good way of describing friends. If I think about my closest friends, they're people that I would stick up for no matter what. […] I'm always defending people who are my friends. It's, like, it's love but in a different way, like… it's not love as in, obviously, not that sort of love but it's like a mutual, like, respect. And that's how you know how your true friends are in jail. That's why if I had a situation where someone died or something, or my kid got ill or something, there's people in here that I know that I can sit down with and tell them the whole situation, and they're not gonna run back and tell everyone my business. (Christopher)

Yet, as suggested here, the framing of friendships in terms of instrumental, physical support often concealed a more complex emotional relationship. Indeed, a significant proportion of these prisoners provided accounts of close and trusting friendships that had been formed over the course of their sentences. For example:

I've made a good few friends [who] I'll be friends with for the rest of my life now, so I'm happy. I couldn't ask for a better friend, you know what I mean? And like we chill, we'll have a laugh, you know what I mean? We know we're one with each other. (Oscar)

Two of my mates know me, know everything about me, my deepest darkest secrets, so there's nothing left to hide. (Shaafi)

I can come off the phone and say, 'My nan, she's worrying me, man, she's getting old, do you know what I'm saying?' And have a conversation like that with a friend of mine, and I'll sit down. You get what I'm saying?
Yeah. So these are proper strong friendships?
Yeah, definitely. In jail you have bonds, it's like being in the army… People that's in the army together if you asked them, they might spend like four years of their life together, but it was so intense [...] that life experience, it bonds them forever. (Asad)

As the final quote here indicates, friendships were shaped and expressed through the intensity of prison life and its mundane, domestic qualities. The amount of time that prisoners spent in close proximity—as well as the shared predicament of deprivation and frustration—meant that closeness could be built up relatively quickly:

So it's quite a deep friendship that you've developed in quite a short…
Yeah, it's weird really. It is. It's come on quite short really.
I suppose you're spending that much time with each other it's…
Yeah, we're at work together, we're on the wing together. We do a lot of things together - listen to music, talk, talk to other people, we have a laugh with them. On the weekends we go to gym together, we work out together. (Aaron)

One interviewee described the way that his friend sometimes ironed his shirt for him, prior to him having a visit, 'cos it's all short sleeve and, like, I can't do this. So he did it for me'. So while the literature commonly characterises friendships between prisoners as reserved and pragmatic, based on defensive or mutual needs (e.g., to prevent exploitation or protect against material scarcity), in this study, we found testimonies of intimacy and affection. While some participants reported having to subdue their emotions for years on end, or at least keep them highly private, others described sharing their feelings in a manner that indicated their emotional vulnerability, their willingness to disclose their sentiments and the sympathy available when they did so:

> Most of the time we're just chatting, just casual chat. [but when] my gramps had died and he was a rock for me verbally, and we'd just sit there chatting. He stayed up all night with me chatting. Because I was fucking wounded by that, do you know what I mean? (Oscar)

> My friend from prison, me and him used to speak about everything. We were locked together in a cell, so when me and my girlfriend broke up and I came back from the visit and I was all pissed off, he was like, 'What's up, man? What's up?'. And I was saying nothing, and he was saying, 'Something is up, man, just tell me'. So I was like, 'Oh, something's not right [with my missus] and I just told her to do her thing'. And he was like, 'So what was she saying?' and I was like, 'Well, she accepted that' and he was like, 'Oh brother! Something's definitely going on, man, I feel for you' and that kind of thing. And it was like what happened in the cell stayed in the cell, so I could speak to him. (Daniel)

Descriptions of these kinds of friendships often hinted at deeper emotional connections. Carl, for example, drew on the analogy of intimate partnership to explain his prison friendships:

> Someone said to me when I was on the outside, 'The best trick of finding out if your girl is compatible, is if you're able to just sit in silence and it's not awkward'. If you can do that with someone where you don't feel like you have to make conversation, but you can just chill and, yeah, it's not awkward', and that's what I've found with a lot of people [in here]. When we can sit in association and just sit and chat, and then there's a dry point in the conversation and it's not a thing where, 'Oh, yeah, I'm going to make a phone call'. When it's not like that, when you're relaxed, then that's how I just like pick my friends. (Carl)

In a similar vein, in the following description of camaraderie and emotional support on the prison landings, it is intriguing to hear Paul comment that he calls one prisoner 'dad', a term which communicates paternal concern:

> You see a lot of emotion. I've seen a lot of emotion in here. [If someone's upset], a couple of the lads'll come in and comfort him or they'll do something to cheer him up. If I'm feeling down they'll do something to cheer me up.
> **What sorts of things?**
> Just being there, d'you know what I mean? Or they'll put their music on. They'll start, like, trying to tell you stuff that are funny or they'll tickle you or… I had one [guy] that lived next door to me that used to pick me up and chuck me over his shoulder and spin me round till I told him I was OK, and stuff like that … and there's a lad on here that I call dad, cos he's always looked out for me. And every time I see him he gives me a hug and stuff like that. […] The last two Christmases we've, sort of, got a bit of food together and everything and had a little get together where everyone's had something to eat and had a bit of fizzy pop and had music and had a laugh too, you know, try and make it feel more like Christmas instead of the concrete walls that we're in.

Even more strikingly, Paul had previously said that he did not have any friends within the prison. Denials of this kind sometimes reflected the difference between boisterous amity and emotional trust. More often, though, they seemed to speak of a reluctance to identify friendships for what they were or an embarrassment about the emotional dimensions of social relations:

> I remember at Christmas, we were talking, and something got said and it made me think about my son and that, and I says, 'Yo, I'll shout you in a minute, innit?' and he's like, 'Yeah, yeah'. And I put my music on loud and I had a cry and that. And then I shouted him up about 20 minutes later… and then we like carried on talking. And then the next day he was like, 'Yo, you had a cry last night, innit?' and I was like, 'Yeah, yeah'. Like, 'Fucking pussy!' and I was just like, 'Yeah, right mate!'. We just had a laugh about it, but obviously I think he sort of knows how I feel and that, do you know what I mean? Because he hadn't seen any of his family for four years being in here. So I think he sort of knew how I felt like about my kid, do you

know what I mean? [...] He knows when I feel down and if I feel bad, he'll sit there and talk to me and he'll let me talk about anything and he won't judge me about how I feel, he's quite good like that. (Harris)

The fact that emotions were jointly concealed and disavowed in this interaction is very different from the implication in a good deal of prison sociology and in masculinities research more broadly that men are so taut with aggression, so fearful of appearing in any way vulnerable or so emotionally repressed that their feelings are nowhere to be found. Rather, what we see here is an almost explicit emotional dynamic, with little sense that feelings of anguish are either deeply suppressed or risky to acknowledge, within limited circles, at least. While the relationships between men in prison often remain bounded and defensive—and are certainly some way from the kinds of inclusive masculinities that Anderson (2008) details—terms such as 'hypermasculine' do little justice to the homosocial dynamics of emotion, support and masculinity among male prisoners that we have described here.

Conclusion

There are methodological barriers to understanding prison masculinities. Not least among these are the discomfort that many men feel when issues of masculinity and male identity are raised explicitly, and the tendency for many male prisoners to limit and disguise the feelings that they express to others. The tendency of prison researchers to portray male prisoners as hardened figures, stripped of their emotionality, and locked in an 'iron cage of masculinity' (Sim 1994: 105), may reflect these obstacles. 'Masculinity' does not always make itself easily known or observed, so that it is all too easy for researchers to identify it in forms that obscure its subtleties and variations. The presentation of male prisoners as 'hypermasculine' risks reproducing dehumanising discourses about these men, presenting them as uniformly regressive and lacking in self-awareness and sensitivity. We do not dispute that imprisonment constitutes a threat to some aspects of masculine esteem, or that it generates defensive responses, particularly in the ways that it places men in environments that feel perpetually threatening. However, our data suggest that the identifications and behaviours of many male prisoners cannot be contained within a framework that reduces masculinity to physical dominance, or the kind of 'no-compromise, hard-man image' (Scraton et al. 1991: 66) that was described in a previous era. Our hope is that prison researchers continue to undertake detailed empirical work on the identities, acts and emotions of male prisoners—sex offenders, older prisoners, white-collar offenders, as well as the 'mainstream' young men who comprise most of the prison population—which will shed further light into this domain.

Notes

1. Participants were from diverse ethnicities and ranged in age from 21 to 70 years old.

References

Anderson, E. (2008). Inclusive masculinity in a fraternal setting. *Men and Masculinities, 10*(5), 604–620.

Anderson, E. (2012). Shifting masculinities in Anglo-American countries. *Masculinities and Social Change, 1*(1), 40–60.

Bandyopadhyay, M. (2006). Competing masculinities in a prison. *Men and Masculinities, 9*(2), 186–203.

Bengtsson, T. (2015). Performing hypermasculinity: Experiences with confined young offenders. *Men and Masculinities, 19*(4), 410–428.

Bosworth, M., & Carrabine, E. (2001). Reassessing resistance: Race, gender and sexuality in prison. *Punishment and Society, 3*(4), 501–515.

Bowker, L. (1983). An Essay on Prison Violence. *The Prison Journal, 63*(1), 24–31.

Clemmer, D. (1940). *The prison community*. Boston: Christopher Publishing House.

Connell, R. (2000). *The men and the boys*. Cambridge: Polity Press.

Crewe, B. (2006). Male prisoners' orientations towards female officers in an English prison. *Punishment and Society, 8*(4), 395–421.

Crewe, B. (2009). *The prisoner society: Power, adaptation and social life in an English prison*. Oxford: Oxford University Press.

Crewe, B., Warr, J., Bennett, P., & Smith, A. (2013). The emotional geography of prison life. *Theoretical Criminology, 18*(1), 56–74.

De Viggiani, N. (2012). Trying to be something you are not: Masculine performance within a prison setting. *Men and Masculinities, 15*(3), 271–291.

Earle, R. (2011). Boys' zone stories: Perspectives from a young men's prison. *Criminology and Criminal Justice, 11*(2), 129–143.

Hakim, J. (2015). Fit is the new rich': Male embodiment in the age of austerity. *Soundings: A Journal of Politics and Culture, 61*, 84–94.

Hall, S., Winlow, S., & Ancrum, C. (2008). *Criminal identities and consumer culture*. Cullompton: Willan.

Hamilton, K. (2012). Low-income families and coping through brands: Inclusion or stigma? *Sociology, 46*(1), 74–90.

Hayward, K. (2004). *City limits: Crime, consumer culture and the urban experience*. London: The Glass House Press.

Haywood, C., & Mac an Ghaill, M. (2003). *Men and masculinities: Theory, research and social practice*. Buckingham: Open University Press.

Hulley, S., Crewe, B., & Wright, S. (2016). Re-examining the problems of long-term imprisonment. *British Journal of Criminology, 56*(4), 769–792.

Irwin, J., & Owen, B. (2005). Harm and the contemporary prison. In A. Liebling & S. Maruna (Eds.), *The effects of imprisonment*. Cullompton: Willan Publishing.

Jewkes, Y. (2002). *Captive audience: Media, masculinity and power in prisons*. Cullompton: Willan Publishing.

Jewkes, Y. (2005). Men behind bars: "Doing" masculinity as an adaptation to imprisonment. *Men and Masculinities, 8*(1), 44–63.

McDowell, L. (2002). Transitions to work: Masculine identities, youth inequality and labour market change. *Gender, Place and Culture: A Journal of Feminist Geography, 9*(1), 39–59.

McDowell, L. (2003). *Redundant masculinities? Employment change and white working class youth*. Malden: Blackwell Publishing.

McDowell, L. (2004). Masculinity, identity and labour market change: Some reflections on the implications of thinking relationally about difference and the politics of inclusion. *Geografiska Annaler, 86*(1), 45–56.

McDowell, L. (2009). *Working bodies: Interactive service employment and workplace identities*. Oxford: Blackwell.

Messerschmidt, J. (2001). Masculinities, crime, and prison. In D. Sabo, T. Kupers, & W. London (Eds.), *Prison masculinities*. Philadelphia: Temple University Press.

Morris, T., & Morris, P. (1963). *Pentonville: A sociological study of an English prison*. Abingdon: Routledge.

Nayak, A. (2006). Displaced masculinities: Chavs, youth and class in the post-industrial city. *Sociology, 40*(5), 813–831.

Newton, C. (1994). Gender theory and prison sociology: Using theories of masculinities to interpret the sociology of prisons for men. *The Howard Journal, 33*(3), 193–202.

Phillips, C. (2012). *The multicultural prison: Ethnicity, masculinity, and social relations among prisoners*. Oxford: Oxford University Press.

Rafter, N. (2006). *Shots in the mirror: Crime films and society* (2nd ed.). New York: Oxford University Press.

Ricciardelli, R. (2015). Establishing and asserting masculinities in Canadian penitentiaries. *Journal of Gender Studies, 24*(2), 170–191.

Roberts, S. (2012). Boys will be boys…won't they? Change and continuities in contemporary young working class masculinities. *Sociology, 47*(4), 671–686.

Sabo, D., Kupers, T., & London, W. (2001). *Prison masculinities*. Philadelphia: Temple University Press.

Scraton, P., Sim, J., & Skidmore, P. (1991). *Prisons under protest*. Milton Keynes: Open University Press.

Sennett, R. (1998). *The corrosion of character*. New York: W. W. Norton and Company.

Sim, J. (1994). Tougher than the rest? Men in prison. In T. Newburn & E. Stanko (Eds.), *Just boys doing business*. London: Routledge.

Sykes, G. (1958). *The society of captives: A study of a maximum security prison*. Princeton: Princeton University Press.

Toch, H. (1998). Hypermasculinity and prison violence. In L. Bowker (Ed.), *Masculinities and violence*. London: SAGE.

Tolson, A. (1977). *The limits of masculinity*. London: Tavistock.

Willis, P. (1977). *Learning to labour: How working class kids get working class jobs*. Farnborough: Saxon House.

Wilson, D. (2004). 'Keeping quiet' or 'going nuts': Strategies used by young, black, men in custody. *The Howard Journal of Crime and Justice, 43*(3), 317–330.

3

Being Inside: Masculine Imaginaries, Prison Interiors

Rod Earle

Introduction

Drawing on personal experience of imprisonment and from ethnographic research in men's prisons, I explore some of the existential predicaments of imprisonment that may be peculiar to men. The situation of the prisoner is unique in throwing men together into an involuntary, highly regulated and confined community. The proximities and intimacies involved represent a paradoxical challenge to conventional notions of insular and autonomous masculinity. The formal institutionalisation of homosociality in prison life (i.e. life lived almost exclusively among other men) generates ironic tensions with the informal way men's public lives often exclude women. This experience can take men in prison inside their own lives in unexpected ways. Differing experiences of gender, race, class and ethnicity shape this journey, and how men think about prison and their own relationship to wider society on the outside. In this chapter, I reflect on ongoing work within Convict Criminology (Earle 2016) that

R. Earle (✉)
The Open University, Milton Keynes, UK

encourages academic reflexivity among those who combine experience of imprisonment and careers in criminology.

Looking Inside Prison

The country singer Johnny Cash is famous for playing a series of concerts to prisoners in Fulsom and San Quentin prisons in the USA. He makes the following address to prisoners in the CD liner notes of the 2006 reissue of the recordings.

> All of you have the same things snuffed out of your lives, everything it seems that makes a man a man – women, money, a family, a job, the open road, the city, the country, ambition, power, success, failure – a million things.

Here is another assessment of imprisonment:

> 'This is the last place', he muttered, 'the very last place in the country'. The convict paused and surveyed the compound yard around us, as if to confirm that he was indeed talking about the prison. 'Here', he continued, 'everything is left behind. There is no beer or tobacco, no women. You cannot see your forest, your rivers, mountains and rocks. You cannot see your children. In this kind of place you are abandoned'. These sad thoughts were followed by silence.

Taken from Adam Reed's *Papua New Guinea's Last Place: Experiences of Constraint in a Postcolonial Prison,* this description also conveys the deprivations that prison imposes, the harshness of men's life there and its exceptional qualities. Both suggest the defining mission of prison life, whether in Papua New Guinea or California, is to isolate a man from society and 'snuff out' the 'million things' that make him who he is. Prison, according to Cash, strips away what makes a man a man. He captures the gender of imprisonment and distils prison's deprivations to a masculine essence.

For the man in New Guinea, a sense of being abandoned is emphasised, and when it comes to abandonment of the poor, and neglect and criminalisation of those at the bottom of social hierarchy, many would

3 Being Inside: Masculine Imaginaries, Prison Interiors

argue that there is nowhere quite like the USA. The historical lineage of abandonment, so often defined by the colour line (Du Bois 1903), runs from the cotton plantations through the southern dustbowl and into the Midwest rustbelt of the 1970s. It ends in the New Orleans of Katrina and the Californian gulag, with the USA accounting for one quarter of the world's prison population from only 5% of the world's population.

In this chapter, I take an autoethnographic approach to examine the ways in which men's experience of imprisonment resonates with wider masculine projects in the imaginary constitution of society (Castoriadis 1997). Drawing from both empirical resources and personal experience, I consider how broader political structures, ethical affects and social ontologies can be paradoxically revealed by being confined inside prison.

Borstal Boys and Beyond

One of the first things I was told by a prison officer, after entering HMP Norwich in 1982, was that I had no rights. I think he only mentioned this because my conviction had some low key political ramifications locally, and he thought I might be a trouble maker. I'd received a three-month custodial sentence for incitement to commit arson, by publishing, in 1981, a slightly incendiary fanzine, just before riots erupted in the streets of Brixton in south London.[1] He quite rightly saw that I wasn't a typical short-term prisoner arriving for a spell behind bars, a spell designed to 'dis-incentivise' a taste for persistent petty theft or minor episodes of violence, the usual reasons for such a sentence. He didn't know how little trouble I could make. I was extremely anxious, wary and confused, and my main priority was to endure the short spell within prison walls without coming to further harm. In that respect, I was much more typical.

I have written elsewhere in greater detail about how my stint in HMP Norwich was a carceral experience I was happy to forget until I started researching prison life (Earle 2016). Since then, my first-hand experience of imprisonment, albeit brief and in the distant past, has become increasingly salient to the way I think about prison and masculinities. Part of the reason for this is that a research project took me to the village of Borstal on the north Kent coast where the original and eponymous prison camp for wayward young men had been established in 1908. Borstals, as these prison camps came to be known, spread across England and much of the British Empire over the next 50 years. As an ethnographic momentum developed in the project and I started to write about the research, it felt like it would take a conscious effort to keep history and biography apart, and that if I did, the result would be dishonest and epistemologically incomplete.

By 2006 when I started my research, the old north Kent Borstal had become Her Majesty's Young Offender Institution (HMYOI) Rochester, a place where about 400 young men aged 18–21 served their sentence before being released or moved on to the adult male prison system. Next to it was the new model, the Medway Secure Training Centre, opened in 1998 as the latest and even more enlightened form of incarceration for troubled and/or troublesome children. Medway STC was a place I had visited soon after it opened, when a child I worked with as a youth justice social worker in the London borough of Lambeth was placed there under a court order. In 2016 the director of Medway STC resigned after the violent abuse of boys at the centre by staff was exposed by a BBC television programme screened in 2015. It is another thread linking the past with the present, places with people, combining to propel me towards autoethnographic methods (Adams et al. 2015; Bochner 2007).

Borstal. Borstals. Borstal Boys. *Borstal Boy*. These are words that have become synonymous with the punishment and discipline of young men in England, and conjure troubling visions of civilising projects spanning the English countryside and the British Empire. This is how the British penologist Alexander Paterson imagined the Borstal boy in the 1930s:

> '…by the end of his training…he will be able to keep any sort of job, however laborious and monotonous it may be. Work arduous and continuous, is the best preparation for the life that ensues… It is the duty of every Borstal officer to preach the gospel of work, not because it is easy or healthy or interesting, but because it is the condition of an honest life'. (Paterson 1932) The Principles [of Borstal], 1932, quoted in Fox (1952: 373)

Borstals have been described as 'the projection of that wholly admirable man, Sir Alexander Paterson'(Alper 1968: 7), a projection that extended to colonial Burma and beyond (Brown 2007). In the country where I was born, Ghana, Borstal Institutions and Industrial Schools were the principle instrument for intervening in the lives of young men until 2003, when the Juvenile Justice Act finally replaced the colonial terminology of the pre-independence Gold Coast state (Ayete-Nyampong 2015; Earle 2015).

From the country I owe my passport, Ireland, there is Brendan Behan's (1958) autobiographical account of how, as a teenage volunteer for the Irish Republican Army, he was arrested and sent to a Borstal. With his description of the 'red and white and pity-coloured flashes' beaten out of him by the blows of the Borstal wardens, *Borstal Boy* established a special place in the public imagination for this peculiarly English institution. Behan's experience is eerily close to that captured on film by the BBC's undercover reporter. What the hidden camera caught on screen in 2015, Behan put into words in 1953:

> My head spun and burned and pained and I wondered would it happen again. I forgot and felt another smack, and forgot, and another smack, and another, and moved, and was held by a steadying, almost kindly hand, and another, and my sight was a vision of red and white and pity coloured flashes. (Behan 1958: 33)

Borstals nimbly combined the athletic ethos and muscular moralism of the English public school system with one of harsh punishments, designed for the benefit of the less privileged and less willing; working-class young men denied access to its system of virtues by an accident of birth. *Borstal Boy* could only have been written by an Irishman who saw its class structures and ambivalent obsessions, with the clear eye of an outsider to whom the colours of the Union Jack (red, white and blue) were also the colours of the 'butcher's apron'.

In the place I call home, England, Borstals are, in most respects, simply distant, semi-forgotten history in that strangely disconnected English, or more properly Whig, sense of being part of a slightly dark past that has given way to an indisputably enlightened present. In 2006 HMYOI Rochester had several architectural traces of its former glory: the imposing brick arch of its front gate and, inside, a series of barrack-style brick buildings and a capacious chapel. The swimming pool that was testimony to its Edwardian predilection for healthy outdoor activity sat empty, neglected and overgrown just beyond the freshly extended and tarmacked car park.

Early in my fieldwork at HMYOI Rochester, a prison officer remarked on the transitional characteristics of the young men inside:

> That's what makes this age group[18–21 years olds] so difficult. Some are just so… so difficult. Especially the 18 year olds. They are the worst I think. Still, emotionally, children really. But in a man's body. I think it's after 21, about 24 I reckon, that you notice change, a bit of sense emerging. (HMYOI Rochester Prison Officer, Unrecorded conversation, Fieldnotes 2nd August 2006)

In an earlier paper (Earle 2011), I develop a gendered analysis of young men's experience of penal confinement at HMYOI Rochester and explore aspects of their sense of who they are in a rapidly changing world. Long-standing shifts in the male labour market since the late 1970s have led to endemic, large-scale unemployment, particularly among young men in the UK, that would once have been regarded a social atrocity. These conditions have, in turn, fuelled a variety of so-called crisis masculinities (Chapman and Rutherford 1989). These masculinities evolve in cultures of prolonged and impoverished adolescence in which some young men's identities get locked into 'the local'. The 'postcode pride' so central to the identity of many of the young men in HMYOI Rochester includes a revolving set of locations: the estate, varieties of homelessness, life 'on road', criminal justice agencies and social services (Earle 2011). Theirs are social relations that may be permeated by violence, both symbolic and physical, and diverse forms of criminalised activity in which excessive drug and alcohol consumption becomes a means of gaining prestige for a masculine identity otherwise bereft of any social value (Alexander 2000). As Morrison (1996: 116) notes in a society which does not require a high level of manual labour, prisons tend to occupy a position of periodic punitive containment where the unwanted men of the economic system are pushed around and recycled: "The simple fact is that those who are currently sent to prison are largely unwanted outside the prison wall and have no skills which are in demand".

The dominant and authoritarian white masculinities of the nineteenth century that openly asserted the patriarchal virtues of 'correct' and virtuous manhood in Borstal Institutions have been destabilised and somewhat discredited, if not dislodged. The explicit gender focus that prevailed upon men to behave in certain ways in Edwardian England was quite candid by today's standards of anxiety and agonising about what constitutes acceptable masculinity (Roper and Tosh 1991). Suitable 'manhood' was widely assumed to be an accomplishment that required explicit guidance, training even; the Borstal Institution openly sought to redress any failures in this accomplishment with an emphasis on 'masculine' activities, health and hierarchy.

Imaginary Masculinities: Mobile and Medieval

In HMYOI Rochester, I identified three themes as distinct but interrelated in the young men's social relations. The first two adopt the young men's invention of the terms 'on road' and 'my boys'. The third, 'postcode pride', is my own but simply refers to the urgently experienced sense of locality among the young men. The term 'on road' resonates powerfully with a paradigmatic form of American masculinity articulated around concepts of freedom, motion and adventure (Ehrenreich 1983). It evokes a masculinity based on flight from domestic settings or commitments and is frequently defined against what women are supposed to stand for in the Western masculine imagination—entrapment, stasis and care. Johnny Cash, quoted above, appears to be particularly fluent in the discourse.

The study I was involved at HMYOI Rochester found the romanticised identification with getting around unencumbered by domestic responsibilities was powerfully evoked in the young men's phrasing and accounts of their lives (Earle 2011, 2014; Phillips 2012). Within the enforced stasis of prison environments, these aspirant, kinetic masculinities were intensely constrained but repeatedly invoked as a kind of ideal state of being, beyond the walls and without walls. It is a self-image entirely consistent with a modernist imagination. Rather than Baudelaire's passively pedestrian 'flâneur', these young men reinvent the vagabond for new times in the city's villages and inhabit the spaces and places between them (Massey 1991; Said 1990).

What was clear from the frequency of the occurrence of the two terms, 'on road' and 'my boys' in the interview data and men's conversations, is that networks of masculine association and friendship were central to many of the young men's social relations and identities, both inside the prison and outside. Here is an example of the way the term featured in the interviews conducted for the study. 'Ajay' is referring to the boasting talk that some of the young men indulged in:

> All the time [they talk], the same things, what they do on road, who they chill with, how big they are, how many straps they got, fire arms, how much money they're worth, how many girls they own, just the same kind of things. They're trying to big themselves up and the people they hang round, they're trying to big their people up, all on road.

Another young man, 'Brian', put it like this: "Well I haven't seen no loyalty in here compared to what I'm used to seeing out on road between me and my boys, you know what I mean".

My interest in a masculine register implicit to the terms 'on road' and 'my boys' derives from Beier's (1985: 9) accounts of vagrancy in medieval England:

> Vagrants were a menace to the social order because they broke with the accepted norms of family life. If the ideal was the patriarchal household, they had no place in it, and for that reason they were considered pariahs.

This prompted a mostly fruitless search for literature on medieval masculinities, a literature which seems to be in an early stage of development. Karras (2003) focuses on the characteristics of European masculinities in three different settings: knighthood, 'the university' and 'the craftsman's workshop'. Unfortunately, falling outside of her remit are the 'master-less men', peasants and agricultural labourers that Beier's study was preoccupied with. However, Rose (1993) reports from an online academic symposium on medieval masculinities. He depicts patterns of itinerant masculine collectivity and 'modalities of being' that have striking correspondence with the accounts of HMYOI Rochester's young men.

According to Rose (1993), to be a man outside the elite in early medieval Europe, it was important to be attached to a 'powerful other', usually in small localised, martial hierarchies, known as *mannerbund*. The *mannerbund* was a crude peripatetic form of virile collectivity offering young men some access to power or at least some level of protection from others. In doing this, young men developed direct, kin-like ties with powerful/heroic men. (See Ehrenreich 2011 and Theweleit 1987 for the mythic appeal these masculinities held for fascist ideology and German Nazism.) They were propelled to do this, Rose argues, by a historical conjunction that witnessed the declining capacity of village communities to provide security, and the impotence of yet to be fully formed urban and State collectivities to offer an alternative. The analysis presented by Rose of the attractions of violent virility and martial activity to these medieval marginal men resonates powerfully with contemporary accounts, critical and otherwise, of young men in gangs (Pitts 2008) and the thrill-seeking, urban edgeworkers discussed by Hallsworth and Silverstone (2009).

Analysis of this kind of historical conjuncture is a feature of Wacquant's (2007, 2009a, b) analysis of contemporary penality, in which certain aspects of a rapidly globalising twenty-first-century modernity are recognised as analogous to those of the pre-modern sixteenth century (see also Retort 2004; Hall 2012). The twenty-first century, it seems, is likely to be an amalgam of rampant nineteenth-century capitalism and sixteenth-century medievalism. It is as if, as Zizek (2015: 10) is so fond of musing, "in a changed historical constellation, a remnant of the pre-modern past can start to function as the symbol of what is traumatically unbearable in extreme modernity".

Armoured Bodies, Penal Masculinities in HMYOI Rochester

During my research in HMYOI Rochester, I was also struck by the young men's descriptions of, and investments in, a type of heavily muscled upper body strength that they referred to as 'hench'. Men's bodies, and particularly young men's bodies, have become established in a new kind of representational practice in popular culture and personal identity work. There is a widespread inclination, particularly among working-class young men, to define themselves through their bodies because of the ways in which social and economic marginality has otherwise reduced their capacity to shape their environment or futures (Gill et al. 2005).

A prison sentence is in itself an explicitly coercive identity project, designed for conformity to rules and obedience to the law as much as rehabilitation. Although men's bodies are no longer the explicit target they were during the Borstal training regime, they remain central to a sense of self-assertion and self-possession. For some young men, muscle and muscularity become almost fetishised as a form of display against the disempowerment and overpowerment that a prison sentence attempts to deliver. Hours of physical training in the prison cell are complemented by activities in the prison gym to present vibrant health, physicality and a well-honed, hard, sculpted body. It is a defiant rejection of the disabling conditions of confinement.

Although an element of relatively straightforward vanity and concern for their health propelled the masculine body projects at HMYOI Rochester, they can also tell us more about the ideological landscape the men inhabit. As Bordo (2003) has argued in relation to women's bodies and society, the shaping of bodies always tells a deeper story about what is dominant and dominating in our material culture. In 'hench', there is the heavy grammar of masculine individualism, strong against the world and the familiar symbolism of a mind-body dualism. The muscular body, armoured and ready for action, the mind less overtly valued and pushed into recess. In prison the grindingly dull routines seem to foster this characteristically masculine polarisation of physical activity against mental passivity (Gill et al. 2005).

The hard-looking sculpted body so highly prized by many young men in HMYOI Rochester (and elsewhere) is one that is apparently impervious to harm, full of extravagantly showy body strength. Generating this semblance of invulnerability is hard, time-consuming work that provides men with a sense of control and potency the experience of incarceration is designed to diminish. In the process, body shape and appearance become the primary locus of affect and experience, the principal means of representing the self to the world (Bordo 2003). It is a defiant gesture of ontological assertion—"I am what I appear to be; no more, no less".

This investment, especially by heterosexual men, in surface definition and appearance is often at the expense of interiors, ambiguity and metaphysical resources. It can foster a mind/body dualism which exacerbates the inner self/outer appearance dichotomy by stressing the image of physical control, a central characteristic of hegemonic masculinity. In prison, the sense of control and self is reduced to mastery of the body, a masculine essence of subjective authenticity (Gill et al. 2005) in perpetual dissonance with the prison's project of control. Even though prisoners might 'live in their head' (James 2013), they often let their bodies do the talking.

There is a stoic, 'trench warfare', mentality imposed by 'doing time' in prison that men may adopt, a way of 'toughing it out', or outdoing the system against all the odds. It is a familiar vision of iconic, heroic masculinity populated by a handful of (relatively) well-known prison survivors, such as Jimmy Boyle, John McVicar and, in film, the characters in *The Shawshank Redemption* and *Papillon* and, more recently, *Starred Up*. They are images of men that tend to perpetuate rather than challenge masculine fantasies to good ideological effect. As Connell (1995) points out, the imagery of hegemonic masculinity involves few actual men, but relies, instead, on models so remote from the possibility of everyday achievement that they remain an unobtainable ideal. Few men live the lives of the screen hero, but many collaborate in sustaining or legitimating those images of masculinity and thus reproduce its patterns of masculine power (Pfeil 1995) and the distribution of its patriarchal dividend[2] (Connell 1995). That this identification with brute strength continues so seamlessly in prison should alert us to the value of taking a gendered analysis of men's imprisonment more seriously.

Being Inside: Losing Without Choosing

One of the principle myths behind both the retributive and deterrent justifications for prison is that it is radically discontinuous with masculine life outside, as Cash, above, describes with his customary eloquence. However, inside prison the relative absence of women, the totalisation of 'public space' and the ensuing constraints on privacy, sensitivity, vulnerability and caring are not necessarily so deeply discontinuous with the lives of many men. Feminist penal theorists critique the masculine and patriarchal authority of women's prison regimes as producing a process of infantilisation among women by depriving them of feminine domestic, private identities and simultaneously rendering them helplessly dependent on a narrow range of stereotypically feminine rehabilitative identities (Carlen 1983; Carlen and Tchaikovsky 1996). For male prisoners, that same authority may also provoke more fundamentally oedipal and existential reactions. Prison, both symbolically and materially, reinforces and validates the process Freud identified as the 'unconscious' becoming part of the alienated self, in retreat and refusing responsibility of 'being for others' as Sartre had it (Connell 1983). In this section, I explore some of these existential dimensions of men's imprisoned life by reflecting on my own experience, the insights of Erwin James and the writing of the formerly incarcerated French philosopher, Bernard Stiegler.

Erwin James served a long prison sentence before developing a successful career as a writer (2003, 2005, 2016). Few others can write on prison with such emotional force, care and sensitivity to its complexities, peculiarities and pains. In a Foreword to a collection of prisoners' writings, he (2013: 7) points out "[W]hoever you are and however long your sentence, in prison you live inside your head". Convict criminologists as social scientists with direct, first-hand experience of imprisonment are well placed to address this aspect of men's experience more closely than most (Earle 2016). Men's interior, subjective worlds are thrown back at them by force of circumstance in a prison sentence, exposing them to both new and familiar challenges of making life liveable, inside prison and into the future when they are out of its clutches.

Prison confronts you with the impossibility of choosing many of the fundamentals of life—your clothes, your food, your home, your friends, the use of your time (Stiegler 2008). The simple question of how to look after your basic needs for food, shelter and hygiene is radically repositioned by the fact that the prison has assumed the elementary functions of welfare provision. These domestic, frequently maternal, roles are radically reconfigured in a paternal register subordinated to the primary penal function of delivering pain. A prison sentence is designed to punish, and punishments hurt the person on whom they are imposed (as well as many others). The symbolism of the liberal, post-war welfare state as the nanny state, the surrogate nurturing mother, is replaced by that of the disapproving, disciplinarian father (Hage 2003). From being a part of family and social networks, however strained or supportive, malign or benign, as a prisoner you belong unequivocally and primarily to the state. It holds you, and in its grip you are fed, clothed and provided with shelter, but excluded from the world of society and deprived of liberty and property. Once you become a prisoner, you become the property of the state. You are brought down close to a feudal form of bondage, being chattel, that is, being owned by someone. This relationship is complex and involves basic functional care and concern, but it is a condition of ownership, of being possessed. For imprisoned men, this relationship is experientially relatively obscure in the modern prison environments I am familiar with, but is no less real for all that.

If you are imprisoned, you are taken away from those you care for and that care for you—your children, your lovers, your family, your friends, your work colleagues, your neighbours. Even if and when your domestic or intimate relations are few, or strained, fragile or fraught, or worse, the secondary pains of imprisonment imposed on family members close or distant have only recently come to be included within penal scholarship (Comfort 2008; Condry et al. 2016). Convict criminologists' direct experience of negotiating these pains and working through their implications can contribute to this new scholarship. To what extent, for example, and how theorised, are our academic interests, careers and appetites conditioned or supported by these personal networks? How are the ruptures to them repaired, remade or abandoned through the transition from prison to university? How, if at all, are these experiences analogous to other transitions?

In prison, even the most widely accepted forms of masculine domesticity, such as gardening and DIY, are often denied to most prisoners. All the treasured fundamentals of the Victorian vision of how a man should be, visions that were channelled through a domestic revolution which trafficked men's identities between the twin poles of 'work-life' and 'home-life', are disrupted and repositioned by a prison sentence (Tosh 1999, 2005; Roper and Tosh 1991). The structured engagement of men with female regimes and power around the home, with children and comfort, are replaced with austere, stripped back, homosocial regulation. Hard time, indeed. By bringing family networks firmly back into the picture, not simply as instruments of rehabilitation but as participants subjected to, and implicated in, the pains of punishment, Condry et al. (2016) have begun to widen the field of opportunity for convict criminology's epistemological contributions.

Out of This World

As I indicated earlier, one of the first things a prison officer said to me in HMP Norwich was "basically, you've got no rights in here. It's not quite that simple, but that's pretty much how it is". Imprisonment institutes an ironic form of self-dispossession where one's rights to oneself are removed and held elsewhere, to be returned, with conditions attached. The political abstraction of the social contract and sovereignty becomes a practical reality for the prisoner, an object lesson in the politics of modernity.

The right to yourself, and its removal, was something that confronted Bernard Stiegler when, as a young man, he served a five-year prison sentence for robbery in France from 1978 to 1983. For Stiegler (2008: 22), it was such an intensely disorienting and profoundly disturbing experience that it propelled him into the arms of phenomenology, philosophy and politics, for survival and comfort:

> I discovered this political theory and practice by chance and by accident, long before studying it in the works of Husserl: I *deduced* it from the situation, I practiced it, in a way, empirically and savagely.

The stage-managed withdrawal of his personal agency by the prison left the robber feeling robbed, violated and undone. Being in prison, Stiegler discovered, takes away the usual human capacity to inhabit a place and to inform its shape with your own: "I no longer lived in the world, but rather in the absence of a world". In phenomenological terms, an active relationship between place and self is the fundamental source of life (Merleau-Ponty 1962), and although its removal in prison is not total, it is very powerful. It is a kind of induced lifelessness that is referred to in the sociological literature as the 'weight' and 'tightness' of a prison sentence (Crewe 2011). It is a state of suspended animation in which life goes on because it is still, just, better than the alternative. For Stiegler, these profound personal ramifications were also intensely political. The absence prison creates, he suggests, is not the mere withdrawal of sociality from the individual, it reveals some of the fundamental features around which modern capitalist society is conceived.

For men in prison, the lack of creative, transactional possibilities between themselves and the immediate environment throws them into themselves, into their heads, as Erwin puts it. The result, according to Steigler (2009), is a profoundly alienating individuation. The ideal man individuated by prison is discrete from his environment, closed off, ontologically still and stable, like the prison. At one level, this is akin to the stoicism described by Toch (1998) as a form of adaptation, but at another, it is a form of half-death, a sacrificing of the vital life, the kind of life lived in a social world which involves perpetual amendment around the flux of social and environmental interaction. It exchanges a multiple world one occupies *with oneself* for a world simply *of oneself*. Stiegler (2008: 24; 32) refers to this perverse transformation as 'the virtue of prison'. It is built on the way prison experience reinforces the classic ontological binaries of Inside and Outside, Spirit and Body, the real and the ideal, or in Stiegler's own terms, 'time and technics' (Stiegler 1998). It lurks forcefully in the prison cell and haunts the landings and corridors. It has all the ghostly characteristics of 'the metaphysics of presence' that Derrida (1978: 279) regarded as 'a full presence which is beyond the reach of play'.

Stiegler organised his prison sentence around reading philosophy, with correspondence tuition from Gerard Granel at the University of Toulouse-Le-Mirail. His prior commitments to the Communist Party he concedes were 'not philosophical in origin', and his erstwhile dogmatic 'materialism' tended towards the Marxist dismissal of philosophy as naive idealism: "The philosophers have interpreted the world in various ways, the point is to change it" (Marx 1969). His five years inside transformed that perspective: "I cannot say that today I am a materialist in that sense, but I must say that I remain a materialist in the sense of a materialism that does not deny that the spirit, while not reducible to matter, is always conditioned by it" (Stiegler 2008: 33). He refers to the difficulty he has in reconciling the prison source of this revelation:

> it became problematic for me to live with the occultation of my past, even if that occultation was part of my existence by choice: I wanted to play not the role of ex-convict but first of all philosopher, discretely, out of this material, in remaining faithful to it but in a sense, without citing my sources. (Stiegler 2008: 33)

The life that requires openness and engagement, that is a vulnerable life and a sociable life, is not for the prison or the men it makes. In stark contrast to the kinetic and liquid properties of modern life, the Western prison persists in stasis and immobility. The emergent social relations of modernity that Marx and Engels (1848/2014) identified with such acuity are turned around to haunt men in prison because 'all that is melted into air' becomes solid, and fluid relations 'are fast-frozen'. The prison world is thus a kind of communist nightmare in which society has withered away leaving only the state and the individual. You don't have to be a communist to find the horror of it palpable, but if you are, it hurts all the more so. Stiegler resisted his prison world by investing deeply in the study of philosophy. Though he didn't turn to criminology, Stiegler's subsequent academic career is a kind of exemplar of the form convict criminology might take, synthesising experience, higher academic study and onward theoretical development.

Existential Staging of the Prison World

When you are in prison, the implications of the daily practice of life in prison pass you by, and it is perhaps only afterwards that it is possible to make sense of it at a different level of comprehension, unless like Stiegler you immediately adopt an overtly philosophical stance to manage and resist the colonisation of your soul. Some of the subtle habituations of prison life ambushed me only on release from my short sentence. Even after just three months inside, I found myself thrown off balance, literally and physically, by the scale and speed of objects in motion, particularly cars and buses, but even people. Everything seemed to move so fast.

It was an unexpectedly physical reaction to the kinetic dimensions of social life that the prison had stilled. The release into chosen rather than frozen relations was sublime.

Prisons are a form of involuntary, immobile human commune where you are forced to live in the kind of close proximity with others that fascinates philosophers and political scientists. Sykes (1958) observed that for prisoners one of the hardest things to bear was being around other prisoners all the time. Prisons, with their potential for solitary confinement ever-present, confront the prisoner with the classic polarities of existential ambivalence: hell is other people and hell is no other people at all. In prison, aged 24, I wasn't much prone to the existential reflection so systematically practised by Stiegler. On the other hand, Samuel Beckett's *Waiting for Godot*, studied at school and memorised for performance, began to make considerably better sense than it did to me at the time. More recently, as a criminologist returning to prison as an ethnographic researcher concerned to integrate social theory into my work, I increasingly found myself recognising, post hoc, in my prison experience various features of modern social life and the classic existential dilemmas that Beckett played with. There are certainly no bars in Godot's staging, only a solitary tree, but Vladimir and Estragon are famously inert, bound to each other and a common predicament. Their proximity to each other is all they have, a destiny ahead of them, somewhere, perhaps. Perhaps not: "Time always takes us where we do not want to go" (Simone Weil, cited in Negri 2015).

Abandoning Prisons and Protecting Ourselves

One of the penal dilemmas that Joe Sim (1994) identified in respect of men and the masculinities prison worlds foster is that prisons are much more in the business of ideological reproduction than personal rehabilitation. The rehabilitation of men as 'men' in prison is likely to emphasise and reinforce notions of personal self-sufficiency, virility and independence, virtues that are central to hegemonic masculinity. Responding to the perverse combinations of homosocial familiarity, gendered estrangement, social abandonment and penal inclusion, men, particularly younger men, are encouraged towards a personal quest for transcendence, to move on, and outward beyond themselves into a new, rehabilitated identity—fit for work, or, in the absence of work, at least family life. As Jefferson (1995) notes, transcendence through some 'extraordinary act' of endurance or daring is one of masculinity's ultimate prized values, the mythic hero transformed by and through adversity. This is a staple ingredient of prison mythology. As men, we find comfort and excitement in fantasies of transcendental omnipotence and invulnerability. In prison, these can become the 'bad soliloquys' of individuation (Stiegler 2009) as much as they become the redemption narratives of desistance.

The prison world presents the man in prison with an implicit sense of being and becoming, and it can be creatively unsettled. The dominant correctional, retributive and penal theme in men's prisons has a distinctly violent, paternal register, but within the walls, the irrefutable interdependencies of human vulnerability (Gilson 2014; Butler and Gambetti 2016) are also exposed and experienced directly by anyone there, prisoner or guard. They reveal the inadequacy of the Enlightenment's penal vision, it's model of 'man' "sprung out of the earth, and suddenly, like mushrooms, come into full maturity without all kind of engagement to each other" (Thomas Hobbes, cited in Benhabib 1987).

Paterson's Borstal institutions were based on the cultivation of virtues anchored in particular articulations of Empire, race, class and gender in a matrix of care and control. The various cults of manliness to which Paterson contributed sublimated complex social and sexual arrangements that the historian Peter Gay (1993) refers to as 'alibis'. These 'alibis' gathered unconscious desires, political projects and social ambitions and channelled them into institutions, such as public schools and Borstals, that are still easily recognisable today in HMYOI Rochester. All too often, the prison world gathers up men with no place to go, who then find themselves in the last place in the patriarchal order. Abandoned but possessed, they find what makes a man a man in the cold intimacies and calculating rationalities of prison life where a million things are snuffed out. It may not be their life, but it is a man's life.

Acknowledgements The author would like to thank the editors for helpful feedback on an earlier draft of this paper and acknowledge their contribution to improving its final form.

Notes

1. The 1981 riots in Brixton, Bristol and elsewhere across England were a response to excessive and repressive policing of areas with large minority ethnic populations. Although not all those involved were black, they were widely perceived as a reaction to racist policing and the policies of the newly elected Conservative government of Margaret Thatcher.
2. This refers to the material pay-off, unevenly distributed, but accruing to men at the expense of women, as a result of their dominant position in global politics and control of the means of violence.

References

Adams, T., Holman Jones, S., & Ellis, C. (2015). *Autoethnography*. New York: Oxford University Press.

Alexander, C. (2000). *The Asian gang: Ethnicity, identity, masculinity*. Oxford: Berghahn Books.

Alper, B. (1968). Borstal briefly revisited – Recollections and some related reflections. *British Journal of Criminology, 6*(12), 6–19.

Ayete-Nyampong, L. (2015). Changing hats – Transiting between practitioner and researcher roles. In R. Earle, D. Drake, & J. Sloan (Eds.), *The Palgrave handbook of prison ethnography*. Basingstoke: Palgrave.

Behan, B. (1958). *Borstal boy*. London: Hutchison.

Beier, A. L. (1985). *Masterless men: The vagrancy problem in England 1560–1640*. London: Methuen.

Benhabib, S. (1987). The generalised and concrete other: The Kohlberg/Gilligan controversy and feminist theory. In S. Benhabib & D. Cornell (Eds.), *Feminism as critique: On the politics of gender*. Minneapolis: University of Minnesota Press.

Bochner, A. (2007). Notes toward an ethics of memory in autoethnographic inquiry. In N. K. Denzin & M. D. Giardina (Eds.), *Ethical futures in qualitative research: Decolonizing the politics of knowledge* (pp. 197–208). Walnut Creek: Left Coast Press.

Bordo, S. (2003). *Unbearable weight: Feminism, western culture and the body*. Berkeley: University of California Press.

Brown, D. (2007). A commissioner calls: Alexander Paterson and colonial Burma's prisons. *Journal of Southeast Asian Studies, 38*(2), 293–308.

Butler, J., & Gambetti, Z. (2016). *Vulnerability in resistance*. Durham: Duke University Press.

Carlen, P. (1983). *Women's imprisonment*. London: Routledge and Kegan Paul.

Carlen, P., & TchaiKovsky, C. (1996). Women's imprisonment in England at the end of the twentieth century. In R. Matthews & P. Francis (Eds.), *Prisons 2000*. London: Macmillan.

Castoriadis, C. (1997). *The imaginary institution of society*. Cambridge: MIT Press.

Chapman, R., & Rutherford, J. (1989). *Male order: Unwrapping masculinity*. London: Lawrence and Wishart.

Comfort, M. (2008). The best seven years I could'a done': The reconstruction of imprisonment as rehabilitation. In P. Carlen (Ed.), *Imaginary penalties* (pp. 252–274). Cullompton: Willan Publishing.

Condry, R., Kotova, A., & Minson, S. (2016). Social injustice and collateral damage: The families and children of prisoners. In B. Crewe & Y. Jewkes (Eds.), *The handbook of prisons*. Abingdon: Routledge.

Connell, R. W. (1983). *Which way is up – Essays on sex, class and culture*. Sydney: Allen & Unwin.

Connell, R. W. (1995). *Masculinities*. Cambridge: Polity.

Crewe, B. (2011). Depth, weight, tightness: Revisiting the pains of imprisonment. *Punishment and Society, 13*(5), 509–529. for special issue on 'Revisiting the pains of imprisonment', In B. Crewe, Y. Jewkes.

Derrida, J. (1978). *Writing and difference*. Chicago: University of Chicago Press.

Du Bois, W. E. B. (1994/1903). *The souls of Black folk*. New York: Dover Publications.

Earle, R. (2011). Boys' zone stories: Perspectives from a young men's prison. *Criminology and Criminal Justice, 11*(2), 129–143.

Earle, R. (2014). Inside white – Racism, social relations and ethnicity in an English prison. In C. Phillips & C. Webster (Eds.), *New directions in race, ethnicity and crime*. London: Routledge.

Earle, R. (2015). Of prison ethnography – Introduction to part III. In R. Earle, D. Drake, & J. Sloan (Eds.), *The Palgrave handbook of prison ethnography*. Basingstoke: Palgrave.

Earle, R. (2016). *Convict criminology – Inside and out*. Bristol: Policy Press.

Ehrenreich, B. (1983). *The hearts of men: American dreams and the flight from commitment*. London: Pluto.

Ehrenreich, B. (2011). *Blood rites: The origins and history of the passions of war*. London: Granta.

Fox, L. (1952). *The English prison and Borstal systems*. London: Routledge.

Gay, P. (1993). *The cultivation of hatred: The bourgeois experience- Victoria to Freud*. New York: W.W. Norton.
Gill, R., Henwood, K., & McLean, C. (2005). Body projects and the regulation of normative masculinity. *Body & Society, 11*(1), 37–62.
Gilson, E. (2014). *The ethics of vulnerability: A feminist analysis of social life and practice*. Abingdon: Routledge.
Hage, G. (2003). *Paranoid nationalism: Searching for hope in a shrinking society*. London: Merlin.
Hall, S. (2012). *Theorising crime and deviance – A new perspective*. London: Sage.
Hallsworth, S., & Silverstone, D. (2009). 'That's life innit': A British perspective on guns, crime and social order. *Criminology and Criminal Justice, 9*(3), 359–377.
James, E. (2003). *A life inside: A prisoner's notebook*. London: Guardian Books.
James, E. (2005). *The home stretch: From prison to parole*. London: Guardian Books.
James, E. (2013). Foreword. In G. Creer, H. Priest, & T. Spargo (Eds.), *Free to write: Prison voices past and present*. Wirral: Headland Publications.
James, E. (2016). *Redeemable: A memoir of darkness and hope*. London: Bloomsbury Circus.
Jefferson, T. (1995). Theorising masculine subjectivity' prison. In T. Newburn & E. Stanko (Eds.), *Just boys doing business*. Abingdon: Routledge.
Karras, R. (2003). *From boys to men: Formations of masculinity in late medieval Europe*. Philadelphia: University of Pennsylvania Press.
Marx, K. (1969). *Theses on Feuerbach (thesis 11)*. Moscow: Progress Publishers.
Marx, K., & Engels, F. (1848/2014). *The communist manifesto*. London: Verso.
Massey, D. (1991, June). A global sense of place. *Marxism Today, 38*, 24–29.
Merleau-Ponty, M. (1962). *Phenomenology of perception* (C. Smith, Trans.). London: Routledge & Kegan Paul.
Morrison, W. (1996). Modernity, imprisonment and social solidarity. In R. Matthews & P. Francis (Eds.), *Prisons 2000*. London: Macmillan.
Negri, A. (2015). *Pipeline – Letters from prison*. Cambridge: Polity Press.
Pfeil, F. (1995). *White guys – Studies in postmodern domination and difference*. London: Verso.
Pitts, J. (2008). *Reluctant gangsters: The changing face of youth crime: The changing shape of youth crime*. Cullompton: Willan.
Retort. (2004, May–June). Afflicted powers: The state, the spectacle and September 11. *New Left Review, 27*, 5–21.
Roper, M., & Tosh, J. (1991). *Manful assertions. Masculinities in Britain since 1800*. London: Routledge.

Rose, G. (1993). *Medieval masculinities discussion archive*. http://www8.georgetown.edu/departments/medieval/labyrinth/e-center/interscripta/archive2.htmlwww.masculintites. Accessed 24 Oct 2008.

Said, E. (1990). Narrative and geography. *New Left Review, 180*, 81–100.

Sim, J. (1994). Tougher than the rest: Men in prison. In T. Newburn & E. Stanko (Eds.), *Just boys doing business*. Abingdon: Routledge.

Stiegler, B. (1998). *Technics and time: The fault of Epimetheus no. 1*. New York: Stanford University Press.

Stiegler, B. (2008). *Acting out*. Stanford: Stanford University Press.

Sykes, G. (1958). *The society of captives: A study of a maximum security prison*. Princeton: Princeton University Press.

Theweleit, K. (1987). *Male fantasies volume 1: Women, floods, bodies*. Cambridge: Polity Press.

Toch, H. (1998). Hypermasculinity and prison violence. Masculinities and violence. In L. Bowker (Ed.), *Masculinities and violence*. Thousand Oaks: Sage.

Tosh, J. (1999). *A man's place: Masculinity and the middle-class home in Victorian England*. Yale: Yale University Press.

Tosh, J. (2005). Masculinities in an industrialising society, 1800–1914. *Journal of British Studies, 44*, 330–342.

Wacquant, L. (2007). *Urban outcasts: A comparative sociology of advanced marginality*. Cambridge: Polity.

Wacquant, L. (2009a). *Punishing the poor*. Durham: Duke University Press.

Wacquant, L. (2009b). *Prisons of poverty*. Minneapolis: University of Minnesota Press.

Zizek, S. (2015). *Trouble in paradise: From the end of history to the end of capitalism*. London: Penguin.

4

"They're All Up in the Gym and All That, Tops Off, Fake Tan." Embodied Masculinities, Bodywork and Resistance Within Two British Prisons

Matthew Maycock

Introduction

Prison masculinities are manifest themselves in a plurality of ways (Maycock et al., Manuscript under review) that include hegemonic (Connell 1995; Connell and Messerschmidt 2005) as well as inclusive (Anderson 2008, 2009; Anderson and McGuire 2010) masculinities. Such presentations have implications for embodied masculinities within prison. Following Gill et al. (2005), I consider a range of bodily modifications, reflecting Shilling's (2003) insight that the more we know about bodies, the more it is possible to change them. These embodied efforts by the men in this study make significant contributions to the performance of 'emergent masculinities' (Inhorn and Wentzell 2011) within prison.

M. Maycock (✉)
The Scottish Prison Service, Edinburgh, UK

The importance of bodies for constructs of masculinity strengthens the view that 'looking' masculine is critical, in addition to 'doing' masculinity (Connell 1983; Drummond 2011). This chapter considers the ways in which the prison context shapes both the 'looking' and the 'doing' of male prisoners' bodies, using data collected from two high-security men's prisons in Britain. I initially examine accounts of the sorts of bodies that prisoners desire and aspire to achieve. I then consider the ways in which specific manifestations of 'bodywork' (Dworkin 1974) and associated performances of certain embodied masculinities constitute resistance to the prison regime.

Embodied Masculinities

The conventional sex/gender dichotomy found in much of the literature on gender has several well-recognised problems. Most fundamentally, such analysis often precludes any focus on the body and its significance in understanding gendered identities. Significant masculinity theorists have engaged with this question, with Connell stating "…gender is a social practice that constantly refers to bodies and what bodies do …it is not social practice reduced to the body" (2005, 71). The following discussion is situated within a framework in which bodies are themselves socially constructed and not 'fixed', following Moore who suggests that "bodies have no sex outside of discourse, in which they are designated" (Moore 1994, 177).

The body, then, becomes a site of potential resistance to certain discourses at certain times. This conceptualisation permits an understanding in which the body is shaped and experienced by gender, rather than the other way around (Moore 2007, 8). Connell has written extensively on the male body, and she and Messerschmidt suggest that: "we need to understand that bodies are both objects of social practice and agents in social practice" (Connell and Messerschmidt 2005, 851). The centrality of the male body to male experience has found expression in a wide range of settings and perspectives. In an analysis that alludes to the contradiction and uncertainty of such experience, Gadd outlines the ways in which bodies can be problematic for men:

> Men's bodies are sources of insecurity and feelings of inadequacy, symbolic purveyors of competence and incompetence, sites through which intimacy is experienced or thwarted. (Gadd 2003, 350)

Men's bodies have an important impact on constructs of masculinity, and vice versa, but this can be in ways that complicate and problematise masculinities. As Waquant illustrates, it is bodies of a certain type that are closely linked to some masculinities:

> …muscles are the distinctive symbol of masculinity …Surveys have shown time and again that men's self-esteem correlates highly with having a muscular upper body. (Wacquant 1995, 171)

Although there are important links between bodies and masculinity, they are not seamless, quite the contrary. As Whitehead suggests: "…many men fail to achieve a seamless, constant, symbiotic relationship between their bodies and dominant discourses of masculinity" (Whitehead 2002, 191).[1] Efforts to create the appearance of continuity between bodies and masculinity are closely associated with masculine subjectivities (Hall et al. 2007, 549).

Thus, whilst certain images and realities of bodies, and certain bodily practices, are associated with certain masculinities, they do not completely determine each other, and there are often negative consequences for having an 'ugly' or 'deviant' body (Garland-Thomson 2009; McDowell 1999). Shilling considers the interplay between bodies and social practices: "This is a dynamic relationship which involves the body both affecting and being affected by social relations" (Shilling 2003, 100). Shilling (2003, 95) also highlights the negotiation of biology in relation to some gendered assumptions, such as attributions of women as 'weak' and 'fragile', with men the opposite. In some ways the body becomes something that must be controlled and sets some of the limits of gender expectations: one must behave 'like a man' *and* have the body expected of a man. One can see this intertwining with Connell's (1995) notion of hegemonic masculinity, as part of the hegemonic position relates to certain bodily expectations that are specific to the hegemonic position.

By exploring the various ways that bodies and gendered identifies influence each other, this section has shown that bodies are a vital part of masculine identities. Therefore, bodies are an important consideration in any analysis of prison masculinities (Author, Manuscript under review).

Embodied Prison Masculinities

In his seminal work, *Discipline and Punish*, Foucault outlines the evolution of the ways in which bodies, and the control and disciplining of bodies, are central to and define the prison experience:

> …distributing individuals, fixing them in space, classifying them, extracting from them the maximum in time and forces, training their bodies, coding their continuous behaviour… constituting on them a body of knowledge that is accumulated and centralized. The general form of an apparatus intended to render individuals docile and useful, by means of precise work upon their bodies, indicated the prison institution, before the law ever defined it as die penalty par excellence. (Foucault 1979, 231)

Foucault's contribution has shaped much of the subsequent theoretical work on bodies and embodiment within criminology. For example, a number of studies principally from the USA indicate that harassment and violence are pervasive within prison contexts. These aspects of prison life in turn shape currents of embodied masculinity (cf. Rosenberg and Oswin 2015; Shabazz 2009; Tarzwell 2006). Within this interpretation of life within prison, Ricciardelli et al. (2015) illustrate the ways in which constructs of vulnerability and risk are critical factors in shaping embodied prison masculinities. For Ricciardelli et al., it is prisoners' constructs of risk that shape performances of embodied prison masculinities. Conversely, Bandyopadhyay (2006) focuses on the ways in which being in prison may in some instances undermine prisoners' masculinities, as a consequence of the collapse of the provider role given the difficulties of protecting and providing for dependants whilst in prison. These quite general reflections on embodied prison masculinities provide a context in which to situate specific embodiments within prison that are considered in more detail below.

Size, Muscularity and the 'Hard' Prison Body

A range of prison research has focused on the importance of muscularity and 'hardness' of embodied masculinities within prison, which signify masculine power in these (and other) contexts (cf. Nandi 2002; Phillips 2001; Ricciardelli et al. 2015; Sabo 1994). Size, strength and muscularity are consistent themes within prison research that has considered bodies. For example, Evans and Wallace state: "the concept of male power embodied in physical size, strength, and violence recurs [in prison]" (Evans and Wallace 2007, 494). Martos-García et al., in research located within the sports Hall of a Spanish prison, make similar observations:

> …in the sports Hall of Varoic Prison, a situated accomplishment of gender identity takes place that is directly related to notions of hegemonic masculinity that are intimately bound to the production of hard, powerful and assertive bodies. (Martos-García et al. 2009, 91)

'Hardness' as an adjective to describe male prison bodies recurs consistently within the prison literature. Sabo considers some of the manifestations of this:

> (T)here are many guises of hardness, which, inside and outside the prison culture, illustrate various ways of expressing masculinity from the honourable to the perverse. Being hard can mean that the individual is toned, strong, conditioned, fit not weak, flabby, or out of shape. A hard man cares for and respects his body. (Sabo 1994, 165–166)

Given the assumed violent and oppressive nature of the prison context, such forms of embodiment have a range of advantages, particularly in relation to being left alone or being seen as someone not to get into conflict with. Sabo goes onto state: "Being hard can also be a defence against prison violence. The hard man sends a message that he is not a pushover, not someone to 'fuck with'" (Sabo 1994, 165–166).

Muscularity and size are key aspects of being seen as 'hard' and subsequently being left alone within prison. As Martos-García et al. indicate, muscularity also has positive consequences for the territory and influence of certain prisoners engaged in bodybuilding:

> [W]ith regard to bodybuilding and the visible display of muscle, one male monitor noted, 'with bodybuilding they also look intimidating to others. Because, the stronger you look, the easier it is for you to define your territory, and nobody touches you'. (Martos-García et al. 2009, 91)

In this chapter I will argue that these studies focusing on muscularity and hardness are describing one (but not the only) hegemonic image of embodied prison masculinity. The findings from these studies do indeed resonate with the embodied experiences of many of the men discussed in this chapter, who had taken part in a physical activity and healthy living group-based programme, delivered within prison gyms. Amongst these men, who had previously not been users of the prison gym and commenced the programme with a plurality of body sizes and shapes, I found a greater plurality of both imagery and performances of embodied masculinity than portrayed in the existing literature. After describing my data collection methods, I present evidence that having a certain body, looking a certain way and trying to conform to facets of the normative images of embodied masculinity are reflections of prisoners' agency within, and resistance to, the prison system.

Methods

The men involved in this research had taken part in pilot deliveries of a group-based physical activity and healthy lifestyle programme which was designed to attract men who were not currently using prison gymnasium[2] facilities. This group-based programme was developed from an earlier community-based weight management and healthy lifestyle programme for men, gender-sensitised in context, content and style of delivery, known as Football Fans in Training (FFIT). FFIT has proved successful in engaging men across the socio-economic spectrum and supporting them in sustained weight loss and other positive changes to their health, wellbeing and lifestyles (Gray et al. 2013; Hunt et al. 2014a, b). The development of this weight management and healthy lifestyle programme for the prison context was a five-phase process over three years, culminating in a ten-week group-based programme (Fit for LIFE), which is being delivered by physical education instructors in all Scottish prisons. It uses behaviour change techniques to support prisoners to increase their physical activity and reduce sedentary time, improve their diet and, if appropriate for them, achieve weight loss.

Prior to undertaking fieldwork, ethical approval was obtained from relevant NHS, SPS Research Access and Ethics Committee and University ethics committees. In this chapter prison names have not been used, to protect the anonymity of those who took part, and participants are referred to only by a unique identifier. As issues of coercion and consent within prison research are particularly complex (cf. McDermott 2013; Moser et al. 2004), every effort was made to stress to participants that they should only take part in the research with full informed consent, and that they understood that they were free to withdraw at any time and only should answer questions that they wished to respond to.

The research was largely conducted within the gymnasiums of two prisons (Prisons A and B) which housed only male prisoners, during the delivery of earlier iterations of the Fit for LIFE programme (between September 2013 and May 2014).[3] Recruitment to the programme in both prisons was undertaken by the physical education instructors (PEIs) who run the gymnasium and delivered the programme at Prison A and facilitated the first delivery in Prison B. The research participants discussed in this chapter were selected from this group of prisoners through post-programme interviews.

This research takes a reflexive ethnographic approach (Hammersley 1992), through which relationships and trust were gradually built with both participants and staff. This leads to insights into changes in performances of masculinity (Maycock et al., Manuscript under review), over the three to four months in which men attended the programme, in the context of prison life more generally for the men taking part. Data were collected through observations of weekly session deliveries, with the permission of participants; all of these were conducted by the same (male) researcher (MM), except two which were conducted by female colleagues.

Semi-structured one-to-one interviews were undertaken with participants in the programme (n = 12 at Prison A; n = 9 at Prison B) immediately after the end of deliveries of these early iterations of the programme, to explore participants' experiences of taking part in the programme in the context of prison life. In addition three interviews were conducted with participants at Prison A 12 months after they started Fit for LIFE to explore their experiences of trying to maintain the changes they had made on the programme, within the prison context.

Interviews were recorded and transcribed with participants' written consent, and these data were analysed using Nvivo 10. For this chapter, coding was structured around three principal emerging themes with many subthemes developed through the analysis 'doing' masculinity within the context of taking part in this programme delivered in prison gymnasiums, participant views of the programme and men's contextualising comments on their life in prison.

Findings

Bodies were consistently referred to and discussed by the men within both prisons. Prisoners were sometimes not discussed by name, or as prisoners, but were actually referred to simply in relation to their bodies. As one man said:

> …there's twenty bodies in there doing a circuit. (Prison B – P11)[4]

The findings in this section are arranged in two main sections that highlight: the importance of bodies in shaping language within both prisons and the embodied experiences of the prisoners in these spaces. Initially I consider the various images, shapes and sizes of bodies that the prisoners who took part in the programme discussed. Subsequently I examine the efforts they made to meet or achieve bodies that correspond with the images that they considered desirable and/or appropriate within prison, and how these efforts might be considered a form of resistance to the prison regime.

Hegemonic Images of the Prisoner Body

Muscularity, Shape and Size

There were conflicting accounts from the participants as to what was considered a desirable body shape. Shape here implies a certain type of muscularity and size, with many participants emphasising the importance of being 'big':

> You've got to get big, aye, you've got a group, your group of guys, that's what they're into, their bodybuilding and their strength, things like that. (PRISON A– P8)

One participant seemed quite cynical about the actual strength of some (particularly younger) prisoners despite their large size. This implies that this might be a kind of façade, disguising the fact that these prisoners are not as strong as they appear:

> Well they [young prisoners] try to big their selves up to look like they've got more than they have. (PRISON B – P12)

Getting and maintaining a certain size was equated with a kind of embodied capital within the prisons. A number of prisoners discussed the ways in which being seen as 'big' was equated with being popular and being seen to have a desirable type of body:

> I actually get people [other prisoners] that go like that, "Oh how long did it take you to get that size?" Guys were all wanting to get like me, and like as big as me kind of thing. (PRISON B – P1)

This quote from participant PRISON B-P1 exemplifies the mainstream image of the desired type of body within these two prisons, which appeared to result in many prisoners wanting to get as big as possible. Being 'big' had a range of consequences, most of which were considered to be positive within the prison. For some prisoners, being big was a means of being left alone:

> ...don't take this the wrong way or that man, because like aye, I'm a big guy, and maybe guys might say, "Oh man, stay away from him, man!", know what I mean? People just...well maybe they know to leave me alone, and be just a little bit wary, know what I mean? Like that, "Well he's a big guy," know what I mean? "He's going to..." But see the way they see it man, "Whoa, he's a big guy man, its going to need about five of us." (PRISON B-P1)

Other prisoners assumed that the bigger a man was, the less likely he was to be the victim of negative banter and to be seen as a target in prison:

> ...'cause people wouldn't, do you know what I mean, try and take the piss or whatever because maybe if you're bigger an' stronger an' that. Think 'cause you're small person, you're a target, know what I mean? (PRISON B – P6)

Persistent bullying could result in prisoners being moved into the protection wing of the prison. It was assumed that if a prisoner was smaller, he was more likely to be the victim of bullying. A number of prisoners recounted tales of how men who had been in protection and moved to other prisons focused on changing their body size:

> People that I know in here that were in protection before, "Oh they made out as if the screws told me I had to go to protection", and all that. Get it together, no they didn't. But as soon as they came out and went to a different jail, then they came back down here and he was away into his gym, pounding the gym, and he's a big, muscly cunt. Know he walks with a swagger and that as if, "I'm getting muscly so that I don't get bullied again." Know what I mean, that's the way it was. (PRISON B – P6)

However, similarly to many aspects of prison life, being or trying to be 'big' had a range of consequences that were in some instances contradictory; being 'big' could also make men more of a target within the prison. For example, one prisoner discussed how being big is not necessarily a protection from all potential threats in prison:

4 "They're All Up in the Gym and All That, Tops Off, Fake Tan."...

But, all it can take is like for…it could be the smallest guy in the Hall, man, could come up and stab you in the neck, or whatever, know what I mean? It's just…that's how easy it can happen in here. (PRISON B – P1)

The focus on getting big within prison influenced the behaviours that were thought to predominate in routine use of the prison gym, resulting in a focus on weight training within prison:

You want everybody tae go into a prison and they all want to do is the weights. They all want to get big and strong. That's what they all want to do. (PRISON B – P11)

The focus on getting 'big' meant that some prisoners were able to make quite radical changes to their bodies during their time in prison:

…you see a lot of people come in here and there not a pick on them [no spare fat], they get out and they're like bodybuilders. (PRISON B – P12)

Age was an important factor in relation to examining the sorts of bodies that are seen as desirable and considered 'manly':

The alpha male culture is alive and kicking. Well, you do have your gym bunnies that, you know, the bigger muscles you've got the more of a man you are. And that's quite prevalent here [in prison]. But they tend not to mind people like me [over 50]. I mean, I don't think they perceive me as a threat. (PRISON A – P2)

This section has illustrated the perceived importance of body shape and size within these two prisons, and indicated some of consequences of being big within prison. It illustrates how discussions of size and muscularity emphasise the desirability of big, fit and muscled bodies within the prisons. However, the reality of embodiment within prisons can be quite different, and the bodies of many participants who took part in the programme were in many ways distinct from these idealised images. For example, the participant below highlights some of the pressures within prison of having to look a certain way. The programme participants engaged in a range of bodywork to try to change their bodies and appearance so that it adhered more closely to the ideals outlined above:

> No matter if it's heavy weight, too skinny, or whatever. But specifically in here [prison], would somebody maybe go…maybe get judged because they're appearance maybe not the same as others? Yes probably. (PRISON B – P8)

In the next section, I consider the sorts of activities that programme participants did, or talked about doing in order to gain, as far as possible, the same physical appearance as the fit, hard bodies of the prisoners who they associated with the gyms.

'Bodywork' Within Prison

Steroids and Supplements

A number of the participants discussed other sorts of bodywork, achieved by taking various steroids and protein supplements (available to prisoners through the canteen list of approved products available to buy), with the objective of increasing their muscle size. Supplements were available in both prisons and were seen as a viable alternative to steroids for some prisoners (supplements were discussed more frequently than steroids). For a number of participants, steroids were part of their pre-prison lives. This participant went on to talk about his experiences of using steroids prior to coming to prison, and steroids were being replaced by the various supplements during his time in prison:

> I used to take that [steroids] before I came in here [prison], (*Int: oh really*), I used to have not a bad build and then I put on a bit of weight in jail and then I sort of managed to trim right back down again, so…just, not for any reason, just to get a bit more shape about me, you know, that's, I'd be happy with that. (Prison B – P11)

The use of supplements was discussed at some length by the same participant; these had a range of consequences for those taking them, including disruption of sleep:

Musclepharm, that's the make of them. A supplement. So it said, it's a good rate, like, but…*Musclepharm*, aye. So I just went and got them yesterday, and yes, I'm not getting to sleep, they kept me awake all night…. Aye, seriously, fucking torture… they're basically the closest thing you'll get to a steroid that's legal. (Prison A – P11)

Protein supplements were seen by some as a shortcut to achieving a muscular body in response to the pressures to attain the sorts of hegemonic (muscular, hard) images of bodies in prison as outlined previously. A number of participants stated that steroids were not commonly found in prison:

It's probably an image thing, isn't, basically? But a lot of them [other prisoners] don't want to come in and do the graft. It's [steroids] kind of far and few between. You really don't get much of that, to be honest with you. You'll get that in other prisons. (Prison B – P11)

These views on steroids and supplements within prison illuminate some body work that some of the participants engaged in, in order to change their bodies so they appeared closer to the normative visions of the male body within prison. There were various manifestations of bodywork focused on looking a certain way that form the focus of the subsequent section.

Looking Good in Prison

For some prisoners maintaining their looks and presenting themselves in certain ways were important means through which to maintain links to outside, pre-prison lives:

…a lot of guys will get slagged and that in the jail because the way they appear, they're like posers, they still think they're outside, know, so, aye a lot of it [attempting to look good] happens in jail as well. (Prison A – P8)

In this sense, maintaining a certain appearance was a potential area of continuity through which to link pre- and post-prison performances of masculinity. Looking a certain way had a significance in prison that reflected the potential for personal control or influence in this aspect of prison life, when many aspects (such as freedom of movement and contact with family and friends) were controlled systematically within the prison system. Consequently, for some prisoners, maintaining certain standards and looking good was part an expression of agency and resistance to the prison system itself. A number of older prisoners viewed this as particularly important for younger prisoners, who it was felt tried particularly hard to maintain their pre-prison standards of looking good:

> I don't know if it's…It's kind of vain, it's like because they're in prison they don't want to lower their standards. It's like, "I can still get this, and I can still get that." Still got all the best clothes. I don't care anymore. Well… I still care, I still, like kind of buy nice stuff. In here, everything, there's quite a lot of vain people in here. I just think they've got in their head it's like, "I'm in prison, I'm going look as best I can. I'm not going let the system get to me."
> *So it's about resisting the system?*
> I think so. (Prison B – P2)

These expressions of agency and resistance were manifested in multiple ways. For example, prisoners wanting to look good in certain ways within prison were able to order certain items from a 'canteen list', an internal system for buying approved products including food items and body products including facial scrub, moisturiser, baby oil and fake tan. Prisoners buying and using these products were sometimes regarded with suspicion, particularly for older men, with potential homosexual undertones:

> Yeah, definitely. There's a lot of people in here do that [want to look good], eh. Definitely. Loads of people. Have you never seen them in there? Their fake tan and all that shite.
> *Fake tan?*
> I'm being deadly serious. There's a moisturiser they buy it's got… it's got like a colour in it. Loads of them up there prancing about with it. Aww, pure gay boys up there like.
> *But are they gay?*
> No, just like…. (PRISON B – P12)

Here there is a form of bodywork that does not relate to size and shape, but rather to more subtle forms of body modification, such as using moisturiser and fake tan. As prisoners are limited in the amount of time that they can spend outdoors, fake tan was a means to achieve and maintain a skin tone that was seen as desirable within the prison, at least by some prisoners.

Bodywork and trying to look good could also extend to smelling a certain way. There were some masculine smells that some prisoners said they missed:

> And that's the thing in here – you don't get your deodorant. You only get, is a roll-in, right? But see when the guys walk by and you can smell their aftershave or their deodorant, I miss all that. You know what I mean? And that's…just 'cause you're in here doesn't mean to say you've got to stop smelling good or whatever, you know? (PRISON B – P4)

Smelling and looking good worked differently in different places within the prison. For example, a number of participants discussed the efforts that some people made to look a certain way, particularly in the gym:

> I don't know. It's like ninety percent of people in here [the prison gym] all kind of look after themselves. I mean you get guys up there buying all sorts of creams, and everything. It's like a lot of guys wear hair gel before they come down to the gym. Honestly it's…You wouldn't believe how vain they are. (Prison B – P12)

These comments suggest that some prisoners were more conscious of looking good within prison, than they might have been on the outside:

> Aye. I think they're a lot more conscious on it, here [in prison]. It's because you've got access to the gym every day of the week, or a couple times a week, know what I mean, that some folk are more conscious about it. (PRISON A– P9)

The potential for change in relation to appearance seemed to heighten the focus on these aspects of prison life for some prisoners. In a context in which prison uniforms restrict expressions of agency and individuality via clothing, personal grooming (and footwear), and 'looking good' more generally, took on greater significance. For some prisoners this meant that they were more focused on these aspects of bodywork, as a consequence of not being able express agency and individuality through other forms of consumption that would be more readily available to them on the outside.

The Social Context of Bodywork

Taking steroids and supplements, and using fake tan and moisturiser, had a range of implications socially within both prisons. For example, these sorts of bodywork could, for some prisoners, have positive implications for their social status within prison:

> When I come in [the prison gym], they say "you look a lot healthier now than you did when you come in [into prison initially]."
> *And how does that make you feel?*
> It feels really good. But then I know I have because I know the lifestyle I was living out there tae now [a chaotic lifestyle of substance misuse]. (PRISON A– P11)

Many participants seemed to want the bodywork they were undertaking, and changes that they were making to their bodies, to be validated by some of their peers within the prison:

> …one or two guys have maybe have says to me like that, "Oh you're looking good for that," That's only guys that like are really dedicated to the gym, like myself, man. They're like that, "Oh, you can see a difference in you," know what I mean? "You've done well!". (PRISON B – P1)

For some men, such as participant P11 at Prison B, getting bigger and building muscle was not about ascending perceived hierarchies within prison, but was in part to get praise for these efforts from other prisoners and more fundamentally to take pride in his appearance in prison:

> *So do you think taking part in this changes, like, the level? You know, if you get stronger you kind o' move up the hierarchy a bit in prison? Or doesn't* (Naw) *it work like that?*

4 "They're All Up in the Gym and All That, Tops Off, Fake Tan."...

I wouldn't say that…that it's like that, that they're a' building muscle to look tough and strong and big and they'll move up the ladder or anything like that. It's just an image thing, basically, for people, innit? To look good about themselves if they've got a bit of size and shape about them and if they're doing the weights and then they've got people saying "Oh, you're looking good." (Prison B – P11)

However, a number of the older participants in the programme seemed unsure about men's motivations for looking good in these ways within prison. These included trying to look good for other men (e.g., as indicated above, this included questioning the sexuality of the men who used fake tan), or it might be using fake tan to look good for their (female) visitors:

There's loads of them up there, you know, they're all up the gym and all that, tops off and all that, fake tan. Maybe it's for their visitors or someone. Or maybe they get released soon, I don't know. (PRISON B – P12)

The fear of being seen as a homosexual was present in these conversations (something that Anderson would identify as 'homohysteria' (2009)),[5] and there was some discomfort in being seen to be overly concerned about using certain products and looking a certain way for other male prisoners. Importantly, though, there were some women within these male prisons, including female prison officers and female visitors, and their presence constituted a motivation for looking good and getting bigger for some prisoners:

I don't know mate, maybe they like some of the female screws. (Laughs) Weird but, but they do it [want to look good for the female prison officers]. (PRISON B – P12)

The social context of bodywork described here both provides an insight into the limited nature of metrosexuality (cf. Hall 2015; Simpson 1999) within prisons and illuminates the ways in which homophobia remains a consistent undercurrent within prison life. Looking good and the bodywork I have described positively contributed to many prisoners getting closer to their perceptions of desired images of bodies in prison.

However, it is important to note that some prisoners rejected these aspects of the performance of embodied masculinity in prison and the associated bodywork and consumption that accompany this. I go on to discuss this next.

Hitting Rock Bottom: Rejecting Efforts to Look Good

The section above illuminates the mainstream currents of bodywork within both prisons. However, there were a small number of participants who discussed prisoners who rejected efforts to 'look good' along the lines outlined above. This could also be considered as a form of protest and resistance to the prison regime:

> But some people don't care about themselves in the jail. Do you know what I mean? It's hard to decide what…whether it'd be 50/50. Some people don't care about themselves because they're in the jail, they've hit rock bottom. (PRISON A– P7)

Prisoners who didn't look after themselves, who had 'hit rock bottom' or who had let themselves go, were considered to have let prison 'get to them'. It was important for prisoners not to be seen as a 'tramp'[6] and to look after themselves as a form of resistance of the prison regime:

> See people say to you, like they'll say, "You're now in prison, you don't, because you're in prison, doesn't mean you have to let yourself go." Like I'm like, I mean I still buy stuff and all that, and, but I wouldn't walk about like dead trampy in here. (PRISON B -P12)

'Tramp' was used as a pejorative term by a number of prisoners, to describe prisoners who through various forms of bodywork did not conform or try to conform to the sorts of embodied masculinities that were predominant with the prisons:

> Because if I, if somebody came in to my peter [cell] and went, "Fuck, you look like a tramp, man!" I'd go, "Who the fuck…?" I'd smack him on the chin. (PRISON B – P6)

Cumulatively these findings illustrate that the bodywork outlined here, which is associated with certain embodied masculinities within prison, is shaped by the prison context in formative ways. Whilst there are opportunities for new embodied performances of masculinity within prison, there are limits to this, and clear boundaries as to what is acceptable within the prison context. These boundaries are specific to the prison context and are drawn in different places outside of prison.

Discussion

Miller's (2000, 3) description of prisons as "sites of sexual and gender complexity" resonates strongly with my research. Some of the men's accounts, as presented in the first section of my findings above, echoes the literature summarised in the introduction, in which embodiment of prison masculinities is closely associated with images of hard, muscly and big bodies. However, as demonstrated in subsequent sections of the findings above, some of the men's reflections on bodywork within prison was contrary to what might be expected from the existing literature. Sabo et al. (2001, 9) indicate that those who are seen to have weak or non-muscular bodies are located towards the bottom of prison hierarchies. However, for some of the participants in the Fit for LIFE programme, there appears to be evidence of evolution of the sorts of bodies that are associated both with the higher, more hegemonic places within masculine hierarchies in prison and the lower parts of these hierarchies. Thus, in these prisons at least, it appears that it is possible for male prisoners to have both hard, muscly bodies and to moisturise and tan their bodies (which resonates with research in schools, for example, where the use of such products point towards changing masculinities (McCormack 2012)). These manifestations of bodywork in prison were more salient amongst younger prisoners, and it is important to note that, where they were apparent, these types of bodywork were still constrained by certain limitations and boundaries.

These men's accounts suggest that there are forms of metrosexuality (Hall 2015; Simpson 1999) that are shaped by the prison context.

However, the forms of bodywork I have outlined do cause some anxiety for some prisoners. There is a consistent tension between certain bodywork and self-care (such as using fake tan and moisturiser) and not wanting to be seen as a homosexual, which reflects wider undercurrents of homophobia within prisons (Author, Manuscript under review). These findings resonate with Anderson's notion of homohysteria ("the cultural fear of being homosexualised" (McCormack 2010, 338). Anderson's theory of inclusive masculinity implies a decline in homohysteria and less hierarchical interactions between masculinities. However, my data indicates that it may be more appropriate to recognise not a decline, but rather a specific manifestation of homohysteria in prison contexts. In this study, heterosexual male prisoners who were engaged in bodywork practices that have previously been associated primarily with women or homosexual men were keen to establish that this did not mean that they were homosexual.

Resistance to prison regimes has been widely analysed within prison contexts (Bosworth and Carrabine 2001; Crewe 2007; Haslam and Reicher 2012; Ugelvik 2014). However, although the importance of clothing as an expression of agency within the prison context has been established (cf. Ash 2010)—with forms of resistance possible through the customisation of prison clothing (2010, 153)—the ways in which resistance might be reflected in the performances of embodied masculinities of male prisoners as I have discussed here have not previously been considered in this literature.

In his influential work on resistance, Scott examines subterfuge through hidden transcripts of the poor and marginalised that often avoid direct confrontation (Scott 1985, 1990). He identifies both a 'public transcript' and a 'hidden transcript' of resistance that is located "'offstage,' beyond direct observation by powerholders" (1990, 2, 4). The bodywork I have considered in this paper challenges this distinction between 'public' and 'hidden' transcripts, as it is at once public *as well as* hidden. With a growing plurality of prison masculinities (Author, Manuscript under review), and accompanying forms of embodiment, there is an associated plurality of potential resistance and compliance to the prison regime and expected behaviours and appearances.

Conclusion

In this chapter I argue that various manifestations of embodiment of masculinity and bodywork create opportunities for resistance to the prison regime, for some prisoners. These forms of resistance that are possible through certain embodiments of masculinity do not replace other forms of resistance within prison, but potentially complement them; instances of other expressions of resistance through bodywork, such as a complete lack of effort to 'look good' or 'dirty protests' (cf. Aretxaga (1995), Coogan (2002)), were also recounted as occasional occurrences within both prisons.

The theoretical framework of embodied masculinity provides a context in which to consider the ways in which bodies are used by prisoners to resist (and conform to) aspects of the prison system. The data presented here suggest that, whilst having a large and muscly body remains an important aspect of performances and embodiments of masculinity within these prisons, there are also more subtle and nuanced means of embodied resistance and compliance with the prison context.

Notes

1. Butler makes a very similar point in *Bodies That Matter*: "That this reiteration is necessary is a sign that materialization is never quite complete, that bodies never quite comply with the norms by which their materialization is impelled" (1993, 2).
2. The term 'gymnasium' is used throughout because it was the term which prisoners and staff used to describe multiple spaces, including the weights/cardio room, sports Hall and changing room.
3. Occasionally interviews took place on the prison Halls where the prisoners live.
4. All quotes have been changed from colloquial English into standard English.
5. Indeed, this pervaded life in both prisons more generally (cf. Author, manuscript under review).
6. The meaning of 'tramp' here implies someone who is homeless and/or does not take care of their appearance.

References

Anderson, E. (2008). Inclusive masculinity in a fraternal setting. *Men and Masculinities, 10*, 604–620.

Anderson, E. (2009). *Inclusive masculinity: The changing nature of masculinities.* London: Routledge.

Anderson, E., & McGuire, R. (2010). Inclusive masculinity theory and the gendered politics of men's rugby. *Journal of Gender Studies, 19*, 249–261.

Aretxaga, B. (1995). Dirty protest: Symbolic overdetermination and gender in Northern Ireland ethnic violence. *Ethos, 23*, 123–148.

Ash, J. (2010). *Dress behind bars: Prison clothing as criminality.* London: I. B. Tauris.

Author. (Manuscript under review). *Performances of multiple masculinities within a health promotion programme delivered in two British prison gymnasia.*

Bandyopadhyay, M. (2006). Competing masculinities in a prison. *Men and Masculinities, 9*, 186–203.

Bosworth, M., & Carrabine, E. (2001). Reassessing resistance: Race, gender and sexuality in prison. *Punishment & Society, 3*, 501–515.

Butler, J. (1993). *Bodies that matter. On the discursive limits of 'sex'.* London: Routledge.

Connell, R. W. (1983). Men's bodies. *Australian Society, 2*(9), 33–39.

Connell, R. (1995). *Masculinities.* Cambridge: Polity.

Connell, R. W. (2005). *Masculinities.* Cambridge: Policy Press.

Connell, R. W., & Messerschmidt, J. W. (2005). Hegemonic masculinity: Rethinking the concept. *Gender & Society, 19*, 829–859.

Coogan, T. P. (2002). *On the blanket: The inside story of the IRA prisoners' "dirty" protest.* New York: St. Martin's Press.

Crewe, B. (2007). Power, adaptation and resistance in a late-modern men's prison. *British Journal of Criminology, 47*, 256–275.

Drummond, M. (2011). Reflections on the archetypal heterosexual male body. *Australian Feminist Studies, 26*, 103–117.

Dworkin, A. (1974). *Woman hating.* New York: E. P. Dutton.

Evans, T., & Wallace, P. (2007). A prison within a prison? The masculinity narratives of male Prisoners. *Men and Masculinities, 10*(4), 484–507.

Foucault, M. (1979). *Discipline and punish : The birth of the prison.* Harmondsworth: Penguin Books.

Gadd, D. (2003). Reading between the lines. *Men and Masculinities, 5*(4), 333–354.

Garland-Thomson, R. (2009). *Staring: How we look*. New York/Oxford: Oxford University Press.

Gill, R., Henwood, K., & Mclean, C. (2005). Body projects and the regulation of normative masculinity. *Body and Society, 11*(1) 37–62.

Gray, C., Hunt, K., Mutrie, N., Anderson, A., Leishman, J., Dalgarno, L., & Wyke, S. (2013). Football fans in training: The development and optimization of an intervention delivered through professional sports clubs to help men lose weight, become more active and adopt healthier eating habits. *BMC Public Health, 13*, 232.

Hall, M. (2015). *Metrosexual masculinities*. Houndmills/Basingstoke/Hampshire: Palgrave Macmillan.

Hall, A., Hockey, J., & Robinson, V. (2007). Occupational cultures and the embodiment of masculinity: Hairdressing, estate agency and firefighting. *Gender, Work & Organization, 14*, 534–551.

Hammersley, M. (1992). *What's wrong with ethnography?* London: Routledge.

Haslam, S. A., & Reicher, S. D. (2012). When prisoners take over the prison: A social psychology of resistance. *Personality and Social Psychology Review, 16*, 154–179.

Hunt, K., Gray, C., Maclean, A., Smillie, S., Bunn, C., & Wyke, S. (2014a). Do weight management programmes delivered at professional football clubs attract and engage high risk men? A mixed-methods study. *BMC Public Health, 14*, 50.

Hunt, K., Wyke, S., Gray, C. M., Anderson, A. S., Brady, A., Bunn, C., Donnan, P. T., Fenwick, E., Grieve, E., Leishman, J., Miller, E., Mutrie, N., Rauchhaus, P., White, A., & Treweek, S. (2014b). A gender-sensitised weight loss and healthy living programme for overweight and obese men delivered by Scottish premier league football clubs (FFIT): A pragmatic randomised controlled trial. *The Lancet, 383*, 1211–1221.

Inhorn, M. C., & Wentzell, E. A. (2011). Embodying emergent masculinities: Men engaging with reproductive and sexual health technologies in the Middle East and Mexico. *American Ethnologist, 38*, 801–815.

Martos-García, D., Devís-Devís, J., & Sparkes, A. C. (2009). Sport and physical activity in a high security Spanish prison: An ethnographic study of multiple meanings. *Sport, Education and Society, 14*, 77–96.

Maycock, M., et al. (n.d.). Multiple performances of masculinity within a health promotion intervention. Manuscript under review.

McCormack, M. (2010). The declining significance of homohysteria for male students in three sixth forms in the south of England. *British Educational Research Journal, 37*, 337–353.

McCormack, M. (2012). *The declining significance of homophobia: How teenage boys are redefining masculinity and heterosexuality*. Oxford: Oxford University Press.

McDermott, B. E. (2013). Coercion in research: Are prisoners the only vulnerable population? *Journal of the American Academy of Psychiatry and the Law Online, 41*, 8–13.

McDowell, L. (1999). *Gender, identity and place : Understanding feminist geographies*. Cambridge: Polity.

Miller, T. A. (2000). Sex & surveillance: Gender, privacy & the sexualization of power in prison. *George Mason University Civil Rights Law Journal (CRLJ), 291*(10), 1–39.

Moore, H. (1994). *A passion for Difference*. London: Polity.

Moore, H. (2007). *The subject of anthropology*. London: Polity.

Moser, D. J., Arndt, S., Kanz, J. E., Benjamin, M. L., Bayless, J. D., Reese, R. L., Paulsen, J. S., & Flaum, M. A. (2004). Coercion and informed consent in research involving prisoners. *Comprehensive Psychiatry, 45*, 1–9.

Nandi, M. (2002). Re/constructing black masculinity in prison. *The Journal of Men's Studies, 11*, 91–107.

Phillips, J. (2001). Cultural construction of manhood in prison. *Psychology of Men & Masculinity, 2*, 13–23.

Ricciardelli, R., Maier, K., & Hannah-Moffat, K. (2015). Strategic masculinities: Vulnerabilities, risk and the production of prison masculinities. *Theoretical Criminology, 19*(4), 491–513.

Rosenberg, R., & Oswin, N. (2015). Trans embodiment in carceral space: Hypermasculinity and the US prison industrial complex. *Gender, Place & Culture, 22*(9), 1269–1286.

Sabo, D. (1994). Doing time doing masculinity: Sports and prison. In M. Messner & D. Sabo (Eds.), *Sex, violence and power in sports. Rethinking masculinity*. Freedom: The Crossing Press.

Sabo, D. F., Kupers, T. A., & London, W. J. (2001). *Prison masculinities /edited by Don Sabo, Terry A. Kupers, and Willie London*. Philadelphia: Temple University Press.

Scott, J. C. (1985). *Weapons of the weak: Everyday forms of peasant resistance*. New Haven/London: Yale University Press.

Scott, J. C. (1990). *Domination and the arts of resistance: Hidden transcripts*. New Haven/London: Yale University Press.

Shabazz, R. (2009). "So high you can't get over it, so low you can't get under it": Carceral spatiality and black masculinities in the United States and South Africa. *Souls, 11*, 276–294.

Shilling, C. (2003). *The body and social theory*. London: SAGE.

Simpson, M. (1999). *It's a queer world: Deviant adventures in pop culture*. London: Routledge.

Tarzwell, S. (2006). Gender liens are marked with razor wire: Addressing state prison policies and practices for the management of transgender prisoners. *The Columbia Human Rights Law Review, 38*, 167–220.

Ugelvik, T. (2014). *Power and resistance in prison: Doing time, doing freedom*. Basingstoke: Palgrave Macmillan.

Wacquant, L. (1995). Review article: Why men desire muscles. *Body & Society, 1*, 163–179.

Whitehead, S. M. (2002). *Men and masculinities*. Cambridge: Polity.

5

"Don't Mess with Me!" Enacting Masculinities Under a Compulsory Prison Regime

Nick de Viggiani

Introduction

It is our nature to conform; it is a force which not many can successfully resist […]. Self-approval has its source in but one place and not elsewhere – the approval of other people […] by the natural instinct to passively yield to that vague something recognized as authority, and […] by the human instinct to train with the multitude and have its approval. (Mark Twain 1923: p. 401)

The need to feel part of the social group, feel socially accepted and fit in can be compelling and seem instinctual. Normative attitudes and behaviours are perceived in all walks of life, from pre-school playgroups to workplace settings. Self-perception and presentation of self operate synergistically, relative to time and place. This dramaturgical perspective—initially developed by Goffman (1956)—seeks to explain social relations in the manner that individuals present themselves to their different audiences. According to Goffman, the 'actor' presents to others

---

N. de Viggiani (✉)
Department of Health & Social Sciences, University of the West of England, Bristol, UK

an idealised impression, attempting to "incorporate and exemplify the officially accredited values of the society" (p. 35). So within any given social situation, individuals act and associate with others according to the interactional *modus vivendi* or 'working consensus' (p. 4), which is shaped to the setting. This consensus is partly governed by normative values associated with what is perceived to be the dominant culture, identified through social signifiers or symbols associated with gender, sexuality, ethnicity, race, religion and/or social class. Furthermore, the setting brings into play the intersection of multiple identities, where gender is not the only signifier (Truong 2006).

Criminal justice settings typify any social situation in which individuals find themselves in a state of interdependence with others, and where social relations may be beneficial or harmful for health and wellbeing (Helliwell and Putnam 2004; Schwarzer and Leppin 1989; Tay et al. 2013). On entering the setting, the individual encounters a social environment in perpetual flux as 'actors' jostle to acquire social literacy, legitimacy and status. This intense social experience can represent a challenge to psychological and social health and wellbeing. This chapter draws upon ethnographic research with male prisoners to illustrate how gender is interpreted, operationalised and enacted in subtle ways to shape and influence social relations. The research findings illustrate how masculinities are enacted, sanctioned and condoned at individual and institutional levels, consistent with historical conventions of gender, power and discipline.

Masculinities—Playing by the Rules

Connell's (2005: p. 19) original discourse on masculinities proposed that gender power operates through varying forms of domination and subordination—or social hierarchy—providing a means to explain social status, subjugation and exploitation within different social contexts. Masculinities describe individuals' social positioning and practices relative to others and to the social system they are part of. 'Hegemonic masculinity' essentially refers to those 'patterns of practice' or 'things done' that position or attribute social status to the individual within the social hierarchy, rather than implying a set of role expectations or identity traits.

They prevail within interpersonal and social relationships as intersubjective power relations between people and groups. At a macro organisational level, this may be understood in relation to the institutionalised gender order, where the system of organisation may empower or disempower its 'subjects,' resulting in social inequities, exclusion or even forms of discrimination. Connell's primary emphasis was on the exercise of power through gender, gender being something socially constructed relative to cultural context. Ridgeway and Correll (2004: p. 510) further argued that gender then functions as 'rules of the game,' influencing behaviour and performance. Connell and Messerschmidt (2005) provide a theoretical lens with which to make sense of hierarchical social relations within transient cultural contexts, where social and institutional environments orientate 'actors' towards normative—yet relational—hegemonic organising principles. Within any given setting, individuals embody masculinities as subjects of those cultural practices that characterise the social environment, whilst simultaneously operating as active agents in these social practices.

West and Fenstermaker (1995) described individuals' attempts to fit in with others, through their attitudes and behaviours, as 'situational accomplishments.' Likewise, Messerschmidt (1997: p. 4) referred to masculinities as 'situated, social and interactional accomplishments.' Rather than passively internalising pre-scripted gender roles or identities, individuals enact gender in interaction with others, relative to the given situation (Renzetti 2013), engaging reciprocally with the social structure. Masculinities then symbolise social relationships enacted by individuals and groups across the infinite range of social contexts, ascribing, reinforcing and supporting normative ideologies of male gender identity and role. Messerschmidt (1993) argued that most social institutions then embody and reproduce a dominant masculine value system that is often heterosexual and reinforces the appearance of a meaningful gender division based on normative 'male' and 'female' positions, to which individuals seek identification, recognition, status and social legitimacy. Men and women—conscious of the need to fit in—regulate their own and others' attitudes and behaviours, participating in forms of interpersonal and social surveillance involving techniques of self-subjectification and objectification (Foucault 1977). Male identity, attitudes and behaviours are explained in relation to a 'broader framework of idealized masculinity' (Collier 1997: p. 94), a series of culturally specific gender reference points with which individuals align themselves to greater or lesser degrees. Individuals derive purpose and meaning from the social setting partly through accessing these symbolic resources for constructing a meaningful social identity (Holstein and Gubrium 2000). This has been observed across many research studies of men where individuals have been described as typically orientating themselves around an ideological 'stake' that compels particular settings-specific conduct (see, e.g., Fielding 1993; Hinojosa 2010; Hockey 1986). Such studies suggest that male-dominated institutions can become centrally orientated around a hegemonic masculine value system, as described by Connell (2005).

Prison Masculinities

Ethnographic research from the mid-twentieth century yielded compelling insight into how gender was perceived to feature within single-sex, usually male, prison contexts. Significantly, Sim (1994) noted that research conducted during this era focused exclusively on men as prison research subjects; women were relatively invisible, reinforcing the perception that being male was a prerequisite for being an offender or a prisoner. Indeed, Chesney-Lind and Pasko (2013) observed that female offending and imprisonment were largely ignored within criminology until the 1970s. Many examples of gender-blind prison-based research focused on prison culture and presumed that studying men in prison was consistent with studying prisoners (see, e.g., Berger and Luckman 1967; Clemmer 1958; Cohen 1979; Cohen and Taylor 1981; Glouberman 1990; Goffman 1961; Mathiesen 1990; Sykes 1958; Towl 1993). Cohen and Taylor's (1981: p. 66–7) study of inmate culture within Durham Prison reported that prisoners tended to identify with a hierarchical social structure defined around 'the man who exemplifies the ideal.' Foucault (1977: p. 305), whilst discussing control and normalisation in 'Discipline and Punish,' inferred a normative masculine role characterised as 'knowable man … the object-effect of this analytical investment, of this domination observation.'

Despite this, some of these earlier studies conveyed the deleterious impact of prison life on the prisoner, characterising imprisonment in terms of its 'deprivations' and progressive assault on individuals' identities. Clemmer (1958: p. 299), for example, described how individuals would assimilate "in greater or lesser degree … the folkways, mores, customs and general culture of the penitentiary [becoming] more deeply criminal [and] antisocial." Sykes' (1958: p. xv) notion of 'prisonisation'—a 'pathological, repressive and depriving system of total power'—described an insidious de-socialisation process that disempowered prisoners through deprivation of self-worth, self-esteem and self-concept:

> The individual's picture of himself as a person of value – as a morally acceptable, adult male who can present some claim to merit in his material achievements and his inner strength – begins to waver and grow dim. (Sykes 1958: p. 79)

These ethnographers inferred that gender is strongly influenced by institutional, ideological and social factors, Sykes (1958) suggesting that single-sex, compulsory custody could degrade a male prisoner's masculine identity. Sykes assumed that all prisoners shared a heterosexual orientation, arguing that enforced, involuntary celibacy would be perceived by prisoners as an assault on their masculinity, which he termed 'figurative castration.' Miller (2000: p. 4) similarly described imprisonment as 'a castrating and infantilising process,' whilst Newton (1994: p. 198) suggested that male prisoners would sense their 'masculinity' being 'besieged' due to sexual deprivation, loss of autonomy and independence, and enforced submission to authority. In his view, this assault on masculinity cultivated attitudes and behaviours designed to conceal vulnerability and exhibit toughness or aggression. Mathiesen (1990: p. 129) likewise argued that single-sex imprisonment could challenge the heterosexual male's sense of 'masculinity':

> Basically, one is shut off from the other sex which by its very polarity gives the world of one's own sex much of its meaning … a diffuse but serious threat is brought to bear on the prisoner's self-image.

Despite these somewhat reductionist, heterosexist generalisations, it could be argued that some male prisoners will adopt maladaptive attitudes and behaviours associated with a normative, hegemonic masculine culture shaped by the prison context. The experience of imprisonment can engender and reinforce values, attitudes and conduct that assist individuals to fit into the social group. Several studies have supported the notion that hierarchical social relations of dominance and subordination occur within male prison populations. Sykes (1958: p. 87) observed self-centred, egotistical 'alienative modes' that included coercion, exploitation, violence and deceit, along with subordinate, servile behaviour amongst prisoners accorded lesser social status. King and Elliott (1977) observed 'active' and 'passive' conduct amongst prisoners, characterised as exploitative ('jailing'), servile ('gleaning') or opportunistic, low profile ('doing your bird'), plus those who took the 'victim' role who were likely to be exploited or to become socially withdrawn. Cohen and Taylor (1981) noted that whilst prisoners viewed friendships with other prisoners as important for 'psychological survival,' they would balance this against maintaining a level of detachment and reserve. Miller (2000: p. 3) more recently argued that prisons should be viewed as 'sites of sexual and gender complexity' that required a much more 'nuanced understanding' than one based purely on dominant-subordinate relations.

Such arguments imply that prisoners have little choice over their circumstances, their identities and their status. Certainly, prisons structure prisoners' lives around strict regimes of compliance, discipline and order, whilst prisoners play an active role in presenting and projecting their values, attitudes and identities (Jewkes 2002). However, criminal justice settings do not operate in a simple, predictable and deterministic way, progressively stripping prisoners of their identities, as many former studies have suggested. Rather, individuals can become involved in an interdependent relationship with these institutions, adapting to and internalising the social structure, yet acting back on and shaping the social structure itself (Jewkes 2002: p. 208). They may actively engage in strategies of 'front management' to avoid being exploited by fellow inmates, endeavouring to "simultaneously maintain a private, 'pre-prison' sense of self *and* a public identity for presentation during social engagement with others" (Jewkes 2002: p. 211), which Goffman (1956) referred to as presenting one's 'backstage' and 'frontstage' selves. So, as Jewkes (2002: p. 211) suggested:

> The tensions associated with sustaining the particular bodily, gestural and verbal codes that are demanded in such an overtly masculine environment are particularly marked, and the necessity for a deep backstage area where one can "be oneself", "let off steam" and restore one's ontological reserves is therefore arguably even greater than in other settings.

It cannot be denied that people in social groups do manufacture roles and responsibilities in response to the circumstances they find themselves in, and therefore experience compulsion to conform and to orientate themselves around what is perceived to be the 'normal' or popular value system. This reflects Foucault's (1980: p. 115) notion of the 'historicisation of the subject,' where, within a prison context, the individual is constituted within a historical context and norms of masculinity then provide the benchmark for the prisoner's conduct. In this artificial world, where responsibility and choice are strictly rationed (and awarded as privileges), dominance and subordination are enacted by individuals, whereby they strive to earn respect, legitimacy and status, from other prisoners, from prison staff and from their families, friends and associates on the outside.

(Un)Healthy Prison Masculinities

The remainder of this chapter presents findings from an ethnographic study undertaken for my PhD research conducted between 1999 and 2003 (de Viggiani 2003, 2006, 2007, 2012). The research employed ethnographic methods to study the experiences of adult prisoners and prison officers in a state-run male-closed category-C training prison[1] in South West England.

The fieldwork was undertaken over eight months on an Enhanced[2] wing, involving participant observation, focus group interviews and one-to-one, semi-structured interviews. It explored how prisoners perceived imprisonment, especially living as men in a single-sex environment, and in terms the perceived effects of imprisonment on their health and wellbeing. Throughout the research, I was granted relatively unrestricted access to prisoners and staff on the wing during association periods (time out of cell) to undertake one-to-one interviews, observation and focus groups. Given the enhanced status of the prisoners, I was permitted to conduct fieldwork unsupervised, in cells or association areas. Part of this time was spent observing and participating in social, educational and employment activities; these included informal social activities (playing board games, pool and darts and engaging in casual conversations), attending education sessions (an anger management programme, an enhanced thinking skills programme, a business studies class, an IT class) and visiting the various employment sites in the prison. Despite this level of freedom, measures were instituted to protect my safety, including undertaking security training, requiring escorts between parts of the prison and staff being aware of my location at all times.

The research design drew upon Hammersley's (1992) reflexive, 'subtle realist' approach to ethnography, which requires striving to build meaningful relationships with research participants in order to elicit rich research data. Over my eight-month period of fieldwork, I became recognised and increasingly accepted by staff and prisoners. This enabled me to gather data slowly and develop an effective snowball sample of 35 prisoners and 4 prison officers. These four male officers comprised the regular wing staff in post for the duration of the fieldwork. All participants were involved in participant observation and the majority also in focus groups, one-to-one semi-structured interviews or both. Thematic analysis, based on constant comparative method, was undertaken using transcribed observation, interview and focus group data. The themes discussed here primarily arose from the semi-structured interview data. Where verbatim quotes are cited, pseudonyms are used to indicate the participant, whilst 'PO' denotes Prison Officer. Abridged citations are marked with [...], with the intention of reducing density whilst not losing the essential meanings of participants' expressions. More than 200 themes were elicited from the data principally relating to social and structural factors associated with imprisonment, some of which are explored elsewhere (de Viggiani 2006, 2007). For this chapter, I discuss the findings that best illustrate how prison masculinities could be seen to manifest within the prison regime and within social relations amongst prisoners and with prison staff.

Prison Regime

In exploring how gender manifested in this prison context, not only was I compelled to seek to understand the values, attitudes and conduct of individuals, but I also wanted to explore how institutional policies and practices operated at an ideological level. This essentially required examination of the character and perceived effects of the prison regime and prisoners' engagement with and resistance to institutional processes. Hence, prison masculinities were evident within the characteristically paternalistic and oppressive policies, regulations and practices of the institution that appeared to privilege or subordinate prisoners and staff.

Good Order and Discipline

Perhaps understandably, prison authorities instinctively seek to control and discipline prisoners on account of their previous offending behaviour. However, in the mind of the prisoner, imprisonment can then be perceived as being primarily concerned with control and discipline:

> … complete control between the prisoner and the staff, that's all prison is about – control. This prison is basically a controlling institution. As long as they can control you, that's it. As far as I'm concerned, rehabilitation and all the rest of it is bullshit. (Jake)

Most prisoners I interviewed spoke of the shock of coming to prison for the first time, and how a 'short, sharp shock' approach was an intentional strategy by prison authorities to engineer control. Many described how, as new prisoners, they had felt vulnerable and fearful of other prisoners, naivety compounding this sense of vulnerability, especially when they did not know the prison rules or procedures, the social mores and language of prison, and thus had to try to adapt quickly. Chris compared the experience with starting a new school, having to learn to fit in, not displaying one's ignorance or naivety and avoiding becoming a target for the bullies. Barry said,

> For that first month you're just in a daze ... You're scared because you've heard bad rumours about prison ... it's the worst feeling you could honestly imagine.

Even the more experienced recidivists conceded that the start of a new sentence was a difficult time; as Pat put it, it was always '... a complete and utter shock to the system.'

During the induction stage of prison, most prisoners admitted they had felt at their most vulnerable and described the experience as intimidating, degrading and incapacitating, and the manner of imprisonment as paternalistic and authoritarian. Many used these kinds of adjectives to characterise prison, where—once inside—they found that they had lost their sense of autonomy, accountability and personal responsibility:

> You've got to get used to *not* thinking for yourself ... You're told when to get up, when to get ready for bed, when to eat, when to go and do exercise, when to go to work ... everything. You've got to work your head around that, big time ... The screws basically think for you. (Pat)

This is compounded by having to endure long periods of forced idleness. Prisoners described this as 'lie-down time,' 'hibernating' and 'living in a dream world,' referring to the sedentary, unproductive periods of 'lock-up' time. Education and employment were perceived as futile or purposeless, as discussed elsewhere (de Viggiani 2006, 2012). Nonetheless, even in a training prison where education and employment are prescribed four days a week, these prisoners had experienced up to 23 hours a day locked up, mostly during the three-day weekend but also during unscheduled 'lock downs,' the statutory minimum time out of cell being 60 minutes of which 30 must be in open air (MoJ 2014).

> You're banged up and you've got four walls and a door, which you can't get through. And you're just staring at four walls. I don't care who you are, people say, "Oh, yeah, I can do my bird, I can do it standing on my head". Put them behind that door and they can snap like that. They're in tears. Nobody can handle staring at walls for twenty-three hours a day. (Jim)

These men also described what they perceived as the physical costs of enforced sedentary time:

> You're lying around in your cell all day. What can you do apart from lay on your bed? So your muscles and your bones are just seizing up, really. (Barry)

Bill had a chronic, painful form of degenerative arthritis, which he claimed had been exacerbated through the long sedentary periods when he had to lay on his bed:

> As I'm talking to you now, my back's aching just sitting here. And I've been getting this back pain a good two and a half years […] I wake up in the morning with a stiff back, so I go over there and ask for a day off work and I'm treated as a fucking malingerer and sent back to work. Obviously, I'm worried about what's going to happen to me …

Despite additional time out of cell being a rationed privilege within this prison, absurdly from a health perspective, certain privileges incentivised prisoners to remain sedentary. One prisoner remarked:

> As far as their idea of rehabilitation goes, the introduction of TVs was just another form of control, another carrot to dangle in front of you to tempt obedience. And PlayStations – prisoners sitting around playing fucking war games – I don't know. PlayStations are there just to keep them calm, keep them fucking cabbaged! (Bill)

Correspondingly, prison officers viewed in-cell television and gaming consoles as a positive intervention that pacified prisoners, reducing episodes of disorder on the wings, especially during lock-down periods.

Divide and Rule

The Incentives and Earned Privileges Scheme (IEPS) operates in all English prisons (MoJ 2011b) and is designed to incentivise individuals towards good behaviour and manage unacceptable behaviour (NOMS 2015). Prisoners perceived this approach towards their management as a strategy of 'divide and rule.' In their view, some individuals were rewarded or favoured, whilst others were not, despite their sometimes being no discernible reason. Prisoners spoke disparagingly about the scheme, arguing that it was unjust, firstly because all prisoners—even if transferred from another prison with a good behaviour record—would enter the prison at the most 'basic' level of regime, a minimum subsistence level, until they had undergone evaluation. Moreover, individuals who lacked the emotional disposition, resilience, motivation or life skills to become incentivised by the regime and to correspondingly make progress could find themselves disadvantaged; so, whilst some prospered, others did not, some shunning incentives for fear of appearing complicit to the regime. Secondly, prisoners perceived the regime as divisive because there was no guarantee a privilege would be granted on account of good behaviour. Prisoners expressed a range of grievances over this perceived source of inequity, referring to injustices they had experienced. They also viewed it as a system of rationing that reduced the incentive to progress and instilled lack of trust in the system:

> I really don't see the incentives any more. The carrot has been taken away. There's no incentive any more to listen to the rules, obey them, and be recognised for it, 'cos there's people coming in now doing things their own way but who are getting the same treatment. So, I'm obeying and respecting the rules and getting no reward for it. (Nige)

Some indeed felt they had been unfairly denied privileges despite consistently good behaviour and rarely received reasons why these had been declined. Darren, for instance, said he was repeatedly refused a Facility Licence to work outside the prison, despite a record of good conduct. Sean claimed he had served three years without any episodes of misconduct, yet said he had been repeatedly refused applications for transfer to move to a prison closer to his family. Barry's account about being refused parole illustrates how such rationing could cause individual prisoners to feel out of control:

> Getting an answer to whether you've got your parole or not would take the stress right off. Either one way or the other, whether it's yes or no, it's not

playing on your mind then, "Am I gonna get it or not?" At least then you can set your mind to what you've gotta face: "I've either got it and I'm out now in a couple of weeks", or, "I ain't, but I'm out anyway in whatever time".

Prison staff admitted that overcrowding and understaffing undermined the effectiveness of the IEPS when prisoners—irrespective of their privilege entitlements—were required to spend long periods locked up or to forgo privileges on account of institutional constraints. Doug (PO), however, said it was more than a case of managing scarce resources, as it was also a necessary technique to prevent social cohesion, cooperation and solidarity:

> If they worked as a team we would be finished. You have to treat each one of them as an individual […], you're playing a game with each one of them really, you're playing them like a fish. You see, prison officers are really extremely two-faced. (Doug, PO)

Dave had seen fellow prisoners singled out in this way:

> You'll get officers that get on your case, like, and they stay on your case for a while. They haven't actually done it to me, but I've seen it with others, where the officers just won't leave them alone. They keep on and on to them. And, like, the inmate's trying to do things and the officers are sort of stepping in their way each time. Like with jobs and that, if an inmate says, "Oh, I'd like to go for that job", the officer'll then turn round and get them totally the opposite job. And, I mean, that's just wrong, it's unfair.

Some officers were seen to operate nepotistically, inequitably favouring or rewarding prisoners. Doug (PO), for instance, admitted he was more lenient towards prisoners who had committed 'grace of God' crimes:

> There are some people in here who are genuine victims themselves, who really have been in the wrong place at the wrong time. They have committed a particular type of offence, which leaves them grieving, particularly manslaughter charges and things like this. And you find that they need help as much as anybody else does.

The Line Between Con and Screw

It was evident that relationships between prisoners and prison officers played a key function in terms of order and control, in particular how privileges and access to resources were apportioned and rationed. Prison staff maintained a discernible 'distance' between themselves and prisoners to enable them to exercise control. Indeed, prisoners shared the view that they should maintain their distance from staff, particularly officers:

> You don't cross that barrier. They are screws, we are cons, and that's it. (Tony)

Prisoners would also reinforce the status gap by only speaking to officers when spoken to and addressing them as 'boss' or 'governor,' rather than by name:

> I'm not up the screws' arses, you know. If they say "Hello" to me, I'll say "Hello" back. They then know me how I want them to know me, if you know what I mean. I do it for my benefit, not theirs. (Pat)

Amongst the inmates, it was important not to be recognised as a 'collaborator':

> If I sat in here for half an hour talking to a screw, the other guys would be asking fucking questions, like. Personally, I wouldn't want to sit and chat to a screw, like. It's not good for your health! The rest of the guys would be thinking you're a bit of a grass or something funny like that. (Len)

Several prisoners admitted that they tried not to get on the wrong side of Doug, the officer referred to previously. Chris and Jim independently remarked that this officer had pushed to have prisoners he had disliked transferred off the wing. Harry admitted that Doug had tried repeatedly to intimidate him, to 'drag me over the edge, just to nick me,' so he chose to keep out of his way.

Prisoners also recounted how they had felt patronised and belittled by prison staff; Barry described this as 'being talked to as if you're a piece of shit.' This 'parent-child' approach—as Stuart described it—served to delineate authority between prison officer and prisoner. Len (PO) said he found it easier to communicate with prisoners by treating them like children. Colin's (PO) view was that prisoners were 'children in long pants that haven't learnt the way of life,' self-centred and lacking in self-awareness, direction and purpose. Doug (PO) argued that an authoritarian approach was the best way to manage aggressive or undisciplined behaviour:

> Inmates that scream and shout are actually the easiest ones to deal with. If you get an inmate where there is a poor relationship, that's got a poor attitude, you can actually use that against him. You'll tend to find they will respond to that.

Speaking about one prisoner in particular, Lance, he said:

> I treat him cruel, but he thrives on it. He actually produces better results being treated like that than he does if you try the caring and sharing approach. He sees that as a sign of weakness, you see. So every time he comes near me, I tell him to hop it.

Jim also described his experience of this 'parent-child' approach:

> He [PO] started speaking to me like a parent, trying to talk down to me, trying to speak to me like a YO [young offender]. But it didn't work. I just spoke back to him as an adult. I could have just shouted back and slammed my door, but when I explained to him what I'd been doing, he just became sort of stuck for words. I think he realized that I was intelligent enough to turn round and say, "Look, I'm an adult, you're an adult …"

Furthermore, Jim said:

> If you're treated like an animal, you start to act like an animal. And when you're acting like an animal, you're being treated like an animal. And it keeps on and on and on. It's just a full circle. You then believe that you're not intelligent. (Jim)

Pat described an instance when he was yelled at by an officer whilst walking to a scheduled appointment at healthcare for his regular insulin injection:

> All of a sudden it's – "Oi!" And I thought, "No, they're not talking to me" … "You, in the fucking blue!", "Me?", "Yeah, you, where are you fucking going?", "Injection, gov", "Who sent you?", "Mr I, the officer on my wing", "What wing are you on?" … and, oh, Jesus! … I walked a bit faster. Their attitude really does stink.

This rather aggressive, authoritarian manner displayed by some officers—which I indeed witnessed—served to inhibit relations between prisoners and staff, fostering lack of respect on both sides and reinforcing the 'con–screw' divide. Prisoners also perceived officers' displays of toughness as attempts to *appear* tough, as Jim inferred: '… they're wanting authority … thinking they're something they're not.'

Prisoner Social Relations

Relationships amongst prisoners can be temporary and superficial, especially where prisoners are not serving life sentences, and given the transience of prison populations with average sentence length in England of 16 months and 57% of prisoners in custody for under six months (Prison Reform Trust 2015: p. 4). On entering prison, prisoners said they endeavoured to remain anonymous and 'keep their head down' to avoid drawing unwarranted attention and risk exploitation or victimisation. This could involve projecting a 'front' as a strategy of self-preservation:

> As soon as that door's open, everyone puts up a front. It's like trying to be something you're not. (Sean)

> Everybody's trying to prove that they're somebody […] all this striving to be noticed, you know, just to be an individual. It's just one big competition to be noticed. (Nige)

Prison Talk: Putting Up a Front

Front projection was particularly evident in the banter—or 'prison talk'—that revealed some individuals' efforts to attain social standing, to fit in and to express confidence. I observed prisoners exaggerating their stories to get their point across, sometimes to outwit or impress. Paul, for instance, was outwardly a joker and crowd pleaser, and used coarse language and anecdotes when with others, which he openly admitted to me was a prison survival tactic, declaring, 'I'm a different person on the out, we all are.'

Such behaviour was also viewed as annoying, provocative or even offensive. Stuart was irritated by the 'incessant talk' he described as 'white van man, Sun reader mentality,' whilst Bill said:

> I don't feel that I fit in at all. You're forced into [...] living with people that you wouldn't normally live with, like, and, I mean, a lot of the talk I hear is just idle fucking chat, you know, just talking for the sake of talking.

Banter was also of a sexual nature, sometimes a means to communicate heterosexual orientation through reference to wives, girlfriends and sexual exploits, coupled with expressions of frustration associated with involuntary celibacy whilst in prison. Some prisoners talked openly about women in a sexual way, using coarse, sexist or misogynistic language:

> A lot of birds want to know when you're getting out, because they know you ain't had none for a while, and that you're really up for it .... (Chris)

Some prisoners used demeaning, sexist language to describe female prison officers. Harry referred to one officer as a 'little woman' and another as a 'little girl.' Nathan referred to a particular female officer as 'a bit of a dog.' Pat had noticed 'one or two tasty screws' in the prison, and Sean's view was that 'all the girls in here are lovely!' The fact that the governor was also a woman was a further point of interest for several prisoners who criticised her managerial style on account of her sex, Jake, for instance, suggesting that "a woman with little experience of the male prison system will have little idea of how to manage one."

Several prisoners described the female prison estate as 'dolls' houses.' One prison officer spoke crudely about the time he had worked at HMP Holloway in London:

> You'd open the door … and there'd be a woman stood there stark naked with a big smile on her face. And quite often you'd walk into their cell and they'd be sitting playing with themselves, legs wide open. So I'd just turn round and say, "I've seen hedgehogs better than that dead on the street!"

Len (PO) made allegations about sexual misconduct perpetrated by female prison staff, which he used to justify his view that all staff should be male:

> We've had female staff shagging inmates. One was suspended and one got the sack about three years ago, a nurse. I mean, even the teachers have done it as well. It's happening all over the place. It happens in all the prisons. That's why I don't agree with female staff at a male prison.

On the other hand, sexist and misogynistic banters were a source of irritation for some prisoners. Bill found the coarse sexual language used by others offensive:

> I've listened to conversations about women and some of them are bordering on rape. They look at them as a piece of meat, and that's it. A woman to them is from the neck down … I never really experienced that sort of attitude until I came here.

Such individuals expressed more positive views of female staff, several suggesting that they reduced tension on the wings:

> I think female officers actually have a positive effect […] they actually help the environment, I think they soften it quite a lot. They do calm a situation quite quickly. (Stuart)

Nearly all the cells I entered had pornographic images from magazines displayed on the walls, which prompted me to ask about this during interview. Derek had a few pictures on his wall but admitted they frustrated him. Sam admitted:

They're there purely and simply because of people coming in here saying, "It's about time you got some pictures up." It's not actually through choice.

Interestingly, I noticed that some officers kept pornographic magazines in the staff room on the wing, presumably for their own use.

Homophobic language was also frequently characterised the informal banter. When I asked directly about this, it tended to trigger the response that same-sex relations were taboo in prison, that gay, bisexual or transgender prisoners were usually invisible and that such individuals should keep this private. Warren remarked:

There's no queers or nothing like that running around. It's just not the done thing, you know. You'd get battered, you'd get proper battered. So there's none of that goes on.

Projecting Toughness and Machismo

In a similar fashion, some prisoners projected a tough 'don't mess with me' front that Jim referred to as 'strutting.' As Bill put it:

Some of 'em will walk about with carpets under their arms …, pushing each other about, and fucking jousting and shadow boxing, and all that fucking nonsense.

Harry admitted:

You've got to sort of build yourself up, you've got to pump yourself up, like, and make yourself look a big guy. It's not necessarily all about muscles and all that. It's a man thing.

Referring to Lance, an ex-soldier, Bill said:

I had this fella in here the other day, an ex-squaddie, and the fucking nonsense he was coming out with! I thought, shall I start arguing with him and giving him my view, but I thought, no, he's too far fucking immersed in it. He was talking about the stuff he wants to do when he gets out, how he wants to die in combat. And I thought, '"Fucking hell!" There was this barrier he was putting up, like. I could feel it, like. I felt that if I said the wrong word, I was going to get fucking floored, like.'

I interviewed Lance, who was indeed heavily built and intimidating in his demeanour. He had his left leg in plaster and admitted with pride in his voice that he had shattered the tibia and fibula doing heavy-weight 'squats' in the gym and refused help from other prisoners to collect his meals from the servery, so as not to appear weak:

> I'm walking on it, but that's just through sheer stubbornness, because I don't want to rely on no one here.

Use of the weights room in the prison gym seemed to be a 'must have' privilege for some prisoners. Tommy painted a rather comic picture, referring to Geoff Capes, the 1980s Olympic Athlete and Strongman:

> You sees people come in skinny as fuck, then six months later you sees 'em looking like Geoff Capes … and their attitude changes with it.

Likewise, Harry said:

> They're building up their bodies trying to look good and eating all the garbage under the sun … They're trying to portray a healthy, fit person, who's not going to be messed with. But, really, they're not projecting a healthy image at all, they're projecting an image of masculinity. (Harry)

Barry described how prisoners who used the weights room would become patronising and sanctimonious:

> You'll get ones coming up, you know, that go to the gym – "Hey, you wanna *eat* some more", or, "You wanna go over to the gym". And you get the ones that try to talk down to you, the bigger ones, and all this. At the end of the day, just because you've got a lot more muscle don't mean you're any bigger or harder than anyone else, you know.

Ewan referred to the weights room as 'very, very macho … everybody trying to outdo everybody else,' and Stuart described it as a 'tense, testosterone-fired' place. Trevor said it 'breeds testosterone [...] you'll get people coming back all hyped up, and that just breeds violent people.' Ken said:

> They go up there, like, to prove theirselves. They do it to pose. They will do one exercise and then they're in the mirror, checking out their muscles.

Stuart admitted that the first time he had visited the weights room, he had been put off by the tense, competitive atmosphere and the poor level of supervision. Others admitted embarrassment or fear of ridicule had prevented them using *any* of the prison sports facilities. Soccer and softball tournaments were periodically organised between wings, which led to pressure to participate. Trevor, who was in his 50s and had a heart condition, had been talked into playing in a softball match. He recalled how, whilst making a run, he was cajoled by the rest of his team:

> It was, "Come on you old fart! You're not gonna get anywhere!" ... and the lads on my team were yelling, "yeah, yeah, go on pops!"

Frank, who was quite heavily overweight, was persuaded to play five-a-side football, despite reservations:

> Why should I join in and then get people saying, "Look at that fat cunt!"? ... I went over to play football last week, and the screw came up to me and said, "Oh, fucking hell, what've we got here, then?"

The Gendered Pecking Order

Prisoners and prison staff—to greater and lesser degrees—evidently strove to project an 'acceptable' façade to others, through language and conversations and in the ways they endeavoured to present themselves physically and emotionally. These responses were crudely aligned with normative and somewhat artificial dominant or subordinate modes of expression, personality, status and identity, whereby individuals would derive respect or distain from others, and/or mete this out to others.

Some individuals referred to their own or others' criminal reputations as a symbol of notoricty or to convey a tough façade:

> I could easily end up back in jail through fighting, like, 'cos I won't take shit from anybody, like. So I suppose that's the main problem I've got to deal with, like. You know yourself, there'll be a lot of times when there are cunts winding you up, and they take great pleasure in it. And they end up hurting and you're locked up. What can you do about people like that, you know, apart from bury them? (Ian)

Dan had a long conviction history for violence, which most prisoners knew about. The officers referred to him as the 'daddy of the wing' on account of this experience and recalled how he would offer advice and protection to new prisoners:

> 'When the younger ones have problems, they'll always go to him for help. Someone will come into the office with a black eye and we'll say, "Oh, so what happened to you?" "Oh, I fell over". And Dan will come down later and say, "It's all right, boss, I've sorted it, enough said". I mean, to be perfectly honest, we know what's going on, but we let it go because we know Dan will calm the wing down. You can turn a blind eye to it. And if we want something sorted, we'll let him go ahead and sort it, so long as he don't assault no-one." (Len-PO)

Less experienced prisoners would seek social recognition from more experienced or respected prisoners, attempting to improve their own social standing:

> If they can be seen as close to him [Dan], then their status is that much improved, 'cos that's what prison's all about, where you are in the pecking order. (Tom PO)

Speaking about Dan, Chris said:

> He's very unpredictable. That's why people respect him. 'Cos they don't wanna get on the wrong side of him. He's got respect 'cos of his age. But I think it's 'cos of who he is as well. He's a nice bloke and all, but he *has* got a

5 "Don't Mess with Me!" Enacting Masculinities...

temper on him. So if you're a bit of a tasty person like Dan, and you're unpredictable, and people are a bit wary of you, they're gonna be nice and polite. People might think he's a wanker, but they won't say it to his face. (Chris)

Thus, a prisoner's offending history, as well as their demeanour in prison, could affect their social standing, criminal notoriety drawing respect. For example, Frank claimed that his conviction for armed robbery raised his credibility. In a similar way, prisoners would endeavour to legitimise their offence either by embellishing or spinning an acceptable version, or by contrasting it with offences perceived to be more heinous, immoral or unacceptable.

> The gangster who blows another gangster's head away and kills him is given higher regard than the lad who knocks over an old woman and grabs her handbag. (Tom PO)

In this regard, sexual offences, especially those against children, were considered the most heinous, attracting the label of 'nonce.'[3] Ian used the term 'nonce' specifically referring to child sex offenders, whom he viewed as 'a separate class of prisoner,' and despite having been convicted for rape and assault, Harry declared: 'The real low-lifes in here are the fucking dirty kiddie fiddlers.'

He found it necessary to put up a 'defensive shield' whenever questioned about his own offence; Dan's response illustrates this, where he referred to Harry:

> Anyone can get done for rape. There's one on this wing, for instance, who had a row with his missus, and she yelled "Rape!" It's so easily done, isn't it? So, I don't believe that rape is so bad. But when it comes to indecently assaulting children, that's bad then, isn't it?

It was common for prisoners to contrive carefully rehearsed accounts of their offences, so that if questioned they had a prepared response:

> You might have assaulted and robbed an old woman in her home, which, in here, makes you scum … There's fucking loads of them who've done that

in here, who go to the elderly because they're easy pickings. But then they'll say they're in for burglary or something like that ... (Harry)

Trevor was serving time for fraud, but being in his 50s and aware of his middle-class accent, he was routinely probed by others about his offence:

You don't go round saying what you've done. But then they'll say, "So, what are you in for?", and I'll say, "Theft". And 'cos I'm older, then I'm hearing comments like, "I'm sure he's a nonce". And then somebody else has picked up on it, so you've got a problem.

Crying Behind Your Cell Door

It emerged that key to social survival was to avoid exploitation or victimisation at all costs, and this was partly achieved through various normative performances of masculinity, where individual endeavoured to fit in socially or through maintaining a low profile, which was characterised as 'keeping one's head down.' This commonly necessitated projecting an uncontroversial, unemotional and confident façade, concealing weakness or potential vulnerabilities. Most prisoners said it was important to stand up for oneself when challenged, not to overreact to being taunted and not to be perceived as a 'push over' (Pat). Chris said he had 'learned the hard way':

I'd be shouted at through the windows, and I was in a pretty bad way. I was weak mentally and I was scared. But I wouldn't show it. I couldn't show it. But I was frightened.

Many, including staff, suggested it was preferable to suffer in silence than to ask for help:

You'll get an inmate with a black eye who comes to the office and says he's being bullied. And when you ask him who's been doing it, he goes, "I'm not a grass. I won't grass on 'em." It's partly fear, but it's also the culture that they have here. Grassing is the lowest of the low, even though you try and explain to him that he's protecting the one who's robbed from his own. They'll still protect the bullies. (Doug, PO)

This usually meant that whilst individuals could have significant personal and emotional issues going on, they would keep this quiet:

> Most of these [fellow prisoners], I think, would cope much better if they faced their problems and had a good cry. Some of them must be really hurting inside, but they won't show it …. (Kieran)

> I'll guarantee you that 80% of [prisoners in] this jail have cried when they're behind that cell door. Every man's had a cry. I've had a cry or two, and I'm not ashamed to admit it. If having a cry's the way you can relieve some tension, pressures, hassles, fucking heartache, whatever, you know, that's what you should do, like, if it helps. (Ian)

Kieran admitted he had attempted suicide in a previous prison when he had been too scared to leave his cell. Warren, on the other hand, admitted he had become increasingly withdrawn and spent as much time as possible in his cell to avoid contact with others. Sam described how he had noticed some individuals would appear withdrawn and detached, adopting various mask-like expressions:

> You get the almost 'autistic' mask, where people don't show any emotion, and then you've got those who wear a 'constantly pissed-off' mask.

Conclusions

A key dimension of 'handling one's bird' lies in the individual's capacity to survive the social environment of prison—imprisonment is indeed fundamentally social. Within this social context, power is exercised through identity, more specifically through signifiers of gender, sexuality, race, ethnicity, religion, class and background. This chapter has focused principally on gender; however, race, ethnicity, religion, class and background constituted key thematic areas within the original research, although there is no scope here to explore these in further depth.

As Foucault argued, power is exercised though the body and is expressed through individuals' "actions and attitudes, their discourses, learning processes and everyday lives" (Foucault 1980: p. 30). Thus by observing prisoners and prison staff, and through listening to their accounts, it became clear to me that the prison social context engendered and perpetuated language, attitudes and behaviours polarised around normative expressions of gender identity. First, at the institutional level, the incentive-based system was employed to appeal to prisoners to conform to good order and discipline. Yet, in my view, this mechanism was flawed and counterproductive, since—according to prisoners and prison officers—it progressively disenfranchised and disempowered individual prisoners by rationing their choices and reducing their capacity for personal responsibility. Essentially, prisoners were treated as docile subjects, impotent within a regime of paternalistic authoritarianism that was enacted through the disciplinarian conduct of staff. This system of control reinforced dissonance towards prisoners' personal rehabilitation goals, especially their desire to rebuild their lives beyond prison, and fostered mistrust in the institution and its staff.

Secondly, within this strongly normative gendered social world, individuals had to learn quickly to fit in and avoid unwarranted attention. Some would play an active and visible role in this regard, whilst others would attempt to 'keep their head down,' maintaining a low profile. The strategies prisoners used to fit into the everyday social life of prison were evident in how they presented themselves to others, both prisoners and staff, especially through use of language (prison talk), their attitudes towards others and their conduct. Close social proximity meant that normative discourses became acute and magnified, orientated around narrow values associated with a heterosexist masculine ideology, which compelled individuals to present a tough façade even if this meant suppressing or concealing their emotions. Carrying this off effectively necessitated adopting 'alienative modes' (after Sykes 1958)—attitudes and behaviours signalling that the individual appears to be in control, loyal to others, prepared to join in and willing to condone normative heterosexist, homophobic and misogynistic values. Conformity in this respect was perceived to be essential to avoid becoming exploited or victimised.

However, it is essential to avoid focusing solely on prisoner identity when endeavouring to theorise about prison masculinities, as this risks shifting responsibility and accountability away from the broader institutional system. Rather than pathologise and problematise the prisoner—or indeed the prison officer—per se, it is important to acknowledge the ideological character of the criminal justice system and of the host society. In this regard, Sim (1994: p. 108) argued that power in prisons should not be interpreted solely in terms of individuals' quests for power, but in terms of society's exercise of its institutional apparatus to manage and 'normalise' individuals whom the state labels 'offenders.' Arguably, then, the criminal justice system materially and symbolically reproduces the ideology of the host society, mediating the identities of prisoners and of prison staff. The efficacy of prisons as mechanisms to improve and rehabilitate offenders is then questionable, given that the system itself—at least as I observed within this prison between 1999 and 2001—can create the ideal conditions for exploitation, nepotism and inequity, via a masculinist ideology of paternalistic authoritarianism. Under this ethos, to survive and thrive, individuals feel compelled to act as they perceive others would expect them to, by adopting the normative masculine apparel. The individual is therefore expected to embrace the identity of 'criminal' and 'offender' and then jostle with the experience of striving to conform, whilst engaging in an existential battle of self.

Prison is undoubtedly a stressful experience, but this extends beyond being locked up and separated from one's family or peer group. Whilst prison is 'designed' to remove an individual's liberty as a free citizen, prison brings into play a range of additional losses, which Mathiesen (1990: p. 138) referred to as deprivations of control, responsibility and choice. Prison forces prisoners to conform, often in unintended ways, whereby they may actively resist the regime to become socially accepted, thereby avoiding a difficult time in prison but forgoing potential opportunities and privileges. Social survival becomes paramount, even if this serves to compromise a prisoner's health, wellbeing and longer term rehabilitation. Prisoners and prison staff become involved in acts of self-censorship, self-subjectification and objectification, acceding to an institutional culture shaped by archaic, artificial hegemonic ideals, where 'masculinities' emerge in the performances of the actors and within the very fabric of the theatre.

You're either up there with the boys or you're down there with the more timid weaker people. You're either popular or you're not. And if you're not, you're in for a hard time, you're in for a rough ride. You're either one of the boys or you ain't. (Chris)

The strongest rule, and the one at the bottom just lies down and they wipe their feet on him. (Doug, Prison Officer)

Notes

1. Closed category-C training prisons are for adult prisoners who are serving medium- to long-term sentences, who are employed in a variety of education, employment and offending behaviour programmes. They accommodate prisoners who cannot be trusted in open conditions but who do not have the resources and will to make a determined escape attempt (MoJ 2011a).
2. Under the Incentives and Earned privileges Scheme (PSO 4000), prisoners are incentivised and rewarded with privileges through good behaviour and performance. Prisoners on enhanced level receive additional visits, better accommodation, additional time for association, more private cash and priority consideration for higher rates of pay. (MoJ 2011b).
3. "Nonce" is defined by the Oxford English Dictionary (2016) as "a sexual deviant; a person convicted of a sexual offence, esp. child abuse." The term may be derived from nance, meaning nancy-boy, or from nonse, the Lincolnshire dialect meaning 'good-for-nothing fellow' (OED 2016). 'Nonce' is also interpreted as an abbreviation for 'Not of Normal Criminal Ethos' (McFarquhar 2011).

References

Berger, P., & Luckmann, T. (1967). *The social construction of reality*. Harmondsworth: Penguin Books.

Chesney-Lind, M., & Pasko, L. (2013). *The female offender: Girls, women, and crime* (3rd ed.). London: Sage Publications.

Clemmer, D. (1958). *The prison community*. New York: Holt, Rinehart and Winston.

Cohen, S. (1979). The punitive city. In J. Muncie, E. McLaughlin, & M. Langan (Eds.), *Criminological perspectives*. London: Sage.

Cohen, S., & Taylor, L. (1981). *Psychological survival: The experience of long-term imprisonment*. Harmondsworth: Penguin Books.

Collier, R. (1997). After Dunblane: Crime, corporeality, and the (hetero-)sexing of the bodies of men. *Journal of Law and Society, 24*, 177–198.

Connell, R. (2005). *Masculinities* (2nd ed.). Cambridge: Polity Press.

Connell, R. W., & Messerschmidt, J. W. (2005). Hegemonic masculinity: Rethinking the concept. *Gender and Society, 19*(6), 829–859.

de Viggiani, N. (2003). *Un(healthy) prison masculinities: Theorising men's health in prison*. PhD Thesis. University of Bristol.

de Viggiani, N. (2006). Surviving prison: Exploring prison social life as a determinant of health. *International Journal of Prisoner Health, 2*(2), 71–89.

de Viggiani, N. (2007). Unhealthy prisons: Exploring structural determinants of prison health. *Sociology of Health and Illness, 29*(1), 115–135.

de Viggiani, N. (2012). Trying to be something you're not: Masculine performances within a prison setting. *Men and Masculinities, 15*(3), 271–291.

Fielding, N. (1993). Ethnography. In N. Gilbert (Ed.), *Researching social life* (pp. 154–171). London: Sage Publications.

Foucault, M. (1977). *Discipline and punish: The birth of the prison*. London: Allen Lane.

Foucault, M. (1980). *Power/knowledge*. Brighton: Harvester.

Glouberman, S. (1990). *Keepers: Inside stories from total institutions*. London: King Edward's Hospital Fund.

Goffman, E. (1956). *The presentation of self in everyday life*. New York: Doubleday.

Goffman, E. (1961). *Asylums*. Harmondsworth: Penguin Books.

Hammersley, M. (1992). *What's wrong with ethnography?* London: Routledge.

Helliwell, J. F., & Putnam, R. D. (2004). The social context of well-being. *Philosophical Transactions of the Royal Society of London. Series B: Biological Sciences, 359*(1449), 1435–1446.

Hinojosa, R. (2010). Doing hegemony: Military, men, and constructing a hegemonic masculinity. *Journal of Men's Studies, 18*(2), 179–194.

Hockey, J. (1986). *Squaddies: Portrait of a subculture*. Exeter: Exeter University Press.

Holstein, J. A., & Gubrium, J. F. (2000). *The self we live by: Narrative identity in a postmodern world*. New York: Oxford University Press.

Jewkes, Y. (2002). The use of media in constructing identities in the masculine environment of men's prisons. *European Journal of Communication, 17,* 205–225.

King, R. D., & Elliott, K. W. (1977). *Albany: Birth of a prison – End of an era.* London: Routledge & Kegan Paul.

Mathiesen, T. (1990). *Prison on trial.* London: Sage Publications.

McFarquhar, H. (2011). *Key concepts in criminology and criminal justice.* Basingstoke: Palgrave Macmillan.

Messerschmidt, J. W. (1993). *Masculinities and crime: Critique and reconceptualization of theory.* Lanham: Rowman and Littlefield.

Messerschmidt, J. W. (1997). *Crime as structured action: Gender, race, class and crime in the making.* London: Sage Publications.

Miller, T. A. (2000). Surveillance: Gender, privacy and the sexualization of power in prison. *George Mason University Civil Rights Law Journal, 291,* 1–39.

Ministry of Justice. (2011a). *Prison service instruction 40/2011: National security framework ref: NSF 1.1 categorisation and re-categorisation of adult male prisoners.* London: Ministry of Justice.

Ministry of Justice. (2011b). *Prison service instruction 11/2011: Incentives and earned privileges.* London: Ministry of Justice.

Ministry of Justice. (2014). *Prison service instruction 10/2011: Residential services.* London: Ministry of Justice. https://www.justice.gov.uk/offenders/psis/prison-service-instructions-2013. Accessed 25 Jan 2016.

National Offender Management Service. (2015). PSI 30/2013 *Incentives and earned privileges scheme.* London: National Offender Management Service. https://www.justice.gov.uk/offenders/psis/prison-service-instructions-2013. Accessed 25 Jan 2016.

Newton, C. (1994). Gender theory and prison sociology: Using theories of masculinities to interpret the sociology of prisons for men. *The Howard Journal, 10,* 193–202.

Oxford English Dictionary. (2016). Oxford: Oxford University Press. http://www.oed.com/. Accessed 25 Jan 2016.

Prison Reform Trust. (2015). *Bromley briefings prison factfile, autumn 2015.* London: Prison Reform Trust. http://www.prisonreformtrust.org.uk/Portals/0/Documents/Bromley%20Briefings/Factfile%20Autumn%202015.pdf. Accessed 21 Jan 2016.

Renzetti, C. M. (2013). *Feminist criminology.* Abingdon: Routledge.

Ridgeway, C. L., & Correll, S. J. (2004). Unpacking the gender system: A theoretical perspective on gender beliefs and social relations. *Gender and Society, 18*(4), 510–531.

Schwarzer, R., & Leppin, A. (1989). Social support and health: A meta-analysis. *Psychology & Health: An International Journal, 3*, 1–15.

Sim, J. (1994). Tougher than the rest? Men in prison. In T. Newburn & E. Stanko (Eds.), *Just boys doing business? Men, masculinities and crime* (pp. 100–117). London: Routledge.

Sykes, G. M. (1958). *The society of captives: A study of a maximum security prison.* Princeton: Princeton University Press.

Tay, L., Tan, K., Diener, E., & Gonzalez, E. (2013). Social relations, health behaviors, and health outcomes: A survey and synthesis: Social relations and health. *Applied Psychology: Health and Well-Being, 5*(1), 28–78.

Towl, G. (1993). Culture' groups in prison. In A. Brown & B. Caddick (Eds.), *Groupwork with offenders.* London: Whiting and Birch.

Truong, N. (2006). Constructing masculinities and experiencing loss: What the writings of two Chinese Americans tell. *Men and Masculinities, 8*(3), 321–330.

Twain, M. (1923). *The complete works of mark twain: Europe and elsewhere.* New York: Harper and Brothers.

West, C., & Fenstermaker, S. (1995). Doing difference. *Gender and Society, 9*(1), 8–37.

6

Saying the Unsayable: Foregrounding Men in the Prison System

Jennifer Sloan

In this chapter, I argue that whilst men comprise 95% of the prison population in England and Wales (MoJ 2017), and dominate the prison and criminal justice systems across the world, they do not dominate the academic and policy discourse surrounding punishment and penal reform. Instead, certain groups such as women, young people, ethnic minorities, religious groups or the mentally ill tend to be given specific attention. Rarely are men in prison as a group foregrounded within critical discourse around penal policy and research; rather, they are 'seen' (whilst simultaneously going 'unseen') as the norm, the stereotype and the population that prison was designed for in the first place.

This chapter questions why it is that men tend to be hidden from view in discussions of prisons and penal policy and research, and the implications of this for both men and for women within (and beyond) the prison system. In particular, it discusses how, ultimately, there are serious implications for feminist thinking in the process of not considering the men at the heart of the prison system. In this chapter, I draw on my research with prisoners undertaken as part of my ethnographic doctoral research in

J. Sloan (✉)
Sheffield Hallam University, Sheffield, UK

2009, funded by the University of Sheffield (see Sloan 2011). All names used are pseudonyms. Where there is a jurisdictional focus provided, England and Wales is the setting, however, arguably this is a global issue as I argue that men dominate the prison systems of the world, but rarely are truly seen in the discourses surrounding them.

As a feminist, I believe in equality, kindness and treating others with respect and dignity, regardless of corporeal composition, clothing or colour. Yet feminism has often been (incorrectly) seen as silencing the voices of men in favour of the oppressed female. As a result, the feminist movement has at times been (inaccurately) positioned as 'anti-men' and as prioritising the needs of women. This process is particularly clear within feminist criminology and in feminist work around incarceration. In December 2013, an article published in the Lancet (Hawton et al. 2013) resulted in the BBC headline 'Self-harm 'four times more likely' in female prisoners' (BBC 2013). The article itself reveals that between 2004 and 2009 '5–6% of male prisoners and 20–24% of female inmates self-harmed every year' (Hawton et al. 2013: 1). Considered merely on these proportions, the statistics suggest a much larger problem in women's prisons. Yet, what the reporting by the BBC masks is the huge scale of the problem of self-harm amongst male prisoners. Indeed, there were 5340 male inmates who self-harmed in 2009, compared to the 1356 female inmates, which prompts the question: why is one group of prisoners privileged in relation to attention, sympathy and outrage about the problem of self-harm in prisons when both groups are suffering (Hawton et al.: 3)?

Men dominate the prison system globally. In England and Wales, there are ten times as many male as female prison institutions. Yet, strangely, this centrality of men in the prison system is almost always pushed aside, with other distinct groups deflecting attention from the male whole. Women's imprisonment, ethnic minorities, sex offenders, young offenders, juveniles, the mentally ill and religious groups tend to dominate academic and policy discourse, whilst all apparently overlooking the numerical dominance of men within prisons. Women are often positioned as different and worthy of special attention due to the fact that they are the minority. For example, Baroness Corston, in her seminal review of women with particular vulnerabilities within the criminal justice system, states:

6 Saying the Unsayable: Foregrounding Men in the Prison System

There are fundamental differences between male and female offenders and those at risk of offending that indicate a different and distinct approach is needed for women. For example: Most women do not commit crime.... (2007: 3)

By contrast, it is rare for men to be given distinct attention as a gender group in prison research and policy-making. There is no equivalent to the Corston Report for men, even though many of the needs and vulnerabilities raised by Baroness Corston in relation to female prisoners are true for men in prison too. For example, following the point that 'most women do not commit crime'[1] (Corston 2007: 3), the report states a range of 'differences' between male and female offenders including the following:

Women with histories of violence and abuse are over represented in the criminal justice system and can be described as victims as well as offenders
   Coercion by men can form a route into criminal activity for some women
   Drug addiction plays a huge part in all offending and is disproportionately the case with women
   Self-harm in prison is a huge problem and more prevalent in the women's estate (Corston 2007: 3)

All of these statements raise issues that apply to both women *and* men in prison. Male prisoners also often have experienced histories of violence and coercion, drug and alcohol addiction, self-harm and mental illness (Prison Reform Trust 2016). However, such perceived vulnerabilities could be said to be in direct conflict with our expectations of what men should be and how they should act (see Sloan 2016). One man that I spoke to in prison, when discussing his self-harming behaviours, made a key observation relating to gendered behavioural expectations of men in prison:

I said [to a member of staff] because to me it's like coping at times. Ok it's not normal to you…I said but you, I said you'd consider me going along and hitting someone else normal behaviour, whereas cutting, hurting myself, that's not normal [...]. (Noah)

In addition, the Corston report states that 'Prison is disproportionably harsher for women because prisons and the practices within them have for the most part been designed for men' and 'Levels of security in prison were put in place to stop men escaping' (2007: 3). What this fails to acknowledge is that prisons and practices were designed to accommodate male prisoners, but, more often than not, with outdated ideals of standards and prisoner needs in contemporary times; that is not for male prisoners *today*. Many prison designs are hundreds of years old. Further, as Young and Reviere note, 'most prisons are built to house violent men' (2006: 2), and the fact that the prison estate was created and designed to prevent men escaping merely highlights the security-focussed nature of imprisonment. This can be felt equally harshly by both women and men—perhaps more so for men at times, bearing in mind the lack of trust that is placed in their gender as a whole (a good example of this can be seen in Jimmy Boyle's account in Smith 1984: 474).

Yet, many may feel it 'unfeminist' (with regard to the fight to bring forward women's voices) to want to foreground the voices of men when women still suffer inequality throughout the world; this is the origin of the chapter's focus on the importance of including men's voices and experiences as unsayable—particularly by a feminist criminologist. In this chapter, I question the lack of attention that has been given to men as a gendered group in prison, considering the ways in which the subject has been avoided in academic discourse in the past, and the reasoning behind this lack of explicit consideration of male prisoners. In addition, I consider the implications for this avoidance, both for men and women in prison and beyond. I argue that, ultimately, it is 'unfeminist' to silence the vulnerable, regardless of their gender or sex, if the feminist struggle is in the name of equality (bell hooks 2000). Indeed, Cohen (2014) recognises that constructing one group as 'normal' relative to another with regard to gender in the criminal justice system can reinforce the hegemonic masculinity that feminists and feminism struggle so hard to push against.

The 'Feminist' Agenda

There is a variety of definitions that are assigned to (or imposed upon) 'feminism'. In this chapter, I draw on the definition of feminism taken from leading feminist bell hooks. She argues that:

6 Saying the Unsayable: Foregrounding Men in the Prison System

> Feminist struggle takes place anytime anywhere any female or male resists sexism, sexist exploitation, and oppression. Feminist movement happens when groups of people come together with an organized strategy to take action to eliminate patriarchy. (2000: xi)

Yet, as a 'feminist' researcher, it always shocks me how little attention men are actually given—both as victims and perpetrators of crimes—and how much attention is diverted from them. Indeed, the very idea of being a feminist researcher who is arguing for the acknowledgement of the needs of men sits uneasily with many staunch feminist academics. Where feminism does engage with prisons, it tends to be for the benefit of the oppressed women—of a variety of intersecting identities—within. For example, Flavin and Huss (2014) draw attention to the reproductive and health rights of women in prison:

> Many mainstream feminist and prochoice groups have been reluctant to adopt intersectional approaches to declare common cause with other progressive movements, Yet the advent of mass incarceration and the prison industrial complex (PIC) makes clear that securing women's reproductive health and rights requires our full-on and intersectional engagement.

I am not wishing to suggest that all feminists divert attention from men—far from it—nor do I suggest that women in prison are undeserving of such attention. What is lacking, however, is any great consideration of the ways in which men's gendered experiences of prison may need just as much sympathetic attention as women's if they are to become less violent or harmful upon release from prison. Such an avoidance of the male subject and his associated potential vulnerabilities is not just limited to the male offender; indeed Cohen makes a similar point in relation to male rape victims, stating that '…the male victim of rape is constructed at present in reluctant and stilted conversation with feminism' (2014: 5–6).

Greer (2012) advocates that women should problematise behaviours, norms and bodies being policed by those in authority (usually powerful men). Such processes, however, also apply to men in prison whose masculinities are often restricted and pushed to extremes of negativity through the imposition of hegemonic norms and unattainable ideals of maleness, *and* social control processes imposed and enforced by a majority-male criminal justice and politico-legal system. As such, men in prisons are subject to the policing of gendered behaviours by other, more powerful men (see Bibbings 2014; Kimmel 1994; Connell 2005). The issue of patriarchy can (and does) affect and impinge upon both women and men.

In addition, the hypermasculine expectations of male prisons tend to focus upon traits of resilience, being able to cope (or at least hide the fact that you can't), not to show weakness or emotions, and to get through your sentence (see Sloan 2011). None of these traits involves men standing up and calling attention to their oppressed situation—indeed, where they do, they tend to be faced with problems and seen to be causing trouble. As one participant in my research said:

> *And you keep complaining they [prison staff] see you as a pest. [...] You know what I mean, you try to stand up, [...] you try to stand up for yourself…they see you as a problem. So you can't win in prison [...] You cannot win. You try standing up for yourself and you start putting in complaints and start, you moan about the food and that…they just see you as a control hazard and everything, you know what I mean. (Gabriel)*

Whereas many women outside of prison will stand up for the rights of women prisoners, men do not readily champion or defend masculinity in the same ways.[2] In fact, to be seen to need such championing would place male prisoners as being in need of help or assistance, thereby undermining what autonomy and power they have managed to retain within the prison (see Sloan 2016), which is so important to the masculine self: as Kimmel notes, 'the hegemonic definition of manhood is a man *in* power, a man *with* power, and a man *of* power' (1994: 125). Self-sufficiency is key to this, particularly to men in prison (Sloan 2011, 2012a).

'Prison damages people' (Behan 2002), but many appear surprised when men are released from prison to commit more crimes, or at the least we seem to be a society resigned to the doomed state of prisoners (by which I mean male prisoners) and the prison system's failings with regard to rehabilitation. But there does always seem to be a sense of 'I told you so' in media reports of reoffending of male prisoners. When inside, there is little focus on what happens to the men, as long as they are kept away from 'us'. Indeed, when it comes to prisons (by which we can generally read 'men's prisons'), security is key, as seen in the first objective of the UK's Her Majesty' (HM) Prison Service, which is:

> To protect the public and provide what commissioners want to purchase by:
> - *Holding prisoners securely*
> - Reducing the risk of prisoners re-offending
> - Providing safe and well-ordered establishments in which we treat prisoners humanely, decently and lawfully. (Ministry of Justice 2015a—emphasis added)

Research on Men in Prison

Most feminist criminological scholars acknowledge the lack of attention given to men within criminological research, in spite of their dominance within the field of offending (Wykes and Welsh 2009; Walklate 2004; Howe 2008). There has been some, albeit not much, attention given to men and criminal justice,[3] and a number of prison scholars have included notions of masculinity in their work (see Aresti 2010; Butler 2007; Crewe 2009; Jewkes 2002a, b, 2005; Moolman 2011; Phillips 2012). Yet, in all of these, maleness is often secondary to another factor which distinguishes or differentiates certain types of men (violence, drugs, the media, sex offending, race, etc.). However, as illustrated by a quote from a participant in my own research, men in prison do tend to go through this process of differentiation amongst themselves, situating themselves as 'different' to other prisoners (see also Sloan 2016):

> [...] me I'm not, I'm, I'm in prison but I'm not a criminal criminal like [...] People out robbing, thieving and, I've never ever gone out robbing...to get money or nothing like that, the only crime I've committed is violence, which is pub fights. (Harvey)

Such approaches of differentiation fail to consider the similarities between prisoners (and people outside prisons)—a tendency that pervades much criminological research more broadly. Human beings tend to look for the things that mark offenders out as 'different'—be that from the 'general public' or from other offenders.

Where masculinity does receive direct consideration, this tends to be framed in negative terms, such as in relation to violence, control, hyper-masculinity (which is seen as being 'over' masculine), being sexually problematic and so on. This is not to say that these issues are not important, but yet again they mark out certain individuals as worthy of special attention, rather than considering the male prison population as a whole. Not all men in prison perform their masculinities negatively—many just want to 'do their time' and get on with their lives. Because such men do not perform their masculinities in highly visible or obvious (i.e. negative) ways, they, in essence, become invisible.

There are many reasons why we fail to *see* men in prison in research, policy or real life, such as the female focus of the feminist research agenda, the resilience and avoidance of vulnerabilities that male prisoners try to show and controlling notions of patriarchy and masculinity more broadly. In addition, however, we can look to three key reasons stemming from the prison experience itself: men's loss of individuality and identity within prisons, the 'normality' of the male prison and the cost and size of the problem.

The Loss of Individuality in Prisons

It has been widely acknowledged that prison can be a dehumanising experience, and many processes are invoked within prisons that erode an individual prisoner's sense of individuality. As one participant in my research said:

> *Well it's coz like they're taking all your identity away and em...they take all your identity away from you, you're just a number in prison [...] Yeah. You're just a number in prison really.* (Elliott)

Arguably many prisons attempt to remove the (sexual) individuality of prisoners through the use of uniforms or generic clothing (Ash 2009), hair cutting processes (Goffman 1961) and restrictions on their ability

6 Saying the Unsayable: Foregrounding Men in the Prison System

to enact expressions of symbolic aspects of gender identity such as fatherhood, employment, 'consumer masculinity' (Crewe 2009: 277) and so on. In essence, the very markers of manhood that are expected in wider society are removed at the gate, leaving only the corporeal available for use—whether that be on the body (such as through tattooing or cleanliness—see Sloan 2012a, b) or by the body (as with violence and sexual harm).

Whilst prisons are seen as extremely masculine spaces (Toch 1998), they are rarely portrayed as positive masculine spaces, or spaces of multiple masculinities. In fact, the prison is generally seen as the sphere of hypermasculinity expressed in negative terms. What tends to be lost is the multiplicity of masculinities that represent men's lived experiences of their sex (Connell 2005), as many men arguably have to conform to the hypermasculine expectations imposed by their audiences in order to fit into the setting (see Schmid and Jones 1991; Sloan 2011; Kimmel 1994).

As such, processes of imprisonment can actually erode gender identity for prisoners. The specific identity of individuals tends to be replaced with the all-encompassing marker of 'prisoner': that is 'prisoner', not 'male prisoner'. By doing so, the female prisoner's sex is presented in a similarly distorted way to those outside—people in prison are 'men'. Women prisoners are 'non-women' who have offended against their female traits.

It is such applications of a non-sexed identity that causes so much consternation about women prisoners, whose experience can be argued to be incompatible with female corporeality (see Finateri 1999; Wahidin and Tate 2005). Hannah-Moffat discusses the issues associated with the idea of women-centred prisons, noting that the very definition of such a thing is difficult:

> because it relies on a problematic category of 'woman'; it is insensitive to wider social, economic, and political cultural relations of power; it sets up a false dichotomy between the woman- and male- centred regimes; and it denies the material and legal realities of imprisonment. (1995: 135)

To change the prison in response to one sex is too simplistic—there are similarities in experiences shared by men and women, yet only the *female* prisoner tends to receive specific attention because of their sex in policy and practice. The nuances of both maleness and femaleness are lost within the sphere of power and control—yet this is rarely acknowledged. There is an assumption that prisons are inherently masculine spaces, reflecting popular discourses around masculinity and femininity which arguably do not do justice to the subtleties of either (see Hayes 2014) and normalise the association between negativity and male prisons. Rarely do we see how men in power actually control and restrict the actions of men in lesser power (Bibbings 2014), albeit this has been significantly theorised in discussions of hegemonic masculinity—for some men to be in power, there must always be others who are subordinate. This occurs within the prison and outside in controlling the actions of certain groups of men (Connell 2005).

The 'Normality' of the Male Prison

The Criminal Justice System is dominated by men: men are the majority of criminals, prisoners, prison officers, judges and police. The terms 'prisoner', 'offender', 'criminal' all tend to be associated by default—consciously or unconsciously—with men rather than women (see also Wykes and Welsh 2009). Heidensohn states: '…females are not only much less criminal than males, they are so much less criminal that whereas convictions are, statistically at least, 'normal' for males, they are very unusual for females' (1985: 2). This is a slightly problematic statement, in that, in mid-2015 there were 32.1 million males in the UK (ONS 2015). Albeit this is inclusive of Scotland and Northern Ireland, we can still see that the number of men in prison (as one branch of the offending population) is an extremely small proportion of the total number of men in the UK.

Popular cultural portrayals of prisons have tended to be dominated by depictions of men, although women prisoners have become more visible in popular culture through *Prisoner Cell Block H*, *Bad Girls*, and *Orange is the New Black*. Even so, there are substantially more films set in men's prisons than in women's (and most of these distort public perceptions through their focus upon high-security prisons in the USA—see Wilson and O'Sullivan 2004).

Despite this, and the fact that most of the infamous criminals in the world are male, thereby ensuring a prominent representation of the male form in popular cultural representations of prisons, still men in prisons are not 'seen'. Instead, the focus is on the surroundings—the violence (again, a male-dominated enterprise, but rarely seen as such), the harm, the fame, the crimes. These all are foregrounded, rather than being subject to any real commentary regarding the maleness of the state of affairs, or the fact that there is such surprise and dismay when women are seen in the same situation. Men in prison are, in essence, invisible in the foreground[4]—be that in research, the media or in popular culture.

The Size (and Cost) of the Problem

The majority of money and spaces that are devoted to prisons are directed towards men. Whereas women's prisons are merely categorised as open or closed (or sometimes, semi-open), by contrast the behaviours and risks perceived to be posed by men in prisons in England and Wales demand a four-tiered categorisation system of A–D status. Category A—high-security prisons—is designed to make escape the hardest and house the most 'high risk' prisoners.[5] Category B is the next grade of security down, following which is Category C, which also often includes 'training prisons' where prisoners can learn trades and skills to aid in rehabilitation and reintegration upon release from prison. Category D prisons are open: men can walk in and out of the prison, and security is much more dependent upon compliance with the rules of the prison.

According to the Ministry of Justice, the prisons which had the highest cost per prisoner in 2014–15 were those holding male young people (ages 15–17) at £87,280 per prisoner and male dispersal prisons (holding the more dangerous prisoners in a way that allows them to be dispersed within the prison estate[6]) at £59,470 per place. The highest overall resource expenditure costs within the system were for male local prisons, housing short-term (not high-security) prisoners and those on remand or awaiting sentence (£1,001,014,792), and male Category C jails (£945,555,027). In comparison, the *overall resource expenditure* of closed (£21,704,972), local (£126,396,164) and open (£7,813,839) prisons *combined* is considerably lower for the women's estate than for the men's (Ministry of Justice 2015c: Table 1).

By giving attention to women and young people, it is clearly visible that something is being 'done' to address the needs of the most vulnerable within the prison system. But does this actually just reflect stereotypical views of vulnerability and victimhood? Those prisoners that do receive focus are often those upon whom the spending of more money from the public purse can be justified according to political imperatives and penal populism (Pratt 2006)—they are the 'ideal victims' of the system (Christie 1986). Of course women and young people need to be given direct attention according to their specific needs within the prison system—there is no argument with that.

What is clear, however, is that male prisoners are rarely constructed as 'vulnerable' (see Sloan 2011), and certainly not in the same way that society sees women and young people in the prison system. This is in spite of the fact that men in prison are actually an extremely vulnerable group, often linked to pre-prison vulnerabilities (such as having a background in the care system). Such 'vulnerability' is in itself problematic, arguably shifting men out of their masculine positionings—men in prison strive not to be seen as vulnerable in order to avoid personal victimisation and perceptions of weakness (McCorkle 1992; Sabo et al. 2001; Sloan 2011).

Why Does It Matter? Why Should Feminists Care?

Men in prison may not receive much direct attention as a gender, but do they really need to? As noted already, they are the 'norm' when it comes to prisons and offending, they receive the resources and 'attention' by default of being the majority, and giving them more direct attention may just divert from those more vulnerable minorities who need distinct attention that they currently do not receive enough. Indeed, men often play a role in women's offending, either through harm or recruitment, and they are also responsible for much female victimisation. However, I would argue that there are numerous reasons why this lack of attention actually matters in reality.

Disproportionate Attention Given to Men in Prison

A key reason why this lack of attention matters comes down to proportionality. More attention is given to the minorities in prison than to the mainstream. Yet this diverts attention from looking at why it is that men are in the majority. The only thing that connects 95% of the prison population, other than criminality, is maleness. By giving disproportionate attention to non-males or minorities of men in prison, we fail to ask the question of what it is about men more broadly that results in their predominance in the system (Wykes and Welsh 2009).

A key reason for many feminists abhorring this group is, of course, due to the fact that many of these male offenders have caused severe harm to women (and other men) and are the epitome of many of the problems feminists are fighting against—male oppression and dominance, violence, sexism and misogyny. But this is surely the most important reason to advocate engaging with men—if we can understand the offenders, then we are one step closer to solving the problem of patriarchy. We must understand the intricacies of the problem in order to address it.

Perceptions of Women in Prison

There are issues with the fact that men are seen as the 'norm' in prison when one considers public perceptions of women prisoners—it can add to the demonisation and 'othering' of female offenders. Women's lack of dominance in the prison system singles them out as the exception, which becomes the focus of the attention, whilst at the same time normalising men's place within the penal sphere. Through the normalisation of maleness of incarceration, too much force is given to the notion that women in prison are 'abnormal', which in turn reemphasises discourses on what women 'should' be and how they 'should' behave in order to be seen as true women (see, for instance, Crewe (2006) regarding female prison officers; see also Heidensohn 1985). Ultimately, engaging with men allows more solutions to be sought to address their harmful behaviours and actions.

Recidivism

One of the justifications that many use for undertaking prisons research is the need to understand offenders and the criminal justice system better, leading, perhaps, to reduced recidivism. Reducing reoffending is a core aim of many penal systems—as illustrated earlier in this chapter by the UK Ministry of Justice's position statement. It is also arguably a gendered process (see Giordano et al. 2002), in that men and women have different access to resources to support desistance. Rumgay posits that 'successful desistance from crime may be rooted in recognition of an opportunity to claim an alternative, desired and socially approved personal identity' (2004: 405). For men, a 'socially approved' self will often depend both on their own perceptions of their masculinity and the opinions of others, particularly other men who ultimately grant them their masculine status (Kimmel 1994). By not focusing upon this one aspect of identity that is so prominent within men's lives, we are missing a huge area of subjectivity and identity through which to address criminality. This is particularly relevant when one considers Messerschmidt's recognition that crime is a resource for doing gender when other resources are unavailable (Messerschmidt 1993: 84) and that 'prison can be a site for changing one's masculine practices' (2001: 71).

This has been attempted on occasions. Potts discusses a prison group run by the Probation Service in West Yorkshire which focused on masculinity in the 1990s (Potts 1996), noting that:

> After all, if we believe that alcohol or drugs related crime can be reduced by work intended to reduce such abuse, then surely gender related crime – and that's most of it – can be reduced by developing interventions which deconstruct traditional masculinity. (1996: 31)

Yet currently, no official offending behaviour programmes focus exclusively on masculinities, although those that look at domestic violence and sexual offenders do give some consideration to male behaviours (which, in turn, makes certain gendered assumptions about these offences). These programmes highlight the key offences against women, but do not actively challenge the structural or less visible forms of domination or control that are in action in everyday life. There is little official recognition of the more general gendered state of reducing reoffending and the importance that masculinities can play in this process. That said, there is a newly emerging focus on masculinities from the perspective of charitable organisations, one example of which is 'Safe Ground'. This organisation runs a number of masculinity-focussed courses, one of which is called 'Man Up' which is:

> A new group-work programme designed to support men and young men to explore the ways in which the concept of masculinity contributes to shaping individual identity. Using active learning techniques, Man Up aims to challenge some of the attitudes and negative outcomes experienced by men as a result of wanting or needing to fulfil stereotypes and expectations. (Safe Ground 2015)

At present, the course is being run in six prisons/young offender institutions and highlights a growing change in approaches to considering masculinity (see further Blagden and Perrin 2015; Safe Ground 2014).

Men Have 'Complex Needs' Too

One of the key reasons for giving specific attention to minority groups such as women in prison is their 'complex needs'. Yet, whilst there are certain needs of minority groups that are distinct to that group, some of these needs may be shared by male offenders, as well as having their own male-centric needs. The Bromley Briefings report that 24% of male prisoners had spent time in local authority care compared to 31% of female prisoners; 27% of men had experienced emotional, physical or sexual abuse compared to 53% of women; 15% of men had symptoms indicative of psychosis compared to 25% of women; and 21% had attempted suicide at some point compared to 46% of women (Prison Reform Trust 2016: 32). Although women had higher percentages, it has to be recognised that women only make up 5% of the prison population, so the actual *number* of men experiencing such problems is substantially higher.

What seems to be forgotten in the arguments about 'complex needs' is that addressing the complex needs of women does not mean that we cannot address the complex needs of men, and the two need not be mutually exclusive.

Concluding Discussion

It is often argued that women are not suited to the current prison system in England and Wales. Evidence shows that women are more able to retain family links and undergo rehabilitation and integration when housed in small units close to where they come from (Corston 2007). However, high rates of recidivism, issues of prison violence and poor mental health show that men also are not suited to the current prison system in England and Wales. Prisons and prison regimes seem to be designed to make inhabitants feel uncomfortable and punished—not just through incapacitation and the lack of physical liberty but also through restricting personal interactions with those outside the prison, subjecting those inside to humiliation and uncertainties which threaten mental well-being and forcing individuals to live together in confined spaces with those that they would not ordinarily choose to associate with (see also Sykes' pains of imprisonment 1958). These conditions apply to both men and women within the prison system, but the feminist voice has tended to prioritise the needs of women in prison more than those of men.

In one sense this is understandable—feminism emerged to fight for female equality and women's rights, and prison does impose inequalities upon women who fall foul of power inequalities within society that often stem from patriarchal and misogynistic institutions and structures. However, male prisoners too suffer from an infringement of their rights, and men in prison are often exemplars of vulnerabilities and the cumulative impact of inequalities over their lifetimes. The forces of patriarchy and hegemony do not solely disenfranchise women: groups of less powerful men—the subordinate and marginalised masculinities (Connell 2005)—are also subjected to structures and practices that put them at a huge disadvantage relative to other men and women. Just because these subordinate/marginalised men are members of a gender group which has framed patriarchy does not mean that (a) these men necessarily benefit from broader patriarchal behaviours—whatever Brownmiller (1975) might argue—or (b) that they are not worthy of a voice or attention. Just because some men make up the most patriarchal and misogynistic dimensions of power structures does not mean that other men do not have issues that need addressing with regard to being disempowered and vulnerable.

This chapter has attempted to highlight the importance of giving feminist attention to men in prison. The sidelining of male prisoners to the realm of the 'taken for granted' or the 'norm' in prison gives disproportionate attention to others and potentially misdirects resources that could actually be used potentially to reduce men's dangerousness (not least towards women). Such disproportionality also leads to a skewed perception of women in prison as being different to other women, and in some ways not 'true' women at all due to their transgression from gendered behavioural expectations. Finally, to ignore the problems that men in prison suffer misunderstands the very nature of imprisonment and those who are subjected to it, and misses the picture of the imposition of unequal power relations and hegemonic power structures upon both men and women. Both men and women are victims of the actions of men (both within and outside of prisons themselves), be that through direct victimisation or through state, political and institutional practices (see also Connell 2005).

This may not be a popular proposition for feminist thinkers who see women as the 'ideal victims' (Christie 1986). However, unless we embrace the problem of men in prison, why they dominate the prison system and what vulnerabilities, behaviours and backgrounds bring them there (and unless we do this with a degree of sympathy and understanding), then it is unlikely that the situation of men always being seen as offenders will change and, in turn, unlikely that women will ever stop dominating the realm of the 'victim' (see also Cohen 2014). This is not to say that women don't matter—far from it: we need to continue working towards advancing the voices and rights of women (both in and out of prisons), which are still pathetically unequal when actually looked at in detail. But one way that we can do this is through looking at the other side of the coin—we need to look at the men.

Notes

1. Most men in society also do not offend.
2. One potential reason for this is the fact that 'prison masculinity' is often seen as 'bad masculinity' rather than being associated with positive connotations.
3. Interestingly, Greer made the observation that 'Probably the only place where a man can feel really secure is in a maximum security prison, except for the imminent threat of release' (2012: 270).
4. Many thanks to Dr. Gwen Robinson for this point.
5. These can also hold prisoners who are classified as Category B. Both prisons and prisoners are categorised—usually these would be matched where possible, but a prisoner will have to be situated in a category of prison equivalent or higher than their own categorisation.
6. All dispersal prisons will be high-security (Category A) prisons, but not all high-security prisons will be dispersals (many thanks to Nicholas Addis for clarifying this!).

References

Aresti, A. (2010). 'Doing time after time': A hermeneutic phenomenological understanding of reformed ex-prisoners experiences of self-change and identity negotiation. Unpublished PhD Thesis, Birkbeck, University of London.

Ash, J. (2009). *Dress behind bars: Prison clothing as criminality*. London: I.B. Tauris.

BBC. (2013, December 16). Self-harm 'four times more likely' in female prisoners. Available at http://www.bbc.co.uk/news/health-25366160

Behan, C. (2002). *Transformative learning in a total institution*. Unpublished MA Dissertation, National University of Ireland, Maynooth.

bell hooks. (2000). *Feminist theory: From margin to center* (2nd ed.). London: Pluto Press.

Bibbings, L. S. (2014). *Binding men: Stories about violence and law in late Victorian England*. Abingdon/New York: Routledge.

Blagden, N., & Perrin, C. (2015). *Man up interim report across three London prisons*. Available at http://www.safeground.org.uk/impact-evidence/full-list-programme-evaluations/

Brownmiller, S. (1975). *Against our will: Men, women and rape*. London: Penguin; New York: Fawcett Books.
Butler, M. (2007). Prisoner confrontations: The role of shame, masculinity and respect. Unpublished PhD Thesis, University of Cambridge.
Christie, N. (1986). The ideal victim. In E. A. Fattah (Ed.), *From crime policy to victim policy*. New York: St. Martin's.
Cohen, C. (2014). *Male rape is a feminist issue: Feminism, governmentality and male rape*. Basingstoke: Palgrave Macmillan.
Connell, R. W. (2005). *Masculinities* (2nd ed.). Cambridge: Polity Press.
Corston, B. J. (2007). *The Corston report: A report of a review of women with particular vulnerabilities in the criminal justice system*. London: Home Office.
Crewe, B. (2006). Male prisoners' orientations towards female officers in an English prison. *Punishment & Society, 8*(4), 395–421.
Crewe, B. (2009). *The prisoner society: Power, adaptation, and social life in an English prison*. Oxford/New York: Oxford University Press.
Finateri, L. M. (1999). The paradox of pregnancy in prison: Resistance, control, and the body. *Canadian Women's Studies, 19*(1&2), 136–143.
Flavin, J., & Huss, L. (2014). Feminism and prisons: Why "Add-Incarceration-and-Stir" doesn't cut It. Available at http://www.truth-out.org/opinion/item/24957-feminism-and-prisons-why-add-incarceration-and-stir-doesnt-cut-it
Giordano, P. C., Cernkovich, S. A., & Rudolph, J. L. (2002). Gender, crime, and desistance: Toward a theory of cognitive transformation. *The American Journal of Sociology, 107*(4), 990–1064.
Goffman, E. (1961). *Asylums: Essays on the social situation of mental patients and other inmates*. Chicago: Aldine Publishing Company.
Greer, G. (2012). *The female eunuch*. Hammersmith: Fourth Estate.
Hannah-Moffat, K. (1995). Feminine fortresses: Woman-centred prisons? *The Prison Journal, 75*(2), 135–164.
Hawton, K., Linsell, L., Adeniji, T., Sariaslan, A., & Fazel, S. (2013). Self-harm in prisons in England and Wales: An epidemiological study of prevalence, risk factors, clustering and subsequent suicide. *The Lancet*. Early Online Publication, 16 December 2013. Doi:https://doi.org/10.1016/S0140-6736(13)62118-2.
Hayes, S. (2014). *Sex, love and abuse: Discourses on domestic violence and sexual assault*. Basingstoke: Palgrave Macmillan.
Heidensohn, F. (1985). *Women and crime*. Hampshire/London: Macmillan Publishers.

Howe, A. (2008). *Sex, violence and crime: Foucault and the 'man' question*. Oxon/New York: Routledge-Cavendish.

Jewkes, Y. (2002a). The use of media in constructing identities in the masculine environment of men's prisons. *European Journal of Communication, 17*(2), 205–225.

Jewkes, Y. (2002b). *Captive audience: Media, masculinity and power in prisons*. Cullompton: Willan Publishing.

Jewkes, Y. (2005). Men behind bars: "Doing masculinity as an adaptation to imprisonment". *Men and Masculinities, 8*, 44–63.

Kimmel, M. S. (1994). Masculinity as homophobia: Fear, shame, and silence in the construction of gender identity. In H. Brod & M. Kaufman (Eds.), *Theorizing masculinities*. Thousand Oaks/London: Sage.

McCorkle, R. C. (1992). Personal precautions to violence in prison. *Criminal Justice and Behaviour, 19*(2), 160–173.

Messerschmidt, J. W. (1993). *Masculinities and crime*. Lanham, Maryland: Rowman and Littlefield Publishers.

Messerschmidt, J. W. (2001). Masculinities, crime, and prison. In D. Sabo, T. A. Kupers, & W. London (Eds.), *Prison masculinities*. Philadelphia: Temple University Press.

Ministry of Justice. (2015a). http://www.justice.gov.uk/about/hmps/

Ministry of Justice. (2015b). http://www.justice.gov.uk/offenders/before-after-release/obp

Ministry of Justice. (2015c). Costs per place and costs per prisoner: National offender management service annual report and accounts 2014–15 management information addendum, Ministry of Justice Information Release. Available at https://www.gov.uk/government/uploads/system/uploads/attachment_data/file/471625/costs-per-place.pdf

Ministry of Justice. (2017). https://www.gov.uk/government/statistics/prison-population-figures-2017

Moolman, B. (2011). Permeable boundaries: Incarcerated sex offender masculinities in South Africa. Unpublished PhD Thesis, University of California, Davis.

Office of National Statistics (ONS). (2015). Population estimates for UK, England and Wales, Scotland and Northern Ireland: Mid-2015. Available at https://www.ons.gov.uk/peoplepopulationandcommunity/populationandmigration/populationestimates/bulletins/annualmidyearpopulationestimates/latest

Phillips, C. (2012). *The multicultural prison: Ethnicity, masculinity and social relations among prisoners*. Oxford: Oxford University Press.

Potts, D. (1996). *Why do men commit most crime? Focusing on masculinity in a prison group*. Wakefield: West Yorkshire Probation Service.

Pratt, J. (2006). *Penal populism*. London: Routledge.

Prison Reform Trust. (2016). Bromley briefings prison factfile, Autumn 2014. Available at http://www.prisonreformtrust.org.uk/Publications/Factfile

Rumgay, J. (2004). Scripts for safer survival: Pathways out of female crime. *The Howard Journal, 43*(4), 405–419.

Sabo, D., Kupers, T. A., & London, W. (Eds.). (2001). *Prison masculinities*. Philadelphia: Temple University Press.

Safe Ground. (2014). *Man up development project evaluation*. Available at http://www.safeground.org.uk/impact-evidence/full-list-programme-evaluations/

Safe Ground. (2015). http://www.safeground.org.uk/programmes-services/man-up/

Schmid, T. J., & Jones, R. S. (1991). Suspended identity: Identity transformation in a maximum security prison. *Symbolic Interaction, 14*(4), 415–432.

Sloan, J. (2011). *Men inside: Masculinity and the Adult male prison experience*. Unpublished PhD Thesis, The University of Sheffield.

Sloan, J. (2012a). You can see your face in my floor': Examining the function of cleanliness in an adult male prison. *The Howard Journal of Criminal Justice, 51*(4), 400–410.

Sloan, J. (2012b). Cleanliness, spaces and masculine identity in an adult male prison. *Prison Service Journal, 201*, 3–6.

Smith, R. (1984). The state of the prisons: Grendon, the Barlinnie special unit, and the wormwood scrubs annexe: Experiments in penology. *British Medical Journal, 288*, 472–475.

Sykes, G. (1958). *The society of captives: A study of a maximum security prison*. Princeton: Princeton University Press. (2007 edition).

Toch, H. (1998). Hypermasculinity and prison violence. In L. H. Bowker (Ed.), *Masculinities and violence* (pp. 168–178, xviii, 267 pp). Thousand Oaks: Sage Publications.

Wahidin, A., & Tate, S. (2005). Prison (e)scapes and body tropes: Older women in the prison time machine. *Body and Society, 11*(2), 59–79.

Walklate, S. (2004). *Gender, crime and criminal justice* (2nd ed.). Cullompton: Willan Publishing.

Wilson, D., & O'Sullivan, S. (2004). *Images of incarceration*. Winchester: Waterside Press.

Wykes, M., & Welsh, K. (2009). *Violence, gender & justice.* London/Thousand Oaks/New Delhi/Singapore: Sage Publications.

Young, V. D., & Reviere, R. (2006). *Women behind bars: Gender and race in US prisons.* Boulder: Lynne Rienner Publishers.

7

Hear Our Voices: We're More than the Hyper-Masculine Label—Reasonings of Black Men Participating in a Faith-Based Prison Programme

Geraldine Brown and Paul Grant

Introduction

> With them, I find it is all about; baring yourself, empowering yourself, finding yourself, knowing yourself, doing yourself mentally, spiritually. So, it is always going to be hard. (Participant, C[1])

This chapter shares the reasonings[2] of men[3] often rendered irrational and voiceless within the criminal justice system. In 2015, researchers based at Coventry University carried out an examination of a faith-based prison intervention (FBPI) delivered by *Bringing Hope*, a third-sector organisation (Brown et al. 2016). The Damascus Road Second Chance Programme (DRSCP) is a personal and social development (PSD) programme delivered by Black men, to Black men in prison. It was initially designed as a 'rites of passage' programme and encourages personal

---

G. Brown (✉)
Coventry University, Coventry, UK

P. Grant
Birmingham, UK

reflection and vulnerability in one-to-one and group settings and has been developed to operate within a specifically Christian framework. The epigram illustrates the programme's core principle: a new value system, based on the principles of responsibility for one's self, family and community, is a foundation for change to take place.

This chapter draws on interview, observational and focus group data to highlight how engagement in the DRSCP (or Damascus) created spaces where Black men could reason together to deconstruct dominant and narrow representations of them as hyper-masculine and 'irrational'. This representation is firmly imposed on Black men's bodies inside and outside prison and has a long history (hooks 2004; Ferber 2007; Clennon 2013). However, the men's talk allowed them to disrupt those representations and how they perform masculinity whilst in prison, 'on the wing', and in the community, 'on road'. They valued the freedom to define their realities, build relationships and share views and experiences on their own terms, and this chapter foregrounds their voices. During the course, the men are invited to discuss the racism implicit in the one-dimensional prism of Black hyper-masculinity, and their critical dialogues undermine its credibility and theoretical usefulness. The men's reasonings show practices of Black manhood and masculinity that are relational, complex, heterogeneous and liberatory. These practices draw on the cultural heritage of African and African Caribbean communities. The programme does not create them, but allows the men to remember and practise them.

Research with Black Men in Prisons

The findings in this chapter are drawn from a wider study that examines Black male prisoners' experiences of a FBPI (Brown et al. 2016). The substantive data is informed by a Black phenomenological perspective, that emphasises individual and groups' perceptions and appraisals of their experiences and situations. Adopting a multi-method approach with an ethnographic dimension allowed the research team to observe and probe views and experiences of those involved in the programme.

The study was conducted in a category B,[4] local prison. The study was undertaken shortly after the publication of the prison's Independent Monitoring Board (IMB) Report (published on 30 June 2015).[5] The IMB reported the following: there were approximately 1450 adult male prisoners, either on remand, awaiting trial or convicted, almost 50% of these identified themselves as non-white, 13.6% identified as Black/Black British, 8% as Mixed Race, 10.7% as Chinese or other ethnic groups and 15.6% as Asian/Asian British. In addition, it identifies a diversity of religions and religious beliefs amongst the men, with a notable number attending weekly worship. The prison housed the highest number of Muslim offenders in the UK (IMB 2015).

The Damascus Road Second Chance Programme (DRSCP)

DRSCP is based on the premises that:

- Transformation is a process that takes time, nurturing and support.
- The need for transformation is the start of the journey.
- The acquisition of a new value system, based on the principles of responsibility for one's self, family and community, is a foundation for such a change to take place.

Bringing hope is a Black-led Christian organisation. The central focus of their work is on transforming individuals' lives, in particular working with those who were previously involved in gangs, drugs and general criminality. Delivered by practicing Christians, DRSCP is a rolling programme that runs over 13 weekly sessions. It is open to participants from all faith groups and operates from a theological framework that roots the activities in a process of group transformation. To aid that process, group sizes are kept to under 15, and participants are expected to 'sign up' for the whole programme and to adhere to a negotiated core set of values whilst on it.

Participants

Participation in FBPI and the evaluation research was voluntary. The study used a non-probability purposive sample comprised of all offenders taking part in the FBPI programme (N = 10).[6] The participants were between 20 and 39 years old and identified themselves with a range of faith groups. The majority were either Muslim or Christian, others identified with Rastafari and some belonged to no faith group or preferred not to say. Seven participants said they were of Caribbean heritage and three of African heritage (within the 'Black/African/Caribbean/Black British' category of the 2011 Census). Seven said they lived in 'single person' households when not in prison, two were 'married or cohabiting with dependent children' and one was married or cohabiting 'without dependent children'. Seven said that their highest qualifications were General Certificate of Secondary Education (GCSE) or their equivalents, and three said they had A Levels or their equivalents. No participants identified as disabled.

Data Collection

The evaluation of the programme utilised multi-methods. It used participant observations, surveys, interviews and a focus group. The lead researcher[7] participated in the programme for 10 weeks and carried out approximately 44 hours of programme participation and observation. This allowed time to build relationships with the three practitioners who delivered the programme, the men participating in it and key prison staff, and to engage in numerous informal and formal conversations. Eight semi-structured interviews were conducted with men on the programme and two with men who had participated in DRSCP, but at the time of the study had been released from prison and were living in the community. Interviews were also conducted with three prison staff, four practitioners and one family member. Interviews lasted between 45 and 60 minutes, and were recorded and transcribed verbatim.

On a weekly basis over the duration of the programme, the men were asked to complete a Warwick-Edinburgh Mental Wellbeing Scale (WEMWBS) (39 surveys completed, but are not reported on in this chapter) and self-directed reflections. They were also encouraged to record their views and experiences in other written forms between sessions, and four men provided written self-reflections. Eight men participated in an end of programme focus group.

Data Analysis

Intersectionality is an approach that allows for centring the experience of people situated in multiple social locations to uncover themes and ideas that direct thinking towards the complexity rather than the singularity of human experiences (Crenshaw 1989; Dill and Zambrana 2009). This approach underpinned the data analysis. Given the breadth of methods used, an open coding system was applied to identify and triangulate themes in the data. This involved sorting data by breaking down, examining, comparing, conceptualising and categorising the responses (Strauss and Corbin 1990: 61). The analysis included identifying variations in relation to age, cultural heritage, religious belief, education background, parental status, familial and intimate relationships. The analytical software tool 'NVivo10' was used to organise and analyse the qualitative data.

Ethics

Following the award of the contract for the FBPI study, an application for ethical approval was submitted to Coventry University Ethics lead. This was approved in August 2013. A National Offender Management application was completed and submitted prior to the start of the study. In line with Research Governance, prior to data collection, participants received an information sheet and were advised of their rights and the research teams' responsibilities. These included the right to question the researcher about aspects of the research and the research process; the right to anonymity and confidentiality; and the right to withdraw from the study at any time without explanation. Participants gave written permission for interviews and focus groups to be recorded and for their contributions to be transcribed verbatim.

Performing Masculinity: On the Wing

Overwhelmingly, the Damascus Second Chance Programme (DRSCP) was a positive experience for those involved. The men spoke candidly about the significance of participating in a programme that was specifically designed, delivered and targeted at Black men. They described DRSCP as unique and empowering. It spoke directly to Black men, understood their lives and addressed both their needs and the barriers they face inside and outside of prison. One of the key themes of the discussions was men talking more openly and critically about their criminal behaviour. This included both coming to terms with the outcomes of their actions, decisions and the wider explanations for their imprisonment. This participant's comments describe the awareness sparked by the space to reason about his life.

> For me, we don't really look at that kind of things… explore, go back as far as when was the first time you did this or the first time you did that kind of thing or when was the first thought of being bad or getting into trouble… Actually opens you mind to thinking, 'Was I destined to end up here from the way I was from the age of 6 or 7, the things I was going on with?' It opens your mind from when you were young to all the years that have gone past and how it has progressed. (Participant, C)

The power of moral and spiritual reflection is also captured in the observational notes of 15 October 2015. These record how a group discussion moved between silent reflection and a shift in group consciousness:

> I observed men sitting silently, reflecting, and listening to a track on a CD made by another young Black male who spoke about his life, love hopes, fears and family. The room is silent and everyone appears to be sharing a moment in time with each other. Emotion, I observed a participant with his head bowed, one covered his face with his scarf, another staring almost without blinking at the ceiling. This is something very powerful …tinged with optimism. There is a lot of love in the room. There is something about the space, people and music playing that is emotional. This is an encounter in which something is openly shared that touches us all. (Lead Researcher)

Sidestepping the charge of sentimentality, these were so-called hyper-masculine Black men dealing with complex emotions and thoughts in a supportive and affirmative manner. The men often shared how the programme inspired them to share their thoughts and ideas and aspects of their identity that they either hid from or were ignored by others. Speaking of the impact of the programme leaders on his personal development, one man said:

> I've been on courses, but I don't stand up and I don't talk. You see the other day, when I got up and talked, you don't know how proud of myself I was because I don't do things like that. Everybody knows me and I don't chat to people like that. I listen and see what is going on and write down what I need to write down. So yeah, I had a good vibe about them and feel they mean genuinely what they say. (Participant, C)

Another participant added:

> It enlightened me about hidden treasures, of certain things I probably knew I had them, but I haven't really put them to use. And I haven't thought about certain things. I've never really looked into certain things before coming on the course, I looked into certain things but I've never really seen it in this mind-set and how I see it now. (Participant, M)

Here there is pride in contributing to group discussions and increasing intellectual and emotional vulnerability. Masculinity here is redefined by the men in terms of critical engagement, of holding each other accountable for keeping things 'real' in the meeting room and in their interactions 'on the wing'. A common theme in over ten weeks of observational data was the sense of togetherness and growing confidence amongst participants. Commenting on the implications of the process of 'checking in' (everyone sharing notable events and emotions at the beginning of sessions), these participants underline the power of reasoning together compared with the practices of 'bottling it up':

> The key thing is how you start it off, like the 'checking in' thing. Like you said, it builds you as a person and it builds confidence as well. So obviously, you may feel not to volunteer, but someone may say something that sparks

you to talk, which is encouraging because you can relate to it. 'And you're thinking' you're going through this and I'm going through that, because what I find is, us as Black men, we carry a lot, you know what I mean, and we don't' let it out. (Participant, C)

It comes out in different ways, maybe anger and whatever else, so we don't express it. I don't like men that chat, but when you're talking about serious situation, issues and feelings, we don't. A lot of us we just bottle things up. I'm talking about myself as well; I'm not expressive like that. I just find a way to deal with it on our own and it helps. (Participant, C)

The men also shared how the programme encouraged critical and analytical reflections that allowed them some space to understand the causes of their circumstances and to challenge stereotypes. For this participant, this promoted and amplified a sense of calm. During his interview, he spoke proudly of the sense of solidarity and camaraderie he felt with the other men in the group and practitioners delivering the programme:

Proved that you don't follow stereotypes. Black people are human beings too. Black boys, Black women as well. I am not racist, if I see someone doing something, I say. I said it to [practitioner] Nah. So don't just think that Black people are just here to cause trouble, because I'm not here just to cause trouble. ...The only reason why I've had to do what I've had to do is because of what I call the Willy Lynch tribute. I call the Willy Lynch-ship have not been able to get a job. I've been brought up where I've been brought up and I've not been able to get a job. I call it the Willy Lynch. I have been fighting my Black brothers because Willy Lynch has made me fight my Black people. I don't want to get too deep, but you know what I'm saying. (Participant, C)

He explained that such relationships and calm and supportive spaces were novelties in prisons, and this view was commonly shared as shown here:

It was surprising, because it [the programme] was calm and there was no arguing, fighting. There wasn't even a bad look. It surprised me. When I went and looked at some of the faces I thought, 'OK'. (Participant, M)

> I try and pride myself to being able to adapt to any situation, so it was not going to be me that was going to see stereotypes be fulfilled and everyone was on the same kind of thinking… I actually made some good friends. I actually made some good friends. So, for me that was an eye-opener in itself, because everyone is slightly stereotypical about each other… not knowing, just hearing, grapevine. I've probably heard something about this guy here, I've heard something about him, but when you actually sit down and get a dialogue and you find out. (Participant, C)

> The first day you might get a nod, the second day you may shake hands or bump fists and by the fourth and fifth day, you're participating in group activities together, so it was a very big eye opener. No one did not care, it was all for the greater good. (Ex-Participant, C)

The Damascus Road programme allowed the men to disrupt expected and accepted patterns of prison relationships, amongst these Black men, and a relatively smooth shift into more open albeit critical friendships allowed them to see themselves as free to think and change for themselves:

> Coming into the room of Damascus, into the programme, there is already an energy that we have already built. An energy that makes you feel free, even though you're not, because you're locked down. But when you come into this room, you feel free. It's not like you're in jail, but you are free to get down to your core problems, free to accept help for progression and free from stereotypes and that is a main thing. (Participant, N)

This freedom to reason with and relate to each other allowed the men to step beyond their views of themselves and each other and to see potential and opportunities within their own lives. This man described being touched and moved to gratitude towards the practitioners and a commitment to change:

> Thank you for helping us to see ourselves in the light that we should see ourselves…This course is touching in many ways…and I have gone back to my cell and thought about the things we have discussed on the course …I know where I am going and that I don't want to be diverted from the path

that I am going down now. I want to thank you for helping me to see myself as the person I want to be. (Participant, M)

The literature relating to FBPI identifies the difficulties in both translating commitment to change into action and measuring the extent of change (see Willison et al. 2010). Nonetheless, it also underlines how significant it is for prisoners to have hope. It eases their willingness to change (Clear and Myhre 1995; Clear et al. 2000). This hope, the help 'to see myself as I want to be', is a key theme in the men's reflections on the programme. As this participant comments on the one-to-one meetings with members of the programme team:

> You can say what you want out there, but when you're in your one-to-one, it's you and that person and you can really express what is going on and how you feel whether you're angry or sad, whatever it is. And, they will take that on board and put that confidence back into you to make you know that you can make it and that is the key goal that you can be a positive successful Black man. (Participant, C)

This man shows how this critical confidence shaped the men's relationships with prison officers and the institution itself:

> I've been in jail a lot of times and I have never allowed authority in jail to treat me a way and me not do anything about it. This time while I've been in jail, before I got on the course, that is what I was on. (Participant, C)

> The support from an officer and the Damascus Project just made me want to show that I can be someone else. So, now what I have figured out about myself, is that I can. That's it actually, [laughs] I can! I can innit. (Participant, N)

On the programme, participants shared their thoughts and feelings around their identities as fathers, sons, partners, entrepreneurs and men of faith. Their reasonings made visible a range of masculine identities that challenge the dominant one-dimensional representations of Black men within prison. The men discussed their experiences of and resistances to these racist caricatures of Black masculinity and families.

Performing Masculinity Outside Prison

A number of men said that the programme gave them support and guidance along paths that they had already decided to take. For these men, the programme encouraged them to think things through together in a much needed challenging, but unthreatening, environment. Some of this reflection work had been started before the course. One of the men shared how he had stated to make some changes in his life before his incarceration:

> No. Before me come onto this course I was already getting on board, anyway, because I wasn't…I was just living very fast and do things on the spur of the moment and that gets me in trouble. But I was on my way to being a better person. I was on my way to knowing what I needed, knowing my priorities and thinking about things. Thinking about how I want my life to go and thinking about other people a lot more. So, the programme has given me more time to think. I think it could be a lot longer. (Participant, M)

Other participants spoke of the need to make changes in how they dealt with themselves and their families and communities. They became aware of the patterns of their behaviour and thinking as men and the cycles of harm that they can reproduce. As this man said,

> The cycle has to stop if we have to make a change. If not for ourselves then for our children. (Participant, C)

> No, I am the sort of person… I bottle up everything me. You wouldn't know what I am thinking or feeling or whatever…if I'm feeling down or whatever or having an off-day. If I go to my mother or brother and sisters… rah, rah, rah. (Participant, C)

> No, I just deal with it. That is just how I was raised. You're a man. You just hold it. That's it. You just deal with it and keep it going. (Participant, M)

> I didn't cry when they found me guilty, but I did feel sadness for my mum and my family. Feeling sad and crying inside, deeply crying inside… emotional feeling down for my mum, not myself. Like I had let them down. I had disappointed them in a way, so that's why I felt sad. (Participant, M)

The observational data shows how the men felt free to discuss the results of their previous strategies of bottling up their feelings, because they were men, and the possibilities of new types of relationships. This participant speaks of the breakdown and rebuilding of his relationship with his mother:

> The disconnect happened when I was on the road and whatever… She used to say, you know, 'Behave yourself and stay out of trouble. Give me your money to save, to hold for you'.
>
> I told her, 'Nah, mum, I'm going about my business' and we kind of broke communication. I used to look after my mum and make sure she's OK, but I feel that I lost connection with her some way down the line and jail has kind of brought it back definitely. Definitely.
>
> 'I love you, mum', I say it to her and she says it back, it wasn't like that back then. I know my mum loves me dearly and does anything for me, but it wasn't like that. The words we don't say, so I say it now normally every day and I just feel good. (Participant, M)

Another shared his efforts to get his life on track following his friends' imprisonment and the derailment of his own plans. Being able to talk allowed him to see some of his issues and the temptations to come:

> It is not scary for me. I'm ready to go and I'm gone. Before I come here, I had settled down, got a girlfriend, moved out to [area] moved out of [area]… driving, working, doing my little thing or what not, because a lot of my friends had got locked up… 14, 15 16 years. So, all my friends had got locked up, so I had no one really. All my friends had gone. So, I went to the [college] and kind of stopped.
>
> Then I got caught up into some stuff and then two years later they just come for me and grabbed me when I was settled down and I was alright. Two years later they grabbed me and now I'm here, but I had broken up with all my friends, but it's mad because we all come out at the same time. So, I don't know what's going to happen, because we are going to link up and what not… but I just want to keep a level head, because I want to go into property development and I'm just researching that now. (Participant, M)

The awareness of new possibilities brings with it the awareness of new obstacles and the results of old decisions. These men show the contradictions between hope based in new relationships and the realities of life outside of prison.

> One of the biggest obstacles is that I have re-educated myself… got qualifications, but no experience. How are you going to get experience if you can't get a job? (Participant, M)

> If I get released today and I don't have a job or have a home, how can I survive? (Participant, M)

Prison is an environment where vulnerability is a 'weakness' and detrimental to safety and well-being. The DRSCP disrupted that truth and promoted group discussion and self-healing. The data shows a connection between the programme and individuals' sense of subjective well-being and evidence of changes from negative thoughts to positive ones, as well as changes in energy, spirits, self-control and willingness to trust.

'Real Knows Real': Making Space for Black Men to Be Men in Prison

A theme in the men's conversations is their candour about the significance of participating in a programme specifically designed, delivered and targeted at Black men. That does not mean that it was easy or comfortable or that the men would have wanted it to be. As this participant said:

> The content is great and I couldn't ask for a better deliverance because it is straight up and raw rather than watered down and diluted type rubbish, like I'm drinking a box drink [carton of juice] rather than a diluted orange squash because you can taste the difference. When they deliver the course it's like richness. Whereas, if it was somebody who have never lived that life or grew up in a certain environment to know that these things happen and it's a way of life when you grow up in a certain environment. (Participant C)

Such praise is hard-earned. During the focus group, the men discussed their experiences of personal social development 'self-improvement' programmes. A common feeling was that these programmes were often more about making the men conform and comply rather than encouraging them to think and reason together. They explained how they were often guarded in what they shared and often did not say much. One participant spoke about initially having low expectations about attending the DRSCP:

> People trying and saying that they want to help and not really doing much, not really saying much, so I had low expectations at first. (Participant, C)

Despite some initial scepticism, the men 'knew' almost immediately and intuitively that the practitioners delivering DRSCP were committed both to the programme and to them. They said that this motivated their attendance and level of engagement. One said:

> I wouldn't really want the course to end. I would just keep on turning, turning up every week. Turning up until I go home, to be honest. Just turn up, turn up. Obviously, you couldn't be on the course until you go home, because nobody else will ever get on it, but it's like, I like this course so much because of the everyday things that I learn is so different. (Participant, M)

Consequently, feeling that practitioners were not just there 'to do a job' was a powerful catalyst for the men's engagement and reappraisal of themselves as Black men:

> When I sat and spoke with them and as soon as they started speaking and I started listening to them. You could tell that what they were saying was from the heart and they were passionate about what they were trying to do and the good they were trying to bring into [names prison]. That was my first memory ... I thought you are the kind of guys I could work with. (Participant, C)

Related to this sense of unconditional and critical commitment, the men underlined the importance of feeling some connection to the practitioners' gender, 'race', experience, place, community and familial connections. This opened the way for participants and practitioners to engage 'on a level', as this man outlines:

> Obviously, it makes a big impact as well, because we can relate to them and coming from their background, the same as our background; area or road whatever. Knowing where they're coming to this and drag it out…Yes, it does, I think. I think it couldn't be any anybody, because nobody would come. They are not going to come, if we can't relate to you and you can't relate to us. It's about relating. They can relate to us. They know our background and they probably know our parents, some of us. We can relate to them and we have an understanding straight away. (Participant, C)

The majority of participants identified themselves as Muslim, but this did not stop them from enjoying the Christian-based programme. The men saw the opportunity to connect with the Christian practitioners as important and valuable. This also applied to the differences in age and educational attainment between the men and the ministers and the men themselves. The participant below highlights the importance of making relationships, finding community, across barriers: talking and learning from each other was positively received:

> After the first session I was 100% down for it, because I felt that the way they approached things and the way they delivered was something that was unique. I'd never… I've done loads of courses in prison and what not, but I had never experienced that kind of… It's more stiff upper lip, kind of 'watch what you say, watch how you live' blah, blah, blah. That kind of way of thinking. (Ex- Participant, C)

> So, their approach I could kind of relate to… I could relate to it definitely. Because they were Black men like myself, first and foremost, and I'd never seen a course delivered by an older Black man ever in my life, you know what I mean? So, I could relate to that aspect and, what they were speaking about wasn't nonsense. It was, you know your kind of stuff, you know, but you kind of leave it in the back of your head and you don't use it. So, that kind of made me think and I was up for it. (Participant, C)

Participants spoke positively about engaging in a programme where they were able to learn from the experiences shared by practitioners.

This included specific experiences of the criminal justice and education systems or personal experiences of being fathers, partners or sons. Practitioners' first-hand lived experiences were important to the positive experiences reported. One participant, who identified as Muslim, summarised the importance of the practitioners' commitment and experience:

> I just say that real recognise real and that's it. They have been there and they have done that and they have worn the t-shirt. Speaking to them, they can relate to the problems that I have faced and the issues that I may have. If they have not been through it, they probably know someone that has been through similar situations.
>
> So, I know that from speaking to them, they give me that…
>
> When they spoke to us and the things that they teach and they say on that first day, it made me know that this is definitely where I want to be, because they are going to teach me things that I didn't know about myself or I probably knew, but I didn't really …
>
> Speaking to somebody that used to do certain things and involved themselves in certain things, when they have taken themselves out and then made a change and, then gone through that all sacrifice period of not falling back into those desires that make them get caught up and could end up back in prison. When you listen to them and they tell you certain things about how it was hard and how it is going to be hard, because nothing is ain't going to be easy, you know that there is a way out for you. (Participant, M)

The support provided within the context of Damascus meant a great deal to the men. Knowing that they were able to access unconditional and non-judgemental practical and emotional support in prison and on release was important to the men's reasoning, reflections and thoughts about their future. This is irrespective of the length and stage of their sentences. One participant, serving an Indeterminate Sentence for Public Protection (IPP), had recently been returned to prison:

> I was in a bad place and needed to get myself on track. I have had battles with them as well, because I would love to do what they are saying, but

sometimes some stuff it is hard to get out of. Sometimes, but you have got to try. (Participant, C)

A man on remand found the programme an important space to think about moving forward:

If I could turn my life around and teach others what they are teaching me now, I will be very pleased within myself to know that I am giving back to the community and I'm helping the community at the same time… and I'm out here struggling to break that cycle no matter how hard it is. I am trying to break that cycle with the youth of today trying to show them a better way. (Participant, C)

One participant, who had been in prison five times and served a total of ten years, spoke about the importance of facing himself and making decisions to deal with what he found there:

I have had to look into myself and find those inner demons and what is hidden in the closet and things that I have never opened, because I probably locked certain feeling in that box. And I've had to open that box and dealt with it as I was supposed to deal with it, if you know what I mean? (Participant, M)

Participants identified the approach, content and delivery of DRSCP as challenging, but also refreshing, creating 'space' for personal reflection and development that was unthreatening. They welcomed the opportunity to speak openly about their experiences and valued the practical and emotional support provided during group activities and during one-to-one sessions. The men found some elements of the programme emotionally challenging, but accepted the reassurances of the 'trusted' practitioners.

In some ways, the practitioners were the programme. They modelled Black masculinities that both engaged with and disrupted the men's perceptions of themselves and their relationships with each other. They offered unconditional and non-judgemental support and were routinely described as 'genuine' men who 'genuinely cared' about the lives of Black men. The need to demonstrate personal investment in participants featured heavily in what the men said. They required that programme staff show their care and concern for their well-being. Once that trust had been established, together with the practitioners, the men developed tools they could employ to navigate and cope with the prison regime and subsequently the world outside. The group created new relationships, perspectives and techniques that allowed them a greater range of creative choices.

The programme's approach offered a 'humanising space' in which learning was reciprocal and dialogic. The group reasoned together, and the men learned from each other, practitioners, guest speakers and prison staff and vice versa.

The association of the faith basis of the programme with values such as unconditional love and critical 'big man' care instilled a sense of hope that helped create a space where all participants could speak openly, emotionally and respectfully to each other.

> With them I find it is all about baring yourself, empowering yourself, finding yourself, knowing yourself, doing yourself mentally, spiritually. So, it is always going to be and, to add to that it is very sure of itself and very confident in what they are saying and allows you to be confident within yourself and to believe in what they are telling you. (Participant, M)

Healing Reasoning

The programme led to creative and positive relationships between practitioners and participants and prison staff and between participants. The focus on self-worth reignited hope and a welcoming of support:

> The opportunity to stop, be calm and to reflect, allows for consideration of an alternative future, both within prison and beyond. Envisioning a future which involves expressing emotion openly facilitates a positive outlook for the future. (Participant, C)

> I know where I'm heading. I'm alright. It's been an up and down week. Mainly this experience of being on the course has humbled me. A lot of

situation I have been in, it's calming me down. I'm thinking about my life, thinking about going back to school, not getting involved in things like I used to. It's humbled me. (Participant, C)

The way the programme opened participants up to thinking about their lives and future in different ways was also noted by a member of the prison staff who also participated in the group discussions:

If I'm walking through the jail now, they'll make a point of coming to say hello… come or waving to me, if they can't come and chat to me, asking me how I am, I think because they know that whatever I have seen there, I've not told anyone else about and I've never laughed about some of the things I've seen up there. And it's a trust thing and I think that is a big thing for the lads, it's trust. (Prison Officer)

Where the humanising space of the meeting room might have been the limit of the men's revisioned masculinity, the prison staff's observations about the men's concerns and trust on wings and landings suggest a wider impact. There is also evidence that indicates the positive benefits of having a programme that supports participants in prison and on release. One participant who had completed the DRSCP, on his release, decided to access further support. He explained that:

I tell you when the fright time is and I feel passionately about this. The fright time is when you are in your resettlement period and when you come to the end of your sentence and when you get out. Those are the times, because I've been through some moment when I have thought, 'Oh, my days! I can't do this. I'm broke. I can't live this kind of life', because it is easy to do what you've always done, as old habits die hard.

I think I have become more open myself to speaking about my emotions and feeling than I was before. I used to be a closed book in that kind of context, but I have spoken in certain kinds of ways and just that reassurance, just that, it just that means such a lot. If you're not around people who are giving you that reassurance that you may need and you have people phoning your phone saying, 'Just come, man! Let's link, man! I can get P [money], you know!'

> When you do so long, the nervous point is you come out and you're not sure about yourself… down to your looks, you're not sure about anything, because all you've been doing is looking in the mirror for an amount of years [laughs] everything is strange, you know what I mean? So when you get out, you're not sure about things so that reassurance can mean a lot. (Participant, C)

Black men are diverse and have diverse needs. However, the data indicates a valuable role for personal social development programmes specifically tailored to engage Black men. They can act as a gateway to building relationships, instilling hope and contributing to recidivism (Burnside 2008). Participants spoke about the lack of attention afforded to understanding the myriad of ways in which Black men may experience discrimination, disadvantage and exclusion, but they also spent time reasoning as men, with men about being men. The participants' experiences of masculinity were diverse, shaped by multiple factors and constructed to challenge notions of hyper-masculinity.

Final Reflections: 'We Are More than the Stereotype': Hyper-Masculinity Masks Black Masculinities

Karp (2010) argues that the cultural, social and material reality of prison life equates survival with the capacity to perform an overtly intense form of masculinity. Hyper-masculinity, then, offers men, and perhaps Black men in particular, the possibility of navigating prison life. Irrespective of the diverse ways that incarcerated men 'be men' in the outside world, the homosocial total institution of prison demands that they become brutal to avoid being brutalised. Not all men have the capacity for such brutality, and where they do, they do not necessarily perform it or perform it in the same ways.

hooks (2004) maintains that Black men are routinely labelled as hyper-masculine regardless of capacity and choice. For her, their very Blackness is the marker for hyper-masculinity, and their masculinity is structured by and against dominant and dominating discourses and practices of masculinity that present white masculinity as 'normal' and 'natural'. For Clennon (2015), the dominant definition of Black masculinity is the outcome of processes that 'fix' and homogenise Black men as essentially big, black and brutal.

According to Carrington, this dominant view of Black masculinity is built on the objectification of Black bodies. Where white men are perceived as variations of rationality—more or less able to think clearly and objectively—Black men are variants of untamed animal urges. Where white men are identified with their thinking organs and moral choices, Black men are reduced to the sum of their sexual organs and perceived as generally 'lacking' in moral values (Carrington 1998). Ultimately, the over-representation of Black men in the criminal justice system is used to evidence the inherent hyper-masculinity of Black men.

This chapter reports on Black men in prison reasoning with each other about their lives within the context of a programme that facilitated the trust, space and confidence for them to reflect on their lives as Black men. They discuss their 'conditioned responses' to their labelling as 'naturally' aggressive, irrational and violent, and share their understandings of what it can mean to be Black men in a racist society. DRSCP encouraged the men to use their 'sociological imagination' (Mills 1959), to connect their own choices and circumstances with wider social processes and the histories of African, Caribbean and British societies. The men's discussions show their exploration of the irrational image that British society forces upon them; that they are unable to succeed on their own, are unsuited for professional careers and cannot think straight. Their perceived hyper-masculinity, instead, predisposes them towards criminality in the public sphere (Kennedy 1997) and absence in the private sphere, as in absent and/or ineffectual fathers and unreliable partners (Allen 2016; Brown 2015; Williams 2015). The power of such imagery drives policies and practices based on the assumption that Black men cannot be trusted and need to be controlled (Ferber 2007). The evidence in this chapter illustrates how the Black men in this study undermine these racist assumptions and all that springs from them.

The decision to focus on their talk in this chapter was in part to disrupt the dominant discourse around hyper-masculinity and Black men in prison. One aim was to demonstrate the power of having access to a humanising space and unconditional albeit critical support from other Black men in allowing 'real talk' to occur. A second aim was to show the sophistication and clarity of these men's reasonings and the grounded moral values and practical ethics that underpin them. The men's observations capture some of this, the quality of thought and rigour of reasoning, but what they do not do reflect are the energy and engagement of the discussions and relationships. The prison officer's comments about the men's behaviour towards her and each other on the wing, and the lead researcher's observations on the moment of silence, from their outsider perspectives, suggest their liberatory capacity. The men were clear about their own choices and acknowledged their agency. They exposed their own failures and scrutinised their criminal and self-defeating practices through reasoning and reflection. They became better men on their terms.

To label this group of Black men as simply hyper-masculine is misleading, and it ignores the different ways Black men perform masculinity in prison. To assume that this small sample is radically and qualitatively different from all other Black men on 'the wing' or 'on road' is a bit of a stretch, if the pun can be pardoned. However, they both contribute to a process that hides the realities of Black men's masculinities and their relationships to multiple systems of power, in order to control and discipline them. One implication of the study is to expose how the concept of hyper-masculinity sustains the disparities and damage that characterise Black men's lives and experiences when they come into contact with institutions such as the criminal justice system (Clennon 2015; Williams 2015). It shows the recreation of different versions of Black masculinity rooted in reasoning, unconditional care, self-discipline, families and communities. These masculinities are not externally ascribed in men's bodies, but emerge from spaces where men set their own priorities and practices of manhood and masculinity rooted in their lived realities of prison and beyond.

Acknowledgement Many thanks to the men participating in the DRSCP who generously gave their time to participate in the study. We would also like to thank Elizabeth Bos and Geraldine Brady for their support with the research.

Notes

1. Participant coding:
   C—Christian
   M—Muslim
   N—No faith group
   R—Rastafari
2. The term reasoning here has its roots in the Rastafari practice of open discussion and debate to come to negotiated group decisions and conclusions. In this context, it underlines a transparent and collective rationality at work in the group that belies talk of Black hyper-masculinity in and of itself.
3. The men on the programme are variously described as men, participants and offenders. They are all of these things. No one term captures their complexities and capacities.
4. Category B prisons are for those who do not require maximum security, but for whom escape still needs to be made very difficult.
5. IMB produces an annual report about the day-to-day life in local prison or removal centre and ensures that proper standards of care and decency are maintained.
6. The data included was collected from ten men who had completed the programme. Two participants has enrolled on DRSCP, but were removed due to commitment and security concerns.
7. Lead researcher, Geraldine Brown.

References

Allen, Q. (2016). 'Tell your own story': Manhood, masculinity and racial socialization among black fathers and their sons. *Ethnic and Racial Studies, 39*(10), 1831–1848. https://doi.org/10.1080/01419870.2015.1110608.

Brown, G. (2015). *Urban gun crime from the margins: An auto/biographical study of African Caribbean communities' understanding and responses to 'urban gun crime'*. Thesis, Coventry University.

Brown, G., Bos, E., & Brady, G. (2016). *Hear our voices: Exploring how bringing Hope's Damascus road second chance programme supports black men in prison and through the gate*. Coventry University.

Burnside, J. (2008). Religious interventions in prisons. *Justice Reflections, 19*, 1–16.

Carrington, B. (1998). Sports, masculinity, and black cultural resistance. *Journal of Sport and Social Issues, 22*, 275–298.

Clear, T. R., & Myhre, M. (1995). A study of religion in prison: The international association of residential and community corrections alternatives. *Journal on Community Corrections, 6*(6), 20–25.

Clear, T. R., Hardyman, P. L., Stout, B., Lucken, K., & Dammer, H. R. (2000). The value of religion in prison: An inmate perspective. *Journal of Contemporary Criminal Justice, 16*, 53–74.

Clennon, O. D. (2013, November 18). What's the problem with black masculinities? *Media Diversified*. https://mediadiversified.org/2013/11/18/whats-the-problem-with-black-masculinities/

Crenshaw, K. (1989). Demarginalizing the intersection of race and sex: A black feminist critique of antidiscrimination doctrine, feminist theory, and antiracist politics. *University of Chicago Legal Forum, 140*, 139–167.

Dill, T. B., & Zambrana, R. (Eds.). (2009). *Emerging intersections: Race, class, and gender in theory, policy, and practice*. New Brunswick: Rutgers University Press.

Ferber, P. (2007). The construction of black masculinity: White supremacy now and then. *Journal of Sport & Social Issues, 31*(1), 11–24.

hooks, b. (2004). *We real cool: Black men and masculinity*. New York: Routledge Taylor Francis Group.

Independent Monitoring Board (IMB). (2015). *HMP Birmingham: The annual report of the independent monitoring board to the secretary of state for justice*. IMB.

Karp, D. R. (2010). Unlocking men, unmasking masculinities: Doing men's work in prison. *The Journal of Men's Studies, 18*(1), 63–83.

Kennedy, R. (1997). *Race, crime and the law*. New York: Vintage.

Mills, C. W. (1959). *The sociological imagination*. Oxford: Oxford University Press.

Strauss, A., & Corbin, J. (1990). *Basics of qualitative research: Techniques and procedures for developing grounded theory*. Los Angeles: Sage Publications.

Williams, P. (2015). Criminalising the other: Challenging the race-gang nexus. *Race and Class, 56*(3), 18–35.

Willison, J. B., Brazzell, D., & Kim, K. (2010). Faced-based corrections and re-entry programs: Advancing a conceptual framework for research and evaluation. Urban Institute, Justice Policy Center, https://www.ncjrs.gov/pdffiles1/nij/grants/234058.pdf.

8

A Framework Model of Black Masculinities and Desistance

Martin Glynn

Introduction

In this chapter, I present a 'framework model of black masculinities and desistance', which is informed by the results and findings of my doctoral study (Glynn 2013), combined with on-going field work in relation to incarcerated black men. Throughout this chapter, I use the term 'black' to refer to individuals of African descent who are living in the UK. Desistance is increasingly conceptualised as a theoretical construct which is used to explain how offenders orient themselves away from committing crimes. Previous studies suggest that successful desistance occurs due to one or a number of factors. These factors include things such as faith (Giordano et al. 2007), gender (Giordano et al. 2002), psychosocial processes (Healy 2010), a rite of passage (Maruna 2010), personal and social circumstances which are space and place specific (Flynn 2010), moral rehabilitation (McNeill 2012), turning points (Carlsson 2012), ethnicity and faith (Calverley 2013), relationality (Weaver 2013), and

M. Glynn (✉)
Birmingham City University, Birmingham, UK

race and racialisation (Glynn 2014). The absence of critical perspectives on race and racialisation when theorising about desistance is problematic for a number of reasons. To address this issue, Russell (2002) has previously called for the development of 'black criminology', while Phillips and Bowling (2003) argue for 'minority perspectives' within in so-called mainstream criminology. Glynn (2017) further states that race and racialisation of the criminal justice system (CJS) invariably impacts on the desistance aspirations of black offenders on both personal and structural levels and calls for a move towards a 'critical race criminology' (CRC) as a possible way forward. The framework that is outlined in this chapter asserts that successful desistance for black men is bound up in navigating a range of masculine transitions within the context of differential racialisation that operates within the wider CJS. Bell (1995) sees differential racialisation as the way the dominant society racialises different groups, in different ways and in different times, in relation to structures such as the CJS. I argue in this chapter that these masculine transitions are situated and contextualised within the worldviews of black men that are shaped by the negative experiences they have faced within the CJS as a whole (Alexander 2010). The findings of my study also reveal how these same black men understand the CJS treats them less fairly (Glynn 2013).

The Importance of Racialised Identities

In this part of the chapter, I give an overview of the evolution of the relevant literature relating to racialised identities. Writing in the 1930s Du Bois (1938) argued that black men struggled with managing a dual masculine identity, referred to as 'double-consciousness' within the confines of the so-called 'American Dream' that legitimised racialised subordination under the US constitution. Fanon (1952) similarly expressed the view that the plight of black men under colonialism was equated with the entrenchment of whiteness that in turn created the conditions for oppositional black masculinities to emerge. Frazier (1957) felt the way to counter the impact/s of subordinate masculine status for black men was through the gaining and sustaining of employment. However, Frazier conceded that the so-called 'American Dream' was beyond the reach of many black men, based on the devastating impact of a racialised history of oppression. Baraka (1963) suggests that many white theorists have little interest in representing the complexities of black masculinities, based on a racist construct designed to maintain and sustain the privileged of some white men in US society. Clark (1965) calls for academic clarity about how black men are looked at, investigated, and understood, in a society that refuses to see who they really are.

Liebow (1967) describes how the lack of employment opportunities destroyed black men's self-esteem, leading to an erosion of their social capital and engagement in criminality as a way of restoring lost masculine pride. Grier and Cobbs (1968) argue that within the confines of a racist society, many black men struggle psychologically to acquire manhood that in turn damages the development, building, and maintenance of social bonds. Majors and Billson (1992) see rebellious masculinity that some black men acquire as a result of rejecting society's rules, as the cumulative impact of racism, denied access, and marginalisation. Hutchinson (1994) also blames the distorted (mis) representation of black masculinities embedded into the psyche of the wider social order via the media compounds black men's ability to build positive masculine resources. Sale (1997) asserts that much of the construction of contemporary racialised masculine identities amongst black men emerged from nineteenth-century slave ship revolts. While Mauer (1999) highlights how the CJS has both labelled and incarcerated diverse black masculinities as an extension of US criminal justice policy following the legacy of historical sustainable white privilege. Hill-Collins (2000) sees the interplay between the two dominant racialised masculine identities as the basis for keeping black and white men apart. Finally, Alexander (2010) sees the expression of 'colour blindness' within the CJS as a way of operationalising the marginalisation and subordination of black men as a key underpinning factor that explains how mass incarceration in the United States can be understood. It is this writer's view that racial caste in a time of globalisation has not ended but has been merely redesigned within the context of the CJS. Alexander's position also provides a cautionary tale for criminology as a discipline that at times operates through a colour blind lens.

Black Masculinities

Connell and Messerschmidt (2005) criticise those social scientists who fail to recognise 'racialized identities' as producing under-theorised models as a whole. Messerschmidt (1993) further argues that power relations exist between different types of men within the CJS and are determined in part as product of masculine responses to crime when other resources are unavailable to accomplish socially acceptable masculine norms, race being one factor. Glynn (2014) similarly points out that criminology seldom addresses the construction of racialised identities when looking at men involved in criminal activity. This paucity of research when theorising black masculinities in the CJS weakens the wider discourse on prison masculinities. Benyon (2002) highlights that social rejection as experienced by some black men can lead to serious violent offending where the structural concerns of white society are internalised by many black men who may feel they are not equal stakeholders in society, and hence the emergence of positive masculine identities is arrested. Marriot (2000) sees the representation and portrayal of black hyper-masculinities as a counter response to a society that attempts to pacify black men's need for validation and self-determination within a white society. However, hooks (2003) challenges Marriot's assumptions and suggests that racist constructs short circuit the development of positive masculinities for black men. hooks concludes by arguing then it may be time for black men to construct new and improved masculinities that can better respond to the increasing social pressures placed upon them. It may be that the internalisation of these hyper-masculine scripts becomes the foundation for nihilistic tendencies amongst some black men. In this chapter, I will explore how this connects to notions of black masculinities and desistance.

A Framework Model of Black Masculinities and Desistance

Owing to the limited amount of research undertaken in relation to the role that black prison masculinities play in the desistance trajectory for black men, this section lays the foundation for further investigation.

As we enter into a new era of racialised existentialism as brought about by the Trump presidency, Brexit, and rise of White supremacy brought about by the rise of far right nationalism, it is evident why criminological theorising, textbooks, and research will at times languish behind the immediacy of social media platforms when looking at, addressing, and mobilising public opinion around on-going issues surrounding 'race and the racialization of crime' (Golberg 2009). This omission makes the current narrative framing of 'crime and punishment' deeply flawed. Gilroy (2008) argues that the racialisation of crime requires a detailed historical investigation that will raise further and more speculative questions. Gilroy goes further and expresses the view that historically 'the left' has failed to appreciate the complexities of black life and discounts the impact of structural racism within its overall class analysis. The need therefore to reinvigorate discussions around the need for a racialised 'counter-narrative' within criminology becomes important. It could be argued that mainstream criminology reproduces a biased account of crime and criminal justice, which in itself does little to ameliorate racial disadvantage within the discipline itself, alongside playing a marginal role in contesting racial disadvantage within CJSs across the world. The need to theorise using racialised paradigms that challenge implicit bias within the discipline of criminology should become a rallying cry for all criminologists who have grown tired of criminological theorising that ignores racialised discourses in areas such as black masculinities.

The Study

My observations and participation in prison rehabilitation programmes targeted at black men over three decades have led me to believe that seldom have the insights, understandings, and 'lived' experiences of the black men who come into contact within the CJS been taken into consideration when contributing to the broader dialogue on the study of both re-entry and desistance. The research operated from an 'interpretivist perspective'. That is, it focused on the meanings that black men gave to their lived experiences in relation to the racialisation of crime and CJSs and its impact on the desistance process (McAdams 1988). Prison was examined as a site where the trajectory towards desistance potentially begins, as a context where for some prisoners 'transformation' and 'change' might occur. The objective here was to push the conventional boundaries of understanding in relation to the study of desistance. I wanted to explore some of the more searching and far-reaching issues concerning the complex nature of desistance trajectories themselves, not just in terms of point of cessation, but other possible influences in relation to black men's desistance, with a specific emphasis on the racialised processes that both inform and govern it. As an 'insider researcher', I was confronted with methodological and ethical issues concerning my own sense of identity as a black man. My 'insider' positioning viewed the research process and products as 'co-constructions' between myself as the researcher and the active 'informants' in the research itself. Such perspectives allow the researcher to conduct research 'with' rather than 'on' their group, which contrasts starkly with 'outsider researcher' perspectives. It was impossible to avoid complete impartiality, but the ethical considerations ensured that there were no improper actions, or the possibility of 'going native'. Being immersed in the world of the research subjects was required in order to access the data, and in doing so generate new insights in an area that is under-researched, under-theorised, and often misunderstood. Reflexivity became an important tool in understanding my own levels of subjectivity in relation to the research as a whole. In presenting a framework model of black masculinities and desistance, the insights and understanding black men possess become important here. It is my view that there is now a pressing need to utilise an improved and more appropriate theoretical lens through which to look at desistance in relation to marginalised populations of offenders in prison such as black men. Intersectionality may provide an enhanced racialised lens and will hopefully engage scholars who are struggling to engage critically around discourses that are raced, classed, and gendered. Intersectionality as Crenshaw (1999) argues is the understanding that human beings are shaped by the interaction of their different social locations which occurs within a context of connected systems and structures of power. Crenshaw sees such processes as being where independent and multiple forms of privilege and oppression are created.

The Framework

Figure 8.1 provides a framework from which to explore some of the issues raised in this section.

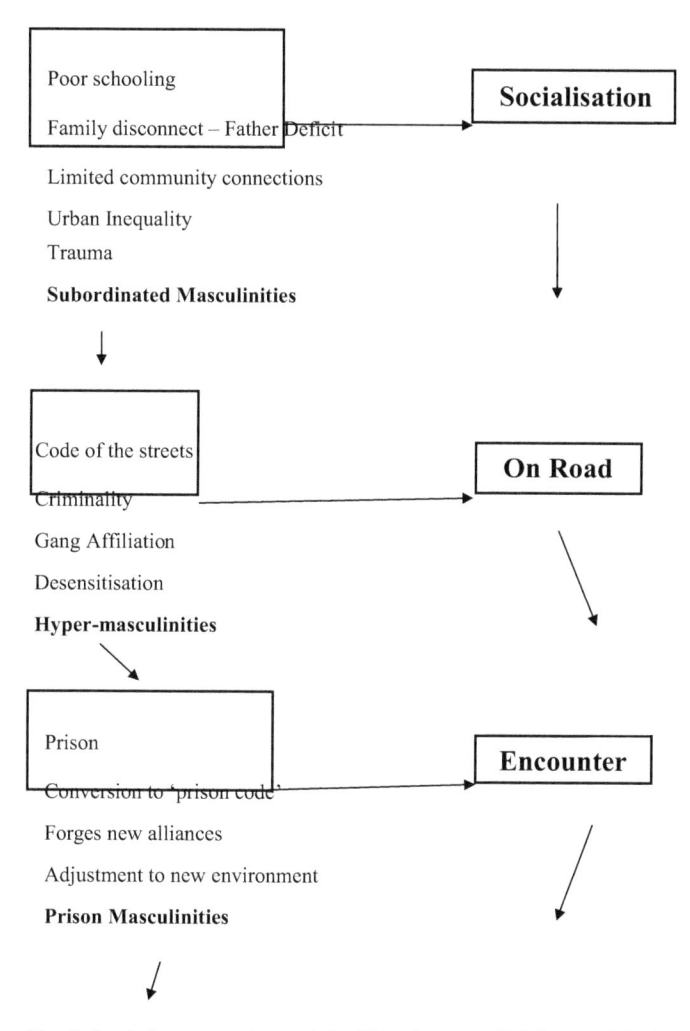

```
┌─────────────────────────────┐
│ Poor schooling              │         ┌──────────────────┐
│ Family disconnect – Father Deficit ──▶│  Socialisation   │
└─────────────────────────────┘         └──────────────────┘
  Limited community connections                  │
  Urban Inequality                               │
  Trauma                                         │
  **Subordinated Masculinities**                 ▼
       │
       ▼
┌─────────────────────┐
│ Code of the streets │                  ┌──────────────────┐
│ Criminality         │─────────────────▶│     On Road      │
└─────────────────────┘                  └──────────────────┘
  Gang Affiliation                                 \
  Desensitisation                                   \
  **Hyper-masculinities**                            ▼
       ↘
┌──────────────────────────────┐
│ Prison                       │          ┌──────────────────┐
│ Conversion to 'prison code'  │─────────▶│    Encounter     │
└──────────────────────────────┘          └──────────────────┘
  Forges new alliances                           /
  Adjustment to new environment                 /
  **Prison Masculinities**                     ▼
       │
       ▼
```

Fig. 8.1 A framework model of black masculinities and desistance (Glynn 2017)

[Physical and psychological isolation]
[Desensitised/Withdrawn] → **Liminality**

Double Consciousness

Crisis

Point of no return

Defiant/Resilient Masculinities

[Fashions a 'new self']

Immersion

Internalisation → **Conversion**

Transcendence

Grounded Masculinities

[Release]
[Re-entry]

Increased communal and social bonds → **Reincorporation**

Purpose and meaning

Commitment to new life

Recovery

Progressive Masculinities

↓

[**Desistance**]

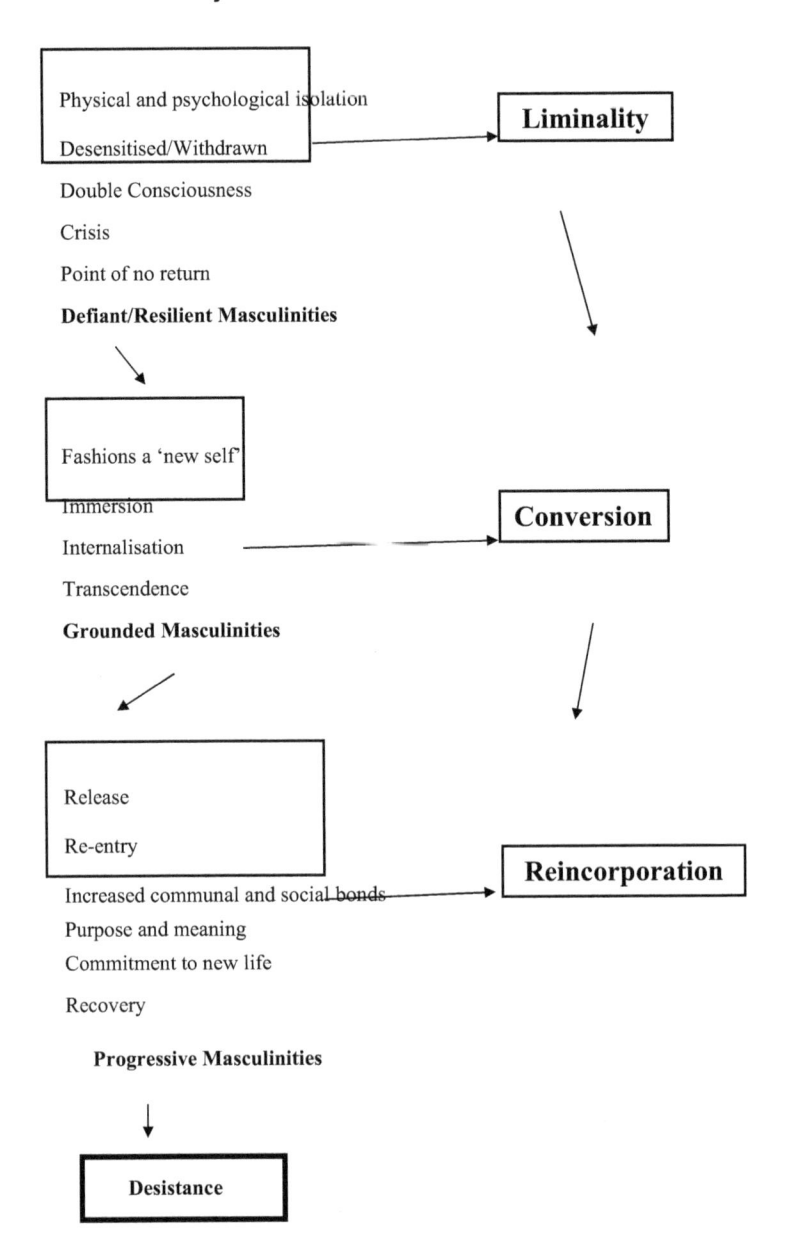

Fig 8.1 (Continued)

Fader and Traylor (2015) suggest that the original formulations in the field of desistance theory are largely, although not exclusively, based on white males. They further suggest that the social location of individuals within interlocking systems of oppression such as race, class, gender, age, sexual orientation, and so on, will expand the conceptual and practical boundaries of research on desistance as a whole. The framework is composed of six elements which are explored in more detail below.

Socialisation

Messerschmidt (2005) argues that when the divisions of labour and power amongst black men are constrained by white privilege, then the outcome may lead to criminal activity. He further argues that social structures organise the way individuals think about their circumstances and generate methods of dealing with them. Therefore, it may be that black men articulate their masculinities according to the context and situation they find themselves in. When men cannot find opportunities to fulfil masculine expectation, then crime becomes an option when other masculine resources are not available. In exercising a choice to commit crime, the prison becomes the space where black masculinities will be constructed, navigated, and expressed. Sampson and Wilson (1995) suggest that research conducted on the individual rarely questions whether community-level processes are influential. They further argue that residential inequality gives rise to social isolation, which in turn leads to structural barriers that undermine social organisation and place limitation on the ability to desist. Sharkey (2008) argues that persistent inequality should be seen as the failure to conceptualise the role that race plays in the production and maintenance of inequality across multiple dimensions. Sharkey further argues that families become connected to places, and these places offer a unique set of advantages within the social structure. If those unique opportunities are blocked, then the life course can be dramatically altered. The growing social and spatial concentration of limited opportunities created a significant set of obstacles for the black men in my study. This structural entrapment plays a significant role in the barrier to desistance for black men. My research indicates that the present concentration on the treatment of individual offenders may serve to obscure much of the truth about the nature of crime and so absolve us of blame for those social conditions and practices which are culpable. In essence, black men will bring the impacts of the racialisation of their socialisation into prison with them. The term used to describe this context is 'on road'.

On Road

Being 'on road' is governed by the 'code of the streets' where respect, toughness, fearlessness, and loyalty are the benchmarks for measuring the masculine resources individuals have to possess in order to be part of criminal community (Anderson 1999). Much of the apprenticeship regarding acquiring such resources is as a consequence of 'differential association', where the code of the streets is learned by affiliation to a group or cohort of individuals involved in criminal activity (Sutherland 1947). The lack of real or meaningful opportunities identified by the black men in my study highlighted many of them had increasingly needed social capital to avoid being trapped by the 'code of the streets' (Anderson 1999). The men in my study talked about the importance of 'street corners', attempting to impress through displays of material success, intimidation, and a disregard for community values and the law. More often, a trail of unfulfilled dreams, broken lives, and jail awaited them. Unfortunately, the engagement with the streets is short-lived, as many were caught, charged, and sentenced. Prison then becomes the next stop on their journey where the outcome places them in a state of liminality.

Liminality

This state of being (liminality) creates anxiety, fear, and delusions, and disrupts the on-going trajectories towards positive masculinities and ultimately desistance. As the primary purposes of the prison environment are confinement, containment, and security, the racialised social order in prison pushed many of the black men in my study into adapting to the

8 A Framework Model of Black Masculinities and Desistance

'prison code'(Sykes and Messinger 1960). This 'prison code' assists in the creation of an informal and hierarchical social structure governed by the prisoners themselves. One prisoner chose to articulate his views using poetry as well as his interview.

Interviewee 1: Too many people seem to have this image that big men don't cry. I personally am not a man to share certain feelings with others. Therefore I tend to bottle up a lot of anger, depression, and regret. This causes me to breakdown at times and cry in private. I feel that crying does relieve us of a little stress and I know that at times I do feel a need to cry. We all have a certain amount of stress inside us and we've all been through different things leaving mental scars and inner pain. A way I can describe it is like this:

In the cell where I dwell
There's a hole in the roof
The roof lets in water and
The rain won't stop
I've got a bucket to collect the water
But it regularly fills and need to be emptied
I empty the bucket 'cos the rain ain't been stopped
And the hole in the roof cannot be blocked

The internalising of anger is all too common a theme that emerged from many of the prisoners in my study. It is also the traditional way that most of them had been socialised. The resulting outcome can push some black men to become desensitised as a survival mechanism, while others can become withdrawn and fearful. In the latter case, individuals can opt to put themselves into a segregated wing, removed from the turmoil of wing politics. However, the collateral outcome was for many of those in my study to feel trapped and unable to find an outlet for positive changes made while being in prison. This pushed many of them to seek outlets for change by undergoing either a 'racialized' or 'spiritual conversion'. Many of the participants in my study who became dissatisfied with their sense of social identity expressed the need to convert their energies into a more holistic spiritual identity, as a way of severing links with a masculine identity they were dissatisfied with.

Racialised/Spiritual Conversion

While change in the environment is tolerated and sometimes welcomed, a change in our identity can be disturbing and difficult. For many black men in study, the desire to change for the better, and not go back to prison, was constantly undermined when a new identity could not be forged. Cross (1991) argues that having a racial identity is essential in enabling black men to transcend the negative impact of racism and white privilege. However, the racialisation of the prison environment can carry many adverse consequences in developing and articulating a new-found 'black consciousness' for prisoners. Indeed as a non-white researcher operating in the same environment, it has been my experience to at times be seen as 'colluding' with my participants, based on nothing other than we share common cultural traits. This position led many of those interviewed to choose a spiritual conversion (mainly Islam) as they felt that the fear of Islam within prisons was enough to provide space and distance between the oppressive nature of the regime itself. In essence, these conversions fulfilled a dual purpose:

1. The individual would experience a new found 'masculine' identity that he felt would be perceived more favourably as it would suggest he had now acquired a new value system, and in doing so have become a new type of 'man'.
2. By 'knifing off' their previous label as 'criminal', they can now be seen to be operating with labels that are more socially acceptable, building much needed social capital in preparation for release.
3. Faith-based activities tend to fall outside of the normal regime delivery. Inasmuch time for prayers, created a communal space that to some extent was viewed by some prison officers as a defiant act and looked upon with scepticism.

I refer to this stage as 'The Golden Fleece', which is a metaphor for not just getting freedom, but more importantly finding it. Leaving the prison gates, a taxi ride home, and driving through the old community that hasn't changed can and does create internal responses that can bring a euphoric moment of release to the realms of self-doubt on achieving freedom.

Reincorporation

Internally, many of those interviewed felt ill prepared to return to their communities, on account of the anxiety brought about by an altered state of their previous identity as an offender. Some deep self-questioning emerges when the enormity of the task (re-entry) begins to set in. In spite of various courses they had been offered in prison as attempts to provide some elements of rehabilitation by the prison, re-established bonds with their friend/family, many expressed a lack of trust in the social structure based on differential racialisation. Many did acknowledge the range of personal and professional support offered while inside was helpful. However, the continuing expressed cynicism regarding the support structures attempt to prepare them for the journey ahead was constantly present. My framework model suggests that the structural context of crime and the level of social disorganisation within the community may be at the core of the problems associated with black men and desistance. Fundamentally, it may be that the community itself needs to change in order to facilitate the changes made by black men who have served their time well while being in prison.

Desistance

The challenge of returning ex-prisoners is much more than their physical relocation into their home community. Instead, the real challenge is reintegrating former prisoners into the community from which they come. Understanding the impact of racism on the desistance process requires regime delivery to play a greater role in equipping black men with the tools required to navigate this hurdle. Healy (2010) argues that when examining desistance, it is important to consider the influence of local cultures and how membership of powerful street cultures fractures the possibility of desistance in inner-city communities. Healy further argues that during emerging adulthood, young people explore a variety of possible… identities, experiment with risky behaviours, and rarely form ties to social institutions. Paternoster and Bushbay (2009) likewise argue that before individuals are willing to give up their working identity as a law-breaker, an individual must begin to perceive this identity as unsatisfying, thus weakening their commitment to it. They further argue that those wishing to quit crime are more likely to be successful at desistance if they are embedded in social networks that not only support their new identities but also protect them from those who would oppose them quitting crime or encourage them to continue in their criminal ways. Successful re-entry therefore must be about providing what has been missing in the lives of most of ex-prisoners; a strong sense of connection to, and respect for, their communities as places to flourish, prosper, and grow. Through the insights coming from black men themselves, my research illustrates that black men's desistance trajectories pose a significant threat to the maintenance and enforcement of white privilege in terms of control and power. Portraying black men as deviant and threatening to the social order protects the interests of white people.

Ibrahim's Story: A Case Study to Illustrate the Framework

I now use a case example to illustrate my theoretical model of masculinities in relation and desistance. If prison is to reduce the continual engagement in criminal activity, then desistance should be a natural outcome of effective rehabilitation and re-entry. However, for many black men in my study who were exposed to the CJS that was racially oppressive, there may be a need to reframe the context in which they desist. The data confirmed that black men understand that the CJS treats them less fairly. The inability to have their masculine aspirations realised may require support services to reframe some of their thinking in relation to what black men need in order to stay crime-free. Webster and Mertova (2007) argue that people make sense of their lives according to the narratives available to them. They also contend that we all have a basic need for story, to organise our experiences into tales of important happenings. In narratives, they argue, our voices echo those of others in the world and evidence membership of society, both through our ways of crafting stories and the content of our stories. A 'critical event', as told in a story, reveals a change of understanding or worldview by the storyteller and becomes almost always a 'change experience'. This 'change experience' can come about as a storyteller encounters some difficulty in integrating their idealised worldview with the reality of their real lived experience. This conflict of belief and experience promotes the development of a critical event as the storyteller struggles to accommodate a change to their worldview. Ibrahim's story could be seen as a critical event within his story, as he contrasts life as a free man and compares it to life as a prisoner (Webster and Mertova 2007).

Ibrahim's Background

Ibrahim (not his real name) is a 32-year-old ex-gang member from Birmingham in the West Midlands. When I got to know him he had served six and a half years in prison for gang-related offences. While serving time, he underwent a faith-based conversion and embraced Islam. On his release, he came back to his old community and faced a range of challenges in terms of re-entry and resettlement issues. Over a period of time, Ibrahim managed to get his life back together, settled down, had a family, and is in a new place working as an advocate around issues of street-based violence and community education. Below I work through the elements of my framework as described above, to structure and illuminate Ibrahim's desistance journey.

Socialisation

When Ibrahim couldn't find opportunities to demonstrate his positive masculine identity, crime became an option as he felt other resources were not available. The pressure of both family and the community expectations was made worse by his access to, and engagement with, the racialisation of social structures that at times prevented meaningful and productive opportunities for him. With severely limited education and skills, Ibrahim had little opportunity to participate in the life of the community, hence he became a product of the streets and indifferent to the laws of society.

Ibrahim: I was crap at school. Always fighting and angry all the time at the teachers. It's only when I left school I found out I was dyslexic. Everyone thought I was stupid. Dad wasn't around. I had lots of brothers and sisters. Plus mum did more than one job. So I never got any attention. No guidance. All my friends at the time were going through the same thing. So it was just a matter of time before I started to stray. I used to sneak out of the house. Back then my brothers and sisters used to tell my mum, which made it worse. Basically I was out of control. That's when the streets called me out.

Ibrahim clearly connected his masculine identity to the streets as a way of challenging the existing social structures that had excluded him. Also evident was the absence of a significant 'male' guardian which he cited as denying him important life guidance. By embracing street life, Ibrahim joined an alternative form of 'social structure', namely, the 'gang'.

On Road

To be immersed and connected to the gang meant Ibrahim had to be prepared to do anything that would cement his place in this extended family. As being 'on road' is governed by the code of the streets, Ibrahim would have to assert a range of manhood goals rooted within using fear, intimidation, and in some cases violence, to maintain his status within the gang. This was expected in terms of the code of the streets, in spite of the risks involved. Here, Ibrahim highlights how a hierarchical trajectory of masculinity is required to move through the ranks of the gang.

Ibrahim: I was about 13 when I started doing robberies and burglary. Never got caught. It wasn't anything major, but after a while

8 A Framework Model of Black Masculinities and Desistance

certain bigger manz (men) in the community heard about what was doing. I suppose I got a bit of a rep (reputation). I wasn't interested in gangs at that point in my life, just making money, coz mum never had any. At school, things got bad and I got expelled for fighting. That's when I decided to join a gang. Never went back to school and got deep into the gang runnings. Had to do some dark stuff to get in, but once I did, they became my new family. Mum went mad, so I left and went to live with my Nan. I never brought no badness to her house, as I respected her. Although she didn't like what I was doing, she did try to talk to me.

Ibrahim highlights how the code of the streets disconnects the individual from the security of their family, into a world full of uncertainty and fear. It could be argued that the absence of positive men in Ibrahim's life fuelled some of his nihilistic tendencies. As he continues:

Ibrahim: Things on road got hectic. I saw things that were horrible, but I became like a mad man. I didn't care about anything. To tell the truth I didn't feel anything either. On road you can't show weakness, so you have to block stuff out, or you can't be a soldier. I was cool for a while. Rollin' with the older guys, doin' all sort of crazy shit. I was makin' money, had nuff (lots) women, and I had the lifestyle. I thought I had it locked. Got away with it. Then some proper madness went down, and then it really hit. When I heard the judge give me 9-year sentence, I was gutted. I saw my family in court, crying. I felt ashamed. Trust me. When they took me down, I knew my nightmare had just begun. But at the time I still thought I was bad man.

Ibrahim's notion of his manhood is now predicated with the word 'bad'. However, without the aid of significant guidance or mentoring, it is challenging to see how Ibrahim could realistically ground himself in a context that would enable him to distinguish between good and bad men.

Liminality

When in prison, Ibrahim made the decision that he did not want to return to a life of crime. The dislike of the prison environment, not wanting to repeat old patterns of behaviour, having acquired new tools and improved confidence through educational qualifications acquired in prison, and his wish to return to the community pushed his inner desire to 'go straight'.

Ibrahim: I hated prison. Reminded me of school. Only this time it was white screws instead of teachers. Plus you had to deal with manz (men) from other endz, as well as beefin' (conflict) with racist prisoners. It was a mad one. Couldn't take the loneliness or isolation. Hardly got any visits and when I did, it was pure arguments with my mum. None of my old crew ever came to see me. Neither did my Nan as she was too upset to see me. There were times when I thought I was goin' crazy.

Ibrahim was clearly overwhelmed by trying to maintain his psychological wellbeing as he reflects on significant relationships in his life.

Conversion

While in prison, Ibrahim spent a lot of time reflecting on, and delving into, his troubled past, as he knew failure to confront his inner demons would result in perpetuating the same type of behaviour that had landed him in prison. It was at this point Ibrahim underwent a crisis that acted as a turning point for his soon-to-be new journey.

Ibrahim: Then I started to read. It was even harder trying to read when I got older, but I had nuff time on my hands. So I went down the prison library and took it slow at first. I was pissed at first, as they had no black books. In fact, the only thing that was black while I was in jail, were the prisoners. After a

> couple of years I started doing some courses and started to get my education sorted. By this time I began to go to the chapel on Sunday, but I wasn't feelin' it. Then one day I met a Muslim and we got talkin'.

Despite the moral panic surrounding Islamic radicalisation emerging from prison, it is clear to see that Ibrahim experienced a strong sense of community that he found favourable. Ibrahim continues:

> All I remember is I started to move with him and his bredrins (friends) on the wing. What I liked about them is the Muslims weren't beefin' (arguing) like we were. So I converted. After that, my life changed. I became a listener, wing rep, and I began to feel useful. I started writing to my mum, and she started to visit more. I felt different. Still used to get beef from my old bredrins (friends) but after a while they left me alone, now I was a Muslim. I suppose in a strange way prison made me think about my life. In some respects it was a good thing, coz I felt I was better than I used to be.

Ibrahim expresses how his identity has shifted, where he perceives himself to be a different person, no longer defined by negative social labels. To Ibrahim, this is a tipping point for personal growth and development, away from an identity associated with crime. This he felt prepared him for his release as he was now a different person with different masculine resources available to him.

Reincorporation

After his release from prison, Ibrahim actively sought out personal and professional support designed to boost his confidence, help him develop new skills, as well as urging him to be compliant with society's rules. However, his former friends did try to tempt him back into street runnings and questioned whether he would be able to stay out of trouble. It is at this moment that the cognitive skills that he developed in prison education become a potential source of assistance.

Ibrahim: I'll be honest, when I knew I was getting released, I felt nervous as hell. It had been a long time. I know I had changed, but while I was inside was all the crap on road. I didn't know what I would be like. Although I'd got qualifications, had a good group of people around me, and I also had good links at the mosque. But I still felt weird. I never felt that nervous when I was on road. I knew I couldn't go back to what I was. I kind of felt with my faith I had nothing to worry about. I knew all I wanted to do is come back into the community and do the right thing. I didn't want no drama in my life. I felt ready.

Ibrahim noticed that the society hadn't changed when he got out of prison, but he had. His thoughts were full of optimism tinged with uncertainty.

Desistance Trajectory

Ibrahim begins to weigh up the pros and cons, and begins to consider his options. He reflects on what his freedom means to him. He also reflects on his skills, abilities, hopes, dreams, and aspirations.

Ibrahim: So I came out. My mum picked me up. I remember I just hugged her. My little sister was there too. I felt good. Trust me. That feeling didn't last long. Things still looked the same. I saw some my old bredrins (friends) standin' on the same corner I stood on all those years back. I felt bad. I couldn't believe it. When I got to my mum's house, there were a few people waiting for me, especially my Nan. I cried. I didn't feel no way. I was so relieved. I'll never forget my first night of freedom. I couldn't sleep. I kept thinkin' about my bredrins (friends) in prison and what my future was gonna be.

Ibrahim clearly wants a better life, but fear of facing his old past makes him nervous. He knows he may be tempted to return to his old

8 A Framework Model of Black Masculinities and Desistance

ways, which has serious implications for his new found masculine identity.

Ibrahim: It took me ages to get work and settle back into things. But my faith kept me goin'. Probation didn't help, plus my old bredrins were trying to rope me back in to the old ways, but I resisted the temptation, when it got rough. Some of the brothers had a barber shop, and I started doin' some trimmin' and made a little change to keep me goin'. Eventually me and some of the other brothers who'd become Muslims opened a little shop, where we cut hair, sold books, and tried to do something in the community. That's how I met my wife. Three years later, I've got daughter, my own place, and I'm goin' back to college to study business. I know there's a possibility that I can always get into trouble, but with the right support, it's possible.

Ibrahim was not only wrestling with a series of personal dilemmas: the difficulty of living, the fear of death, the uncertainty of the future, combined with a significant amount of recurring existential crisis. He was faced with the uncertainty about pursuing a new future (desistance), or staying on the familiar road of re-offending. Ibrahim knew if he continued to commit crime, he could not go back to a free life. Therefore, within the frame of his new-found masculine identity, Ibrahim was able to make new and improved life choices that pushed him towards sustaining his desistance trajectory leading to a life filled with new hope. A range of key issues emerge from Ibrahim's narrative that are explored in more detail in the discussion.

Discussion

How do prison services engaging with men like Ibrahim call upon their insights and understandings of their attitudes and behaviours in relation to his engagement with the CJS? Accessing these insights and understandings should not purely centre on further diagnosis, risk, or needs assessment. It should be a way of restoring some much needed humanity back to MEN such as Ibrahim, whose future away from offending requires the community, services, and in some cases the man's victims to play an active role in his desistance. This would suggest that this type of intervention required for black prisoners like Ibrahim need to promote an individual's assets as well as managing and reducing any risks posed. This requires the holistic reconstruction of the self that requires practitioners to consider and address individual, relational, and community-wide factors, attending to both personal characteristics and social environments.

The Structural Context

The structural context of Ibrahim's lived reality and the level of social disorganisation within the community is at the core of some of the problems he faced. It could be argued that he could benefit from a process referred to as 'knifing off'. 'Knifing off' is about the means by which individuals are thought to change their lives by severing themselves from detrimental environments. It is also important to consider the influence of local cultures and how membership of powerful street cultures threatens the possibility of desistance in inner-city communities. Before black men like Ibrahim are willing to give up their working identity as a lawbreaker, they must begin to perceive this identity as unsatisfying, thus weakening his commitment to it.

Social Networks

Unless black men like Ibrahim are embedded into new social networks that not only supports a new identity and tastes, but can also isolate them from those who would oppose them quitting crime or induce them to continue in his criminal ways, then desistance is highly unlikely. These aspirations are built on two premises: first, all men have skills, abilities, and talents that can and should be used for the benefit of the community; second, rather than seeing black men as 'community liabilities', the communities need to view, enlist, and deploy these men as 'community assets'. Enabling and supporting men like Ibrahim to desist is about providing them with what has been missing from their lives. To promote a successful, positive change, the community must confront their negative value system in ways that will increase their appreciation for the challenges facing the communities they have affected, connected to real and meaningful opportunities.

Conclusion

Future dialogue around understandings of desistance must locate its vision around researching and theorising how rehabilitative processes can create greater opportunities to black men like Ibrahim to prevent them from re-offending. McNeill and Weaver (2010) note that achieving desistance is often very difficult and requires the building of both human and social capital. These other dimensions of offender cognitions may be useful in understanding the psychological aspects of desistance from crime. Using the 'narrative' of reformed offenders such as Ibrahim is intended to enable them to narrate, to interpret events, and to bring coherence to how they see their future concerns (McAdams 1985). This 'narrative' must also challenge dominant social and cultural assumptions regarding young offender's capacity to shape their own reality. The challenge for returning offenders is much more than their physical relocation into their home community; instead, the real challenge is reintegrating former prisoners like Ibrahim back into the community. Understanding the impact of racism in the trajectory towards desistance also requires the prison regime delivery to play a greater role in equipping black men with the tools required to navigate this hurdle. Through the changes Ibrahim made in prison in relation to education and religion, it is evident that improvement in self-confidence is possible as a term in prison. This chapter raises critical questions on prison masculinities. How can we view black men's experiences of prison and associated desistance journey with a lens which can both contest and challenge the racialisation of CJSs? How can black men like Ibrahim speak for themselves on issues where historically they have been rendered invisible? It is to this end that I envision that a possible way forward is in the development of a 'community led model of desistance' for black men. This model would critically assess how this intersection enhances or impedes the cultural functioning of black offenders, in relation to offenders as a whole. Freire (1970) points out that the oppressed are better placed to understand their oppression and argues that their voices must be heard. It is hoped that by using intersectional approaches when conducting future inquiries into desistance will be possible to eradicate the multiple oppressions faced by black men like Ibrahim and the communities they come from.

References

Alexander, M. (2010). *The new Jim crow – Mass incarceration in the age of colorblindness*. New York: The New Press.
Anderson, E. (1999). *Code of the street*. New York: Norton.
Baraka, A. (1963). *Blues people: Negro music in white America*. New York: William Morrow & Company.
Bell, D. (1995). *Critical race theory: The key writings that formed the movement*. New York: The New Press.
Benyon, J. (2002). *Masculinities and culture*. Buckingham: Open University Press.
Billson, J. (1996). *Pathways to manhood – Young black males struggle for identity*. New Jersey: University Press for New England.
Brown, K. (2002). *The colour of crime*. New York: New York University Press.
Calverley, A. (2013). *Cultures of desistance: Rehabilitation, reintegration, and ethnic minorities*. London: Routledge.
Carlsson, C. (2012). Using 'turning points' to understand processes of change in offending. Notes from a Swedish study of life-courses and crime. *British Journal of Criminology, 52*, 1–16.
Clark, K. (1965). *Dark ghetto – Dilemmas in social power*. New York: Harper and Row.
Connell, R. W. (1995). *Masculinities*. Cambridge: Polity.
Connell, R., & Messerschmidt, J. (2005). Hegemonic masculinity – Rethinking the concept. *Gender & Society, 19*(6), 829–859.
Crenshaw, K. (1999). Mapping the margins: Intersectionality, identity politics and violence against women of colour. *M Stanford Law Review, 43*, 1241–1299.
Cross, W. E. (1991). *Shades of black: Diversity in African-American identity*. Philadelphia: Temple University Press.

DuBois, W. E. B. (1938). *The souls of black folk*. New York: Norton.
Fader, J., & Traylor, L. (2015). Dealing with difference in desistance theory: The promise of Intersectionality for new avenues of inquiry. *Sociology Compass, 9*(4), 247–260.
Fanon, F. (1952). *Black skin, white masks*. London: Pluto.
Flynn, N. (2010). *Criminal behaviour in context – Space, place, and desistance from crime*. Devon: Willan Publishing.
Frazier, E. (1957). *Black bourgeoisie*. New York: Free Press.
Freire, P. (1970). *Pedagogy of the oppressed*. London: Penguin.
Gilroy, P. (1987). 'The myth of black criminality', in 'There Ain't no black in the Union Jack. London: Routledge.
Giordano, P., Cernkovich, A., & Rudolph, J. (2002). Gender, crime, and desistance: Toward a theory of cognitive transformation. *AJS, 107*(4), 990–1064.
Giordano, P., Longmore, M., Schroeder, R., & Seffrin, P. (2007). *A life course perspective on spirituality and desistance from crime*. Bowling Green: The Center for Family and Demographic Research: Bowling Green State University.
Glynn, M. (2005). *Passages – Black men, masculinity, and the search for a contemporary rite of passage*. MA Thesis, U.C.E.
Glynn, M. (2013). *The racialisation of crime/criminal justice systems and it's impacts on the desistance process*. Doctoral Thesis, Birmingham City University, Birmingham.
Glynn, M. (2014). *Black men, invisibility and crime – Towards a critical race theory of desistance*. London: Routledge.
Glynn, M. (2017). Towards a crirical race Criminology (Unpublished Paper).
Golberg, D. (2009). *The threat of race: Reflections of racial neoliberalism*. Oxford: Blackwell.
Grier, W., & Cobbs, P. (1968). *Black rage*. New York: Basic Books.
Healy, D. (2010). *The dynamics of desistance – Charting pathways through change*. Devon: Willan Publishing.
Hill-Collins, P. (2000). *Black feminist thought*. New York: Routledge.
hooks, b. (2003). *We real cool: Black men and masculinity*. New York: Routledge.
Hutchinson, E. (1994). *The association of black male image*. New York: Simon & Schuster.
Liebow, E. (1967). *Tally's corner – A study of negro corner men*. Maryland: Rowman and Littlefield.
Lipsitz, G. (2006). *The possessive investment in whiteness – How white people profit from identity politics*. Philadelphia: Temple.
Majors, R., & Billson, J. (1992). *Cool pose: The dilemma's of black manhood in America*. New York: Touchstone.

Marriot, D. (2000). *On black men*. Edinburgh: Edinburgh University Press.
Maruna, S. (2001). *Making good – How ex-convicts reform and rebuild their lives*. Washington: American Psychological Association.
Maruna, S. (2010). Reentry as a rite of passage. *Punishment and Society, 1*, 1–26.
Matua, A. (2006). *Progressive black masculinities*. New York: Routledge.
Mauer, M. (1999). *Race to incarcerate*. New York: The New Press.
McAdams, D. (1985). *Power, intimacy, and the life story*. London: Guildford Press.
McAdams, D. (1988). *Power, intimacy, and the life story*. London: Guildford Press.
McNeill, F. (2012). Four forms of offender rehabilitation: Towards an interdisciplinary perspective. *Legal and Criminological Psychology, 17*(1), 18–36.
McNeill, F., & Weaver, B. (2010). Travelling hopefully: Desistance research and probation practice. In J. Brayford, F. Cowe, & J. Deering (Eds.), *What else works? Creative work with offenders*. Cullompton: Willan.
Messerschmidt, J. W. (1993). *Masculinities and crime*. Lanham: Rowman & Littlefield Publishers.
Messerschmidt, J. (2003). *Masculinities and crime in criminological theory past and present, Cullen and Agnew* (pp. 430–440). California: Roxbury Publishing.
Messerschmidt, J. (2005). *Masculinities and crime – Beyond a dualist criminology*. Los Angeles: Roxbury.
Paternoster, R., & Bushbay, S. (2009). Desistance and the "feared self": Toward an identity theory of criminal desistance. *The Journal of Criminal Law and Criminology, 99*(4), 1103–1156.
Phillips, C., & Bowling, B. (2003). Racism, ethnicity, and criminology: Developing minority perspectives. *British Journal of Criminology, 43*(2), 269–290.
Pietila, A. (2010). *Not in my neighbourhood*. Chicago: Ivan R Dee.
Russell, K. (2002). Development of a black criminology: The role of the black crimnologist. In S. Gabbidon, H. Greene, & V. Young (Eds.), *African American classics in criminology and criminal justice*. New York: Sage.
Sale, M. (1997). *The slumbering volcano*. Durham: Duke University Press.
Sampson, R., & Wilson, J. (1995). *Toward a theory of race, crime, and urban inequality*. California: Stanford University Press.
Sharkey, P. (2008). The intergenerational transmission of context. *AJS, 113*(4), 931–969.
Sutherland, E. (1947). *Principles of criminology* (4th ed.). Philadelphia: Lippincott.

Sykes, G. M., & Messinger, S. L. (1960). The inmate social system. In R. A. Cloward (Ed.), *Theoretical studies in social organization of the prison* (pp. 5–19). New York: Social Science Research Council.

Weaver, B. (2013). Desistance, reflexivity and relationality: A case study. *European Journal of Probation University of Bucharest, 5*(3), 71–88.

Webster, C. (2007). *Understanding race and crime*. Berkshire: Open University Press.

Webster, L., & Mertova, P. (2007). *Using narrative inquiry as a research method: An introduction to using critical event narrative analysis in research on learning and teaching*. London: Routledge.

West, C. (1993). *Race matters*. Boston: Beacon Press.

West, C. (2004). *Democracy matters*. Harmondsworth: Penguin.

West, C., & Zimmerman, D. (1987). Doing gender. *Gender & Society, 1*(2), 125–151.

Winlow, S. (2004). Masculinities and crime. *Criminal Justice Matters, 55*(1), 18–19.

9

Sporting Masculinities in Prison

Hannah Baumer and Rosie Meek

Sport plays a key role within discourses of masculinity in Western contemporary culture. Throughout mainstream prison research however, the male offender is recognised (or perhaps unrecognised) as the non-gendered offender. This failure to treat the gender of male subjects as problematic has long been highlighted by some academics (Morgan, 1986; Newton, 1994), and increasing numbers of contemporary researchers are beginning to acknowledge and respond to the omission of their predecessors. Nonetheless, this explicit recognition remains relatively unusual in academia, as within the prison walls there still exists an apparent silence around gender and masculinity (Sabo 2000). Johnsen's ethnographic study of sport, masculinities and power relations in a Norwegian prison revealed that few male prisoners view themselves as gendered men or have a "conscious relationship to the concept of masculinity" (Johnsen 2001, p. 108), instead appearing more at ease discussing femininity and their gender in relation to women (Johnsen 2001). So, although research is now serving to objectify male prisoners as gendered subjects, for the most part male prisoners seem to be subjectively unaware of their gender,

---

H. Baumer • R. Meek (✉)
Royal Holloway, University of London, Egham, UK

except perhaps, in the context of sport. When referring to young offenders (aged 15–21 years old), it is also important to consider that adolescent boys may experience masculinity in a somewhat different manner to adults, particularly in British society where masculinities of young men are often presented as being problematic (Frosh, Phoenix & Pattman, 2001). The criminality of young offenders suggests that their experience of masculinities has been more negative than most, leading them to construct a masculinity which conflicts with social norms and laws. Although there is limited research which focuses on the role of sport in debates of masculinity in prison, this chapter will consider literature on sporting masculinities across the community and the prison estate where possible, in the context of both adult prisoners and young offenders, making inferences where research does not exist.

Weightlifting and Masculinity in Prison

With the decline of physical labour and warfare across economically developed societies in the Global North throughout the twentieth century, the relevance and meaning of the muscular body changed from being practical to a tough, macho and powerful symbol (Messner 1990, p. 213), and in this sense, the muscular and athletic body of a professional sportsperson is often seen as the masculine ideal. McNay's exploration of feminism and the body draws upon the work of French philosopher, Michel Foucault, and his notion of the body as the point where power relations are most prominent. McNay considers how the inferiority of women is naturalised on the basis of biology, with women's bodies marked as inferior by being compared to dominant perceptions of men's bodies such as firmness, aggression and strength, features which are all related to masculine characteristics (McNay 1992). Extracts from Johnsen's (2001) study reveal that this association between the typical male body and masculinity also exists within Norwegian prisoner discourses, where a distinct connection is made between masculinity and muscles, together with an assumption that a fit body is attractive to women, thus enforcing the heterosexual image attached to the hegemonic masculinity that exists within the prison. In some cases, the link between masculinity and sport is so strong that it appears exclusive; one prisoner in Johnsen's study claimed that he was not masculine *because* he did not exercise (Johnsen 2001, p. 109). Therefore, sport as means to achieve certain forms of masculinity becomes pivotal in prison settings where embodied masculinities are struggled with, due to a lack of ways to overtly display heterosexuality (Bandyopadhyay 2006; Riciardelli 2013). Riciardelli et al. (2015) suggest that within this context, muscularity, coupled with physical prowess and ability, is a signifier of power, dominance and manliness amongst prisoners, and that this transcends ethnicity. Through the use of their bodies then, men in prison can affirm their gender and sexuality through sport (Sabo, 2001; Nandi 2002).

Combat sports are viewed as one of the ultimate exhibitions of masculinity. Woodward's (2004) ethnographic study in a boxing gym in Sheffield, England, claims that boxing offers a site where the hegemonic masculinity is heterosexual, to the subordination of masculinities constructed as weak, fearful or lacking courage (Woodward 2004, p. 7). Indeed, Woodward reported that women were banned from the gym altogether, and the boxers found the thought of women's boxing as dangerous and unacceptable, stating "It isn't right. It isn't natural. They might get hurt" (Woodward 2004, p. 5). Considering its macho image, perhaps it is unsurprising that boxing was found to be the most popular sport in a survey of young prisoners choosing the focus of a sporting academy (Meek 2014). Pierre Bordieu, a renowned French sociologist, attributes the popularity of combat sports to the visible signs of manliness and testing of manly virtues (Bourdieu, 2001). The latest available instruction released by the National Offender Management Service (NOMS) for England and Wales advises that *"Establishments must not deliver any supervision, training or instruction to prisoners in combat sports such as boxing, boxercise, martial arts or any similar activity"* (National Offender Management Service, 2011, p. 11), although it should be noted that the expiry date for this instruction is October 2015. There are examples of prisons providing forms of martial arts which comply with NOMS' instruction, such as Ashfield prison and young offender institution (YOI), which ran a *non-contact* boxing academy for young offenders for eight years, ending due to the closure of the prison in 2013 (Groombridge 2016, p. 126). Her Majesty's Prison (HMP) Doncaster, in the north of England, used boxing as part of its rehabilitation programme for non-violent offenders only, but focused on coaching and training others to box, rather than teaching prisoners themselves to box. This programme was recently suspended following the release of a report by the All-Party Parliamentary Group for Boxing who are campaigning for violent offenders to take part in this form of non-contact boxing within the prison, arguing that they would benefit more from participation than non-violent offenders (All-Party Parliamentary Group for Boxing 2015). As a comparison, access to physical activity programmes or equipment in American prisons is far more restricted, with prisons prohibited from purchasing "*any instruction (live or through broadcasts) or training equipment for boxing, wrestling, judo, karate, or other martial art, or any bodybuilding or weightlifting equipment of any sort*" (United States Government 1997, p. 110).

In a typical depiction of the average prison gym in England and Wales, one would see a range of free weights and weight machines of varying conditions, with various cardiovascular machines around the outside, including a couple of treadmills, exercise bikes and perhaps a rowing machine. There would also be a sports hall for team sports, usually football, maybe tennis or circuit training, and an outdoor pitch or two for rugby or football. So perhaps it is a consequence of the limited cardiovascular equipment and space available within a typical prison gym that weight lifting is the most popular physical activity amongst prisoners who are regular users of the gym, in particular bench pressing, which focuses on increasing muscle around the upper arms, chest and shoulders.

Observations and discussions with Physical Education (PE) Officers in YOIs across England and Wales have revealed that, despite complaints about the weight restrictions placed on free weights for young offenders and juveniles, many of them would still prefer to use the limited free weights to the machines without any restrictions placed on them. One might conclude from this that despite the opportunity to lift heavier weights and potentially grow stronger, these young men would rather lift lighter weights which are visible, and provide a better opportunity to exhibit manliness. As Johnsen (2001) attests, prisoners who are regular gym users are very vocal about lifting heavy weights, and, through word of mouth, everyone knows who has lifted the most; indeed, some adult prison gyms in England have notice boards which display the names of those prisoners who have lifted the heaviest weights. There is a lot of pressure to participate in weight training amongst prison gym attendees, and the hierarchy which pre-exists in the weights room can be a particularly tough place to integrate into, particularly for newcomers who are likely to feel overwhelmed with feelings of insecurity, uncertainty and emotional exposure (Riciardelli et al. 2015). As Sabo et al. report "One way to avoid a fight is to look as though you're willing to fight – as a result prisoners lift weights compulsively, adopt the meanest stare they can muster, and keep their fears and pain hidden beneath a tough guy posture" (Sabo et al. 2001, p. 10), although perhaps this image of prisoners in the gym is a little exaggerated. Many of the reasons for weight lifting present in prisoner discourse do not reflect this masculine 'tough guy' ideal, instead there is a recognition that there is not much else to do, but the 'challenge' associated with lifting weights appears important, as well as the 'high' or 'feel good' factor associated with lifting more, promoting self-confidence and alleviating tension (Riciardelli et al. 2015; Johnsen 2001). The lack of free time and social isolation can fuel the emotional vulnerability of prisoners and result in extreme levels of anxiety and poor mental well-being in general. It is thought that dominant forms of masculinity legitimise violence as an acceptable way of dealing with such emotions in circumstances in which asking for help would lead to a 'loss' of masculinity (Evans and Wallace 2008). As an alternative to violence, regular participation in sport can help alleviate such stresses by enabling individuals to feel empowered and enhance feelings of self-worth, self-esteem and achievement, in turn giving them the ability to manage emotions by forgetting or suppressing them, thereby potentially diminishing anxiety and even depression (Hassmen et al. 2000; Salmon 2001). Although more research is needed on the relationship between mental well-being and sport in prisons specifically, accounts from prisoners in the research considered thus far suggest that weight lifting may be a way for them to deal with the stresses of incarceration through the emergence of new, positive masculine ideals.

Sporting Masculinities and Empowerment in Prisons

The Body as Social Capital

As a fundamental material and symbolic signifier of how we see ourselves as gendered, the body plays a pivotal role in the construction and reconstruction of masculinity (Shilling 1993; Gordon et al. 2000; Connell 1995). We are more or less consciously aware of the significance and resource which our bodies hold in various social settings, referred to by Shilling (1993) as 'physical capital'.[1] And as Swain's exploration of the role of sport in the promotion of masculinity in a junior school concludes, this physical capital has the potential to empower individuals with resources of influence such as power and status (Swain 2002). The prison gym is an exemplar of how a fit body can act as social capital within social relations (Johnsen 2001).

The Ministry of Justice instruction on PE for Prisoners in England and Wales (2011) states that "*PE makes a major contribution to the physical, mental and social wellbeing of prisoners and positively impacts on the good order and discipline within establishments*" (Ministry of Justice, 2011, p. 2). Sabo (1994) reports that prison officials view prisoners' involvement in sports as making them more compliant, whilst others suggest that there is an implication within the prison service that PE can be used as a means to control prisoners' construction of masculinity, using it as a mechanism for regulating prisoners' attitudes and bodies (Carrabin and Longhurst 1998). Johnsen (2001) proposes that in spite of this attempt at control by prison management, prisoners in the Norwegian prison which was the focus of her research seem to be using the gym as a 'heterotopia' (Foucault 1991) of sorts in which to 'do masculinity' (Johnsen 2001, p. 23) and develop an excessively macho and muscular body, consequently representing a challenge to the prison's ideal of disciplined minds and controlled bodies. This process can be understood as a form of protest masculinity, the method of using your body to claim a gendered position of power (Connell 1995). This form of 'protest masculinity' as it is practised within prison gyms is a pronounced example of the power of the body as a tool of social practice.

Masculinity and Negotiating Risk in Prison

Whilst serving a prison sentence, a prisoner's personal (legal, physical and emotional) safety is continually perceived as being at risk. Riciardelli et al. (2015) propose that previous research has failed to address the way in which prisoners' reactions to such risk and uncertainty can shape and conflict with their masculinities, stressing that whilst confronting these personal challenges, prisoners wish to come across as empowered rather than submissive. Riciardelli et al. outline masculinities as fluid and transient, arguing that there are nuanced variations of gender in prison and those best able to manage 'penal uncertainties', such as the arbitrary nature of decision making or involuntary prison transfers, hold the most empowered position. Avoiding confrontation with other prisoners or officers is important to avoid potential emasculation or subordination; consequently, those who can negotiate themselves to evade such confrontation are most protected against the unpredictable situations which may arise and therefore, as Riciardelli et al. see it, constitute hegemonic masculinity. An example of a prisoner who is successfully negotiating their position in prison and would therefore fit this idea of hegemony is reflected in Johnsen's (2001) portrayal of a Norwegian prisoner on the 'contract wing' who was afforded enhanced privileges due to good behaviour, and in his words, had learnt to play the 'game' (Johnsen 2001, p. 137). There are many perspectives on what constitutes hegemonic masculinity in prisons, but what remains constant is the idea that the construction of masculinity is under continuous influence from changing socio-environmental factors—whether that be moving from a single-occupancy cell to a shared cell in a prison, or the arrival of a new prisoner—and these changes prompt a renegotiation of power relations, and as such, the idea of an 'empowered' prisoner changes from one context to the next.

Prison Gyms and Empowerment[2]

According to Swain (2002), hegemonic masculinity "wields the single greatest power and authority, is able to regulate, influence and shape action" (Swain 2002, p. 3) and to quote Connell, is the most 'idealised' form of masculinity in any setting (Connell 1990, p. 83). Since the overt authority in a prison setting lies with officers and management, empowerment is attributed even greater importance for the configuration and practice of masculinity amongst prisoners. Bandyopadhyay (2006) suggests that it is possible to present two versions of hegemonic masculinity: the official ideal male prisoner, and one who has successfully mastered manipulation of the rules and achieves a well-balanced relationship with prisoners and staff alike. However, in the context of a prison gym, it is arguable that these versions of hegemonic masculinity cannot mutually exist. The potential risk associated with embodying the 'ideal' male prisoner as recognised by other prisoners is that behaviours associated with the embodiment of hyper-masculinity include being strong and aggressive, and could be interpreted as challenging the prison service's ideal of good order and discipline, thus resulting in punishment.

Punishment has a direct impact on exercising masculinity through sport with the prison system in England and Wales, as those demoted to the basic level of the Incentives and Earned Privileges (IEP) scheme[3] for poor behaviour will have their access to the gym limited to as little as once a week. Some UK prisons will prevent those on the basic level from accessing weights in the gym at all, instead limiting them to physical activity in the sports hall such as team sports or circuit training. Conversely, across many prisons and YOIs in England and Wales, prisoners who 'play the game' and are rewarded with enhanced level status are permitted to access the gym on a regular basis, sometimes even daily. Therefore, in order to maintain the embodied manifestation of hegemonic masculinity in the form of a muscular body which requires regular attendance at the gym, prisoners must also conform to the requirements of the prison management system through good behaviour and active rehabilitation. Thus, through the use of the IEP scheme, prison authorities are able to regain some control over prisoners' use of the gym and participation in sport, but not at the expense of the prisoners' freedom to express their masculinity.

Challenging Hegemonic Masculinities in Prisons Through Sport

The importance of challenging existing hegemonic sporting masculinities within prisons lies not only with the prevention of subordinating other groups, but also in the protection of prisoners who continuously strive to achieve hegemonic status to the detriment of their well-being. Any strategy for the maintenance of power, such as embodying the hegemonic masculinity of a prison gym, is likely to involve a subordination of other groups, leading to a diminished sense of empathy and emotional relatedness within the self (Schawalbe 1992). Furthermore, maintaining a body image which reflects the male ideal requires a tremendous amount of self-discipline, and the rewards of status and power afforded through this image are not guaranteed and always up for contestation, requiring constant negotiation of one's power relations with others. Therefore, maintaining the embodiment of hyper-masculinity in prison is likely to have a detrimental effect on mental well-being.

Hardness–Softness Dichotomy

'Masculinity' is a discursive construct which unfolds and changes through time, culture and context (Morgan 2000; Connell and Messerschmidt 2005). It is imperative to bear this idea in mind when describing masculinities in the context of prison gyms in general, as one must not fail to recognise the variations that are likely to be found within and between institutions. For instance, a prisoner's construction of masculinity in the context of the prison gym is likely to differ from the masculine ideal they present in the visits room in front of their loved ones. Likewise, the factors which constitute hegemonic masculinity in a Mexican prison, where good behaviour is not recognised and gangs have more authority than prison officers, are unlikely to mirror those found in an English prison which exercises a privilege scheme and presents an opportunity of early release or removal to a lower category prison for good behaviour.

As part of an ethnographic study exploring how men in a prison in Kolkata, India, deal with the 'less than a man' image which prison imposes on them, Bandyopadhyay (2006) concludes that hardness and softness are not traits 'inscribed onto maleness', but that they vary with circumstance. This alternation is described by Sabo (1994) as a 'hardness-softness dichotomy', which stimulates and mirrors feminine and masculine stereotypes. The construction of masculinities which express 'hardness' is centred on a male code for acting tough, which includes being prepared to fight, minding your own business, suffering in silence, avoiding feminine behaviours and never admitting you're afraid. These traits of 'hardness' and 'softness' are often understood through personal appearance and thus can be amplified through sport or exercise. A perfect illustration of this is found in the way a male athlete constructs himself as muscled, aggressive, competitive and emotionally controlled (Messner & Sabo, 1994). In terms of prisons, Riciardelli et al.'s (2015) interviews with men across prisons in Ontario, Canada, suggest that the presence of a softer masculinity can be found in low secure settings where violence is less of a risk. They suggest that prisoners in these settings tend to reflect compliance and a submission of 'tough-guy' behaviours in order to avoid transfer to a high secure prison, by acting stoically, avoiding attention, attending prison programmes and refraining from violence. In contrast, they also argue that those in more secure prisons where violence is rife use sport as a means of expressing hardness by displaying a penchant for body building not only as a way to appear muscled and competitive but also as a way to "alleviate tension and feelings of isolation and limit physical vulnerability by spending more time away from other prisoners or in supervised settings" (Riciardelli et al. 2015, p. 500). Thus, sport can be used by prisoners as a means to control emotions and stay out of trouble, whilst maintaining a 'hard' masculinity.

Prison Management and Masculinities

Researchers propose that more focus is needed on the management of prisons as organisations, with "a clearer focus on the activities of the powerful and their interactions with the relatively powerless" (Carrabin and Longhurst 1998, p. 163). To this end, it would be ill-informed to discuss sporting masculinities within prison without mentioning the PE Officers who form such a crucial part of the prison management system.

The wings of a prison have been described as lacking in autonomy for prisoners who feel that prison officers make the decisions for them, whereas the gym or sports halls are thought to weaken these negative feelings somewhat (Riciardelli et al. 2015). Perhaps this feeling of increased autonomy can be attested to the fact that prisoners who find themselves in the gym have chosen to be there, and have some freedom over the equipment they choose to use, or which exercise class or sports programme they are participating in.

Johnsen (2001) found the discourse on masculinity within a prison to reflect the authoritarianism alongside which an idealised form of masculinity operates, which is considered essential in the control of prisoners. However, this sense of authoritarianism in prison management can be lessened in the context of a PE Officers' construction of their own masculinity, who arguably have the opportunity to embrace a softer masculinity within the context of prisons. Direct observations, discussions with staff and a review of reports reveal that, across prisons and YOIs in England and Wales, violent incidents are less likely to occur in the prison gym than elsewhere in the prison. This may be unsurprising as the gym is more often occupied by prisoners on the enhanced regime than the basic regime and prisoners are not in the gym for extended periods of time; moreover, prisoners who do attend the gym are often doing so by choice and it is probable that they are unwilling to jeopardise their access through bad behaviour. It may also be a consequence of physiological effects of regular exercise such as an enhanced tendency to suppress anger and hostility (Hassmen et al., 2000) and reduced anger expression (Buchman et al., 1991). Regardless of the cause, this reduced tendency for violence means that PE Officers in England and Wales are not required to impose overt authority on prisoners under their care as often as other prison officers, and are thus able to develop a relatively untarnished relationship with them that fellow officers may struggle to achieve. It also stands to reason that prisoners who enjoy spending time in the gym will spend significantly more time with the PE Officers than wing officers, who are not engaged with prisoners for extended periods of time, and this may strengthen the relationship between PE staff and prisoners further. Through her exploration of the role of physical activity in correctional settings across England and Wales, Meek is able to provide an example of improved relationships between prisoners and PE Officers as a result of increased time spent together through sporting academies, "Lads see us differently – rather than screws we are screws with individual personalities and interests" (Meek 2014, p. 106). Meek also found that when discussing their relationship with PE Officers, prisoners often refer to them as being unlike the officers 'in blue'. Those 'in blue' being uniformed officers in English and Welsh prisons, differing in appearance from the PE Officers who wear casual sports clothes. This is an important distinction in terms of embodied masculinities and the authoritarian masculinity represented by the officers' uniform. Conversations with prisoners and prison officers in prisons and YOIs in England and Wales revealed that prisoners have a tendency to view those in uniform as the opposition and adopt a strong 'us versus them' mentality when referring to them. Young offenders in particular, however, tended to refer to PE Officers in general with more warmth. These lower rates of violence and increased opportunities to develop relationships and build trust and respect from prisoners provide PE Officers with a chance to construct a softer masculinity where appropriate, which is perhaps a luxury not afforded to wing officers in prisons across England and Wales who face overcrowding and high rates of violence, and may perhaps feel that a less than macho image leaves them vulnerable. Whatever the cause, this mutual respect present in the prison gym is crucial when managing large groups of muscular and potentially aggressive male prisoners, and perhaps there is something to be learnt from this positive relationship in terms of prison management strategies in general.

PE Officers take on an extensive range of responsibilities, as a Senior Manager at a prison describes in Meek's book, 'Sport in Prison', "PE officers have to be able to organise and supervise offenders who display challenging behaviour. They teach PE, deliver vocational courses, coach a range of different sports, provide remedial treatment programmes for prisoners, mentor and influence prisoners in the unique custodial setting" (Meek 2014, p. 15). In order to perform such diverse tasks, PE Officers are required to display an assortment of masculinities ranging from the hegemonic macho masculinity, which enforces authority on challenging individuals, to masculinities constructed by more 'feminine' qualities such as caring and understanding in the role of mentor. These masculinities require a careful balance, particularly in contexts such as the classroom where it is crucial to control disruptive individuals at the same time as creating a rapport which encourages them to engage with the sessions. Controlling a class of juvenile offenders can be a particularly problematic task, as a result of the prevalence of attention deficit/hyperactive disorder and conduct disorder (Foley et al., 1996). It could be reasoned then that PE Officers are in a key position to undertake the task of leading and educating offenders through a deconstruction of hyper-masculine bodies and macho masculinities to reconstruct positive masculinities which will help prisoners through their time in incarceration.

Gym Orderlies

Johnsen's study of Norwegian male prisoners indicates a threat of subordination surrounding the prisoners should they choose to ask another for advice or an opinion on how best to train, prompting them to learn through observation rather than risk emasculating themselves (Johnsen 2001, p. 60). Prisons in England and Wales may have found a way to avoid such threats through the employment of gym orderlies, that is, prisoners given the job of working in the gym, often on a daily basis, to provide sport and exercise-related support and advice to other prisoners. Here, orderlies and PE Officers are both on hand to provide support to prisoners who may need it. It is conceivable that because it is their *job* to provide sport-related advice, prisoners do not feel the same threat of subordination as observed by Johnsen when asking other prisoners (the Orderlies) for the same type of advice. This is reflected in accounts of orderlies and PE Officers alike in English and Welsh prisons who recall frequent conversations with prisoners seeking advice or support for getting 'bigger', managing their weight or trying something new.

With typically no more than six to eight orderly positions offered in total across prisons in England and Wales, being an orderly is arguably the most sought-after job for prisoners in the entire prison, representing a tremendously privileged position which enables more time in the gym than any other prisoner. As a result of their increased time spent working out, orderlies are often amongst the largest and most muscular of all prisoners; they are the true embodiment of the physical hegemonic masculinity within the prison gym. However, in non-corporeal terms, a typical orderly's nature is in stark contrast to macho characteristics such as dominance and aggression. Only the best behaved of those on the enhanced regime will be afforded the privileged position of gym orderly, and in the majority of cases, if an orderly is involved in a negative incident anywhere in the confines of the prison, then their role will be revoked. This is a rare occurrence it seems, with orderlies representing one of the most trusted groups in prison. In terms of the orderlies' relationships with other prisoners, PE Officers and prisoners who attend the gym will place them amongst the most respected and well-liked within the prison. Such a social standing is likely to be a result of sporting masculinities, as constructed by the orderlies, impacting on the strategic power relations between them and other prisoners. Interestingly then, it would appear that the prisoners who are viewed as the most masculine within the prison are also amongst the best-behaved and most well-liked, contesting any aggressive masculinities in the gym and instead presenting a positive example of hegemonic masculinity for others to aspire to.

Non-Competitive Sporting Activities

Competitive sports have been described as providing 'the quintessential manifestation of the masculine ethos' (Gilbert and Gilbert 1998, p. 60). It would make sense then that when trying to challenge and contest such masculinities through sport, the competitive edge should be lessened from any typically competitive sports. As Connell and Messerschmidt (2005) explain, hegemonic masculinities can be positive, and this is a key strategy for contemporary efforts at reform in the criminal justice system. The capacity to deconstruct gender binaries and criticise hegemonic masculinity is the basis for many successful educational interventions and change programmes including non-competitive sporting environments. Discussions with PE Officers in England and Wales who have worked with Young Offenders (aged 15–21 years) report developing the strongest rapport with prisoners when on trips outside of the prison in non-competitive sports programmes, such as completing the Duke of Edinburgh award,[4] taking part in running events, raising money for Troopaid[5] and in particular the Airborne Initiative—a weeklong, hard-hitting residential course delivered for young offenders in Dartmoor, in the south of England, designed specifically to challenge young offenders to achieve their own personal success (https://airborneinitiative.org).

Throughout the course of these non-competitive programmes, the dominant masculinities constructed through hardness, such as acting tough, avoiding intimacy, minding your own business, suffering in silence, avoiding feminine behaviours and never admitting you are afraid, are all contested. The reconstruction of masculinities necessary to achieve success on these courses includes teamwork and intimacy, as well as an understanding of others' needs. Through the embodiment of these new masculine ideals, young offenders are able to achieve success at levels they may have never felt before. PE Officers involved in the Airborne Initiative openly admit that there are tears of joy from both sides on completion of the week, which is a fantastic example of how masculinity can be partially constructed by typically feminine characteristics. It is this overlap that exists between feminism and masculinity which Riciardelli et al. (2015) argue the majority of masculinity research has failed to acknowledge. The acceptance and construction of such empowering masculinities which contest masculinities characterised by isolation and poor coping mechanisms can aid prisoners when dealing with negative emotions once they return to prison following temporary release on these sports-based excursions.

Under the management of NOMS in England and Wales, prisoners who wish to engage in activities in the community require the approval of a Release on Temporary Licence (ROTL) application (National Offender Management Service, 2015). These applications are generally used towards the end of a prisoner's sentence as a rehabilitative aid and are approved by the prison governor, who manages the prison. Prisoners in high-security prisons (category A) and those on remand are amongst those who are not entitled to apply for ROTL. Following a ROTL review in July 2013 as a result of "instances of serious offending on ROTL" (NOMS 2015, p. 1), the stringency of ROTLs was increased. Furthermore, the Criminal Justice Act 2013 (Legislation.gov.uk 2017) expanded on the offences eligible for Multi Agency Public Protection Arrangements (MAPPAs), which are imposed on violent or dangerous offenders by the courts, preventing them from taking part in activities outside of the prison at any point during their sentence. To date, research into the positive impact of non-competitive sporting initiatives for offenders held outside of prison is very limited. Dubberley, Parry & Baker's evaluation of the impact of the Duke of Edinburgh Award on young offenders (aged 14–21 years) found an improvement in participants' attitudes towards victim hurt denial and perception of current life (Dubberley et al. 2011, in Meek 2014). However, because different participants were used for the original cohort and the follow-up group, comparisons between the two groups should be considered with caution.

Sporting Academies for Young Offenders

Team sports such as football and rugby are immensely popular amongst prisoners, in particular young offenders (15–21 years old; Meek 2014). Although such sports have the potential to provide positive outcomes in terms of team building and developing social skills, it would be misguided to label team sports as all-inclusive and assume they always encourage social integration. Team sports have a real potential to highlight tensions between contrasting styles of masculinity or to encourage the subordination of non-hegemonic masculinities; therefore, it is important to challenge and contest existing competitive masculinities and promote the construction of positive masculinities that team sports can facilitate such as socialisation and teamwork.

Sporting academies which bring together YOIs and external organisations, such as rugby or football clubs, community-based voluntary sector providers and charities in the UK, are tremendously popular amongst young offenders who are interested in sport. The National Alliance of Sport for the Desistance from Crime has partnered with charities and the criminal justice system in the UK to support organisations which use sport to prevent offending and rehabilitate offenders, and they have been instrumental in supporting a number of programmes which bring external organisations and prisoners together, including Saracens Sport Foundation supporting young offenders through rugby academies at Portland YOI in the South West of England and Feltham YOI in London, Cricket for Change using cricket to support people in custody in Jamaica, and the 2nd Chance Foundation using sport to promote desistance from crime in Portland YOI with participation from London-based football club Chelsea and the Rugby Football Union in the UK (http://www.nasdc.org/power-of-sport/case-studies).

Meek's evaluation of four football and rugby academies run at HMP and YOI Portland, involving 79 young offenders, found sustained improvements in measures of belief about aggression and self-esteem (Meek 2014). This contestation and reconstruction of hegemonic macho-masculinities is well illustrated through a comment provided by a Prison Gym Staff member on the academies, "It creates good behaviour around the jail, through the perceived standing of the lads involved, leading to them openly challenging others' inappropriate behaviour either on the pitch or on the wings [residential halls]. Lads involved with this academy have openly stopped violent incidents and been strong enough to say why and lead others" (Meek 2014, p. 105). This open challenge by young offenders of others' violent acts exhibits the powerful potential for sporting academies to nurture new masculinities which contest existing, damaging masculinities within the prison.

It is increasingly popular for sporting academies aimed at young offenders inside prisons to include classroom-based sessions involving peer-review work and presentations from external speakers to promote the development of adaptive skills and thinking skills, challenging existing masculinities centred on aggression and egocentrism. The Prisoner's Education Trust (PET) advocates the use of sport in prisons as a 'hook' to engage prisoners in education, publishing the 'Fit for Release' research project which examines the value of sport as a rehabilitative tool in prisons, particularly in relation to educational and employment opportunities (Meek et al., 2012).

The positive feedback and accounts of those working closely with sporting academies and non-competitive sports programmes outside of the prison are encouraging. Nevertheless, it should be noted that prisoners are not afforded the privilege of participating in such schemes unless they are on the enhanced level of the IEP scheme. As a result, the most disruptive and reluctant to engage do not currently have the chance to experience the related benefits directly. Such individuals reflect the epitome of the 'hard' masculine ideal outlined by Messner and Sabo (1994)—being prepared to fight, minding your own business and suffering in silence, behaviours which create barriers to earning privileges in prison.

In addition, the very act of having more restrictions placed on them as 'men' is likely to create a greater desire to enact their masculinity in other ways which are interpreted as inappropriate, such as overt sexism, homophobia or aggression. For this very reason, it could be argued that those on the basic IEP regime are in most need of an intervention which will challenge their masculine ideals in positive ways.

As illustrated by the following quote from a young offender who had previously conformed to this 'hard' ideal and struggled with behaviour issues, the sporting academy had been for him an effective way of encouraging good behaviour, "Behaviour wise, when I was first sent down [to prison] I was always on basic [regime] for messing around. With the academies you have to be on enhanced [regime] so you have to be well behaved and work your way up, so they give you an incentive to behave" (Meek 2014, p. 105). More research is needed on the impact of incentive schemes within prisons generally, perhaps with a focus on sporting interventions for persistent non-engagers on the basic regime.

Masculinity and Participation in Sport

Masculine Ideals and Inequality of Participation

Although the prison service imposes some restrictions on the type of sport and exercise available to prisoners based on their conviction,[6] for the most part the specification for PE in prisons as outlined by the Ministry of Justice for England and Wales is centred on the "*equality of access to PE programmes and resources to meet the requirements of all prisoners, through identifying and giving full considerations to meet specific needs of their gender, religion, age, disability, race and sexual orientation*" [Ministry of Justice (England and Wales) 2011, p. 6]. Somewhat inevitably, however, given the competitive masculinities which dominate the spaces in which exercise is performed inside prisons, this equality is threatened. A Senior Prison Manager quoted in Meek's research on promoting diversity in prison gyms revealed that "Some prisoners, individuals or groups, may want to influence and dominate sports provision at the expense of others"

(Meek 2014, p. 37). For other prisoners, it may be a general fear of appearing as a 'loser' which prevents participation (Johnsen 2001), or the *public trial of bodily presentation* which participation in sport carries with it (Wellard 2002, p. 236).

Discussions with gym orderlies across prisons and YOIs in England and Wales revealed that regular users of the prison gym routinely associate with other 'regulars', in some instances finding it almost impossible to name someone they know who does not use the gym. When we consider that non-gym users could include as much as half of the prison population, this constitutes a clear divide within prisons. Average monthly participation levels for prisoners in juvenile and young offender estates in England and Wales vary from 50% to 100%, whereas those in adult establishments (excluding immigration removal centres) vary from 48% to 63% (Meek 2014). In the case of young adults and juvenile offenders (14–21 years old) in England and Wales, we must be mindful that the guidelines for prisons from the Ministry of Justice differ for young adults and juvenile offenders, and adult offenders: for example, those under 18 are required to participate in physical education as part of their academic timetable. Even so, these variable participation levels are of concern, and when facing a prison population with an increasing multiplicity of requirements due to age, obesity, mental health, substance misuse and disability, there is an important need to ensure equitable provision of sport and exercise. Those who regularly attend the prison gym seem to benefit from the existing sport provision in positive ways, but the question of who is choosing not to participate in sport within prisons and their reasons for this is an important one. Unfortunately, to date this has received little academic attention.

As Sabo et al. (2001) suggest, men's behaviour in prison can be viewed not as deviant but rather an exaggeration of many culturally acceptable forms of masculinity. Since particular performances of masculinity are manifested in boys through sports at school from a young age (Swain, 2002), there are arguably similarities to be drawn from research into sport and masculinities in schools and in prisons. Swain's study of the promotion of masculinity through sport amongst upper middle-class school boys (Swain, 2002) identified a number of masculine practices present in the school that were ordered in terms of power and standing; many of these mirror those found within prisons. These included "competitive team games, strict discipline, a strict code of dress/uniform, divisions of labour and patterns of authority" (Swain 2002, p. 6). Through the consideration of these masculine practices, Swain identifies three types of masculinity when explaining reasons for non-participation in sport: personal, subordinated and liminal.

For Swain, personal masculinity is associated with boys who choose not to participate in sports because they are simply unable to do so due to a lack of physical resource. He argues that these boys construct their masculinity in personalised ways, but do not feel subordinated as they do not aspire to, or wish to challenge, the hegemonic masculinity displayed by the 'sporty' boys. Subordinated masculinities represented a small minority of boys who did not seem to put in any effort and were also seen as 'outsiders' for reasons not related to sport. These subordinated boys were isolated from their peers and regularly subordinated as the object of homophobic harassment. Finally, Swain described liminal masculinity an aspirant type of masculinity seen in those boys who aspire to idealised masculinities but who do not possess the personal resources to succeed in performing these. They were good at sports, but not quite good enough; in other words, in Adler and Adler's terms they are the 'Wannabes' (Adler and Adler, 1998). Through consideration of the type of masculinities outlined by Swain (2002), it may be possible to identify groups who exclude themselves from sport in prison and use the characteristics of such groups to inform programmes which encourage engagement. Typically, evaluations of sports programmes in prison to date have focused on opportunity samples of prisoners who opt to participate, with little evidence for the impact of such programmes when motivation or ability is low (Meek, 2014). However, there are examples of sports initiatives in prisons targeting those who do not normally play, by teaching basic skills for football, volleyball and basketball (Meek 2014, p. 38), and many prisons in England and Wales do offer special time slots in the prison gym for 'poor copers' who are vulnerable to self-harm and bullying. One such scheme within a YOI was highlighted in Lewis and Heer's practical toolkit for improving the health and well-being of young people in secure settings (2008), and was aimed at engaging the most vulnerable young people in custody in a range of physical activities designed to build confidence and trust in others. The benefits of this approach are demonstrated through positive outcomes including an increase in motivation and self-esteem, more frequent attendance at the gym, and a reduction in self-harm and suicide.

Contesting Masculinities and Increasing Engagement

Wellard's (2002) exploration of 'exclusive masculinities', which can prevent participation in sport for gay and straight males from school right through to adult sports clubs, concludes that a review of contemporary sporting practices is key in increasing participation from subordinated groups. In the context of prisons, this means establishing *alternatives* to the existing and established practices of team sports or the competitive weights room, not merely making existing spaces more inclusive so that those who are less macho are invited to engage in macho behaviours. It is also important to challenge the assumption that the dominating hetero-gender order is the 'natural' order, as this forms the basis for homophobic taunts experienced by subordinated heterosexuals and non-heterosexuals alike, both in and outside of sporting contexts. Anderson (2011) believes that approaches to gradually diminish homophobia will eventually allow for the construction of an 'inclusive masculinity', in which multiple forms of masculinity can exist without gendered policing. On a broader level, by allowing diverse forms of masculinity to co-exist their qualities can be harnessed in ways which promote difference further; ideas should be based on acceptance and accommodating difference where winning or losing, or dominating an opponent, is not a key component. There is currently limited provision of this type within the criminal justice system for young offenders in UK in the form of the Airborne Initiative or the Duke of Edinburgh Award, but an apparent absence of anything similar for adults. Such programmes are in a position to not only encourage engagement from otherwise subordinated men in prisons, but also support the deconstruction of maladaptive coping mechanisms which are embedded in existing hegemonic masculinities in order to recreate positive and beneficial masculinities which will support prisoners throughout their time in incarceration. PE Officers are in the ideal position to facilitate and develop this type of programme to greater numbers of young offenders and juveniles, and consideration should also be made for adults to be given the same opportunities. However, this is only possible with the support of prison management to help provide appropriate resourcing and opportunities for release where necessary. Perhaps policy makers and prison management would respond better to a greater body of psychological and sociological research which validates the impact and importance of such programmes in terms of addressing exclusion from sport and reconstructing masculinities in a more inclusive way.

Through consideration of academic research, literature, direct observations and discussions, the present chapter has outlined the influence of sporting masculinities on prisoners' well-being, from both negative and potentially positive perspectives. There is a need for prison management, practitioners and the sports development sector more broadly to consider the potential that exists within the prison gym, and through sport in prisons more generally, and to challenge hegemonic masculinities where they are having a negative impact on well-being. In doing so, prisons should aspire to develop an environment which promotes inclusive and diverse masculinities and increased well-being through sport and exercise.

Notes

1. As drawn from Bordieu's idea of 'embodied' capital as a subdivision of cultural capital (Bordieu 1986).
2. Empowerment, as recognised in this chapter, is the development of internal power, strength and confidence, in particular, feeling in control of one's own life and rights.
3. The IEP scheme currently running in prisons across England and Wales operates three privilege levels: basic, standard and enhanced. Prisoners must display good behaviour and work towards their own rehabilitation if they are to earn privileges and gain enhanced level status.
4. The Duke of Edinburgh Award is a programme which invites young people to complete a series of challenges across five sectors (volunteering, physical, skills, expedition and residential), and there are three levels of award which increase in duration and difficulty.
5. Troopaid is a charity raising money to support injured troops returning from conflict across the British Armed Forces.

6. For example, sex offenders are forbidden from completing a sport-based qualification on the basis that they may use this following release to gain employment which enables them to work inappropriately closely with individuals who they may regard as potential targets for a sexual offence.

References

Adler, A., & Adler, P. (1998). *Peer power: Preadolescent culture and identity*. London: Rutgers University Press.
All-Parliamentary Group for Boxing. (2015). *Boxing: The right Hook*. [Online]. Available at: https://appgboxing.wordpress.com/2015/03/17/boxing-the-right-hook/. Accessed 26 Jan 2017.
Anderson, E. (2011). *Inclusive masculinity: The changing nature of masculinities*. Oxon: Routledge.
Bandyopadhyay, M. (2006). Competing masculinities in a prison. *Men and Masculinities, 9*(2), 186–203. https://doi.org/10.1177/1097184X06287765.
Bourdieu, P. (2001). *Masculine domination*. Cambridge: Polity.
Buchman, B. P., Sallis, J. F., Criqui, M. H., Dimsdale, J. E., & Kaplan, R. M. (1991). Physical activity, physical fitness, and psychological characteristics of medical students. *Journal of Psychosomatic Research, 35*(2–3), 197–208.
Carrabin, E., & Longhurst, B. (1998). Gender and prison organisation: Some comments on masculinities and prison management. *The Howard Journal, 37*(2), 161–176.
Connell, R. W. (1990). An iron man: The body and some contradictions of hegemonic masculinity. In M. A. Messner & D. F. Sabo (Eds.), *Sport, men and the gender order: Critical feminist perspectives*. Champaign: Human Kinetics.
Connell, R. W. (1995). *Masculinities*. Cambridge: Polity.
Connell, R. W., & Messerschmidt, J. W. (2005). Hegemonic masculinity: Rethinking the concept. *Gender and Society, 19*(6). https://doi.org/10.1177/0891243205278639.
Evans, T., & Wallace, P. (2008). A prison within a prison? The masculinity narratives of male prisoners. *Men and Masculinities, 10*(4), 484–507.
Foley, H. A., Carlton, C. O., & Howell, R. J. (1996). The relationship of attention deficit hyperactivity disorder and conduct disorder to juvenile delinquency: Legal implications. *The Bulletin of the American Academy of Psychiatry and the Law, 24*(3), 333–345.

Foucault, M. (1991). Space, knowledge and power. In P. Rabinow (Ed.), *The Foucault reader: An introduction to Foucault's thought*. London: Penguin Books.

Gilbert, R., & Gilbert, P. (1998). *Masculinity goes to school*. London: Routledge.

Gordon, T., Holland, J., & Lahelma, E. (2000). *Making spaces: Citizenship and differences in schools*. Basingstoke: Macmillan Press.

Groombridge, N. (2016). *Sports criminology. A critical criminology of sport and games*. London: The Policy Press.

Hassmén, P., Koivula, N., & Uutela, A. (2000). Physical exercise and psychological well-being: A population study in Finland. *Preventive Medicine, 30*(1), 17–25. https://doi.org/10.1006/pmed.1999.0597.

Johnsen, B. (2001). *Sport, masculinities and power relations in prison*. Oslo: The Norwegian University of Sport and Physical Education, Norges Idrettshøgskole.

Legislation.gov.uk. (2017). *Criminal Justice Act 2013*. [Online]. Available at: http://www.legislation.gov.uk/ukpga/2003/44/schedule/15. Accessed 26 Jan 2017.

McNay, L. (1992). *Foucault and feminism*. Boston: Northeastern University Press.

Meek, R. (2014). *Sport in prison: Exploring the role of physical activity in correctional settings*. Oxon: Routledge.

Meek, R., Champion N., & Klier S. (2012). *Fit for release*. London: Prisoners Education Trust.

Messner, M. A. (1990). When bodies are weapons: Masculinity and violence in sport. *International Review for Sociology of Sport, 25*(3), 203–219.

Ministry of Justice. (2011). *Physical Education (PE) for Prisoners. PSI 58/2011*. National Offender Management Service. Available at: https://www.justice.gov.uk/downloads/offenders/psipso/psi-2011/psi-58-2011-physical-education.doc. Accessed 26 Jan 2017.

Morgan, D. (2000, March). Problems with masculinities. Lecture at the seminar "Researching Masculinities" in Trondheim, 20–23.

National Offender Management Service. (2015). *Release on temporary licence. PSI 13/2015*. Available at: https://www.justice.gov.uk/downloads/offenders/psipso/psi-2015/psi-13-2015-release-on-temporary-licence.docx. Accessed 26 Jan 2017.

Newton, C. (1994). Gender theory and prison sociology: Using theories of masculinities to interpret the sociology of prisons for men. *Howard Journal, 10*, 193–202.

Riciardelli, R. (2013). Establishing and asserting masculinities in Canadian penitentiaries. *Journal of Gender Studies*, 1–22. https://doi.org/10.1080/09589236.2013.812513.

Riciardelli, R., Maier, K., & Hannah-Moffat, K. (2015). Strategic masculinities: Vulnerabilities, risk and the production of prison masculinities. *Theoretical Criminology, 19*(4). https://doi.org/10.1177/1362480614565849.

Messner, M. A. and Sabo, D. F. (1994). *Sex, Violence & Power in Sports: Rethinking Masculinity*. Freedom, CA: The Crossing Press.

Sabo, D. F. (2000, October 13). Prison masculinities: Issues for research on men, masculinities, and gender relations. Lecture in Oslo.

Sabo, D. (2001). Doing Time, Doing Masculinity: Sports and Prisons, In Sabo, D., Kupers, T. A. & London, W. (eds) *Prison Masculinities*. Philadelphia, PA: Temple University Press.

Salmon, P. (2001). Effects of physical exercise on anxiety, depression, and sensitivity to stress. *Clinical Psychology Review, 21*(1), 33–61. https://doi.org/10.1016/s0272-7358(99)00032-x.

Schawalbe, M. (1992). Male supremacy and the narrowing of the moral self. *Berkley Journal of Sociology, 37*, 29–54.

Shilling, C. (1993). *The body and social theory*. London: Sage Publications.

Swain, J. (2002). The role of sport in the promotion of masculinity in an English independent junior school. *Sport, Education and Society, 11*(4). https://doi.org/10.1080/13573320600924841.

United States Government. (1997). *104th Congress Public Law*. Accessed at: https://www.gpo.gov/fdsys/pkg/PLAW-104publ208/html/PLAW-104publ208.htm. Accessed 26 Jan 2017.

Wellard, I. (2002). Men, sport, body performance and maintenance of 'exclusive masculinity'. *Leisure Studies, 21*(3–4), 235–247. https://doi.org/10.1080/0261436022000030641.

10

Inhabiting the Australian Prison: Masculinities, Violence and Identity Work

Katie Seymour

That men's prisons are grounded in, and dominated by, a narrowly conceived ideal of masculinity is a widely accepted "truth". Representing the antithesis of the feminine, made real through the exclusion of women and of "weaker" men, the masculinity of the prison—of physicality, toughness, control and aggression—has endured, remarkably consistently, over time and across a range of institutional forms and structures. Nonetheless, the truth about masculinity, and prison masculinities in particular, is—like all "truths"—considerably more complex and nuanced. This chapter explores the complexities and contradictions of the prison as the setting in which some men are compelled to live and other men and women choose to work. The discussion incorporates two, interrelated, themes; firstly, I consider the ways in which masculinities are invoked within the prison, in and through relations within and between prisoners and prison officers, with particular focus on the multifarious manifestations and performances of masculinities in this context. Hierarchies of difference constitute the structural and cultural context for violence, in

K. Seymour (✉)
College of Education, Psychology & Social Work,
Flinders University, Adelaide, Australia

prisons as in society; thus while violence is not inherently male, it is closely intertwined with relations of power including those of gender, "race", ethnicity, class, sexuality and so on. Accordingly, the latter part of the chapter focuses on the significance of discourses of violence for identity work in prisons, specifically in relation to the ways in which these reflect and maintain certain discourses of masculinity.

Imprisonment in Australia

In Australia, we are fortunate to be able to draw upon the comprehensive research of the Australian Prisons Project (APP), funded by the Australian Research Council between 2008 and 2010. As a "multi-investigator" project, the APP sought to provide a national picture of Australian imprisonment through analysis of penal trends and developments across the diverse "social, political and cultural contexts" (Baldry et al. 2011, p. 25) of Australia's eight states and territories. The project findings are extensive and its conclusion—regarding the 'revalorisation of the prison in Australian culture and society' (p. 24)—sobering. Here I draw attention to just a few of the issues highlighted by the APP.

Increasing imprisonment rates are a global, but not uniform, trend, varying greatly between and within regions and countries (Penal Reform International 2015, p. 8). In Australia, the rate of imprisonment has risen markedly in recent years; the national rate, for example, rose from 157.9 prisoners per 100,000 adults in 2005–2006 to 190.3 in 2014–2015, an increase of 20.5% (Australian Productivity Commission 2016, p. 85; see also Cunneen et al. 2013). Whilst Australia's *overall* rate of imprisonment has increased, however, this varies greatly across jurisdictions and communities and is reflected in the overrepresentation of certain groups in the criminal justice system. An especially significant finding of the APP is the extent to which Australia's increased use of imprisonment has targeted "particular racialized groups" and other marginalised people including those with mental health disorders and alcohol and other drug dependencies (Cunneen et al. 2013, p. 4; Baldry et al. 2011). Recent statistics show, for example, that although Aboriginal and Torres Strait Islander (AATSI) adults make up only 2% of the Australian population, nationally they account for just over a quarter (27%) of the prisoner population (ABS 2015).

The APP has also drawn attention to "changing sensibilities about both race and gender" (Baldry et al. 2011, p. 28) as evident in the "extraordinary growth" (Cunneen et al. 2013, p. 14) in use of imprisonment for women and for AATSI women in particular, with a 46% and 49% rise, respectively, in the numbers of non-Indigenous and AATSI female prisoners over the period 1996–2010 (Australian Prisons Project n.d., p. 32). The Australian prison population nonetheless remains overwhelming male: 90% of both AATSI prisoners and non-Indigenous prisoners are male (ABS 2015). The APP also names the increased imprisonment of men and women with mental health issues as a critical concern. The normalisation of "warehousing" via the 'effective transfer of large numbers of the mentally ill [from mental institutions] to prison' (Baldry et al. 2011, p. 29) is seen as representing "significant cultural change" in Australia. This is especially apparent given the relative lack of debate concerning the appropriateness of the prison as an "institutional response to mental illness" (p. 29). Whilst the patterns and practices of punishment vary considerably across the country, the "broader picture" of penality in Australia is dominated by the "relentless expansion" of—what Baldry et al. (2011, p. 36) refer to as—the "imprisonment machine".

Inhabiting the Prison

Prisons are all about power and authority; indeed, despite recognition that offenders are sentenced to imprisonment *as* punishment rather than *for* punishment, it is clear that prisons, in the public imagination, exist to control and discipline—to put offenders "in their place"—and not just to accommodate and segregate. It is testament to the "punitive power" of imprisonment, Roberts (2004, p. 2) argues, that 'to the public, nothing appears to punish like prison' (see also Brown 2009). Similarly, offenders are expected to leave prison having "learnt their lesson" and nowhere is this more evident than in the intensity of public criticism regarding the perceived failures of the prison system. In other words, the depth of our attachment to the *idea* that punishment—and prisons—"work", in Australia as elsewhere, is laid bare in the vehemence of our outrage when these are seen to "fail". Ironically, then, while the claim that prisons are too "soft" often lies at the heart of such debates, Halsey and Harris (2011), in their study of young Australian prisoners, observe that it is this very insistence on harshness that functions, in effect, to sabotage the possibilities of rehabilitation. That is, those opportunities for developing the capacities associated with caring in 'non-violent and durable ways for self, other and future', arguably the very essence of rehabilitation, are "radically reduce[d]" (Halsey and Harris 2011, p. 75) in this conceptualisation of prisons and punishment.

Anyone who has spent time in a prison, whether in the capacity of prisoner, worker or visitor, will likely have experienced the sensation of unease, the simmering resentment or undercurrents of tension which ebb and flow. One is struck by the precariousness of civility and order, the feeling that, at any moment, chaos could break out, juxtaposed with the mundaneness of daily routines, repeated ad infinitum. Visibility, or at least the sense of this—of being observed, scrutinised in fact, of impressions made and stored away for later use—is a constant, no matter who you are, whether prisoner, officer or visitor. Foucault's (1977) panoptic power is, of course, relevant here. Equally critical to note, however, is the complexity of power relations that this suggests and the ways in which these transcend and cut-across the boundaries of status and (formalised) authority. This is not to say that the power associated with authority is irrelevant. Rather, in paying attention to the range of "players" and stakes involved, a more nuanced understanding of prison masculinities is possible, one that acknowledges the complex, dynamic and contingent alignments of gender, class, "race"/ethnicity and so on.

Performing Masculinity: "Real" Men

The performance of hegemonic masculinity is central to the hierarchical dynamics of prisons (Crewe et al. 2014), operating on a sliding scale of power, status and entitlement. Towards the bottom of the hierarchy are the "non-men" (by implication, feminine), including those men who deviate from "normal" (i.e., dominant) masculinity. The "homosocial prison culture", as observed by researchers such as Karp (2010), is one that values "emotional stoicism", dominance and "stratification" (p. 80).

It is not, however, exclusive to the prison but rather is a culture shared—indeed, generated—by broader society. Paradoxically then, and despite their association with "deviance" and non-conformity, the masculinities embodied and reproduced within the prison are more likely to resemble "normal" and everyday ways of being a "man". Moreover, acknowledging the continuum of normative masculinity practices, notwithstanding the considerable diversity that exists within *and* between groups of officers and prisoners, there is no absolute distinction between (so-called) "prison masculinities" and ordinary, everyday masculinities.

Discussions about prison culture are often framed in ways that suggest that "prison culture" and "prison*er* culture" are, essentially, the same thing, as if those who *work* in this environment are incidental and of peripheral interest only. This is not to say that "officer culture" goes unacknowledged but, rather, that this tends to be presented as entirely separate, as a "thing" in and of itself. Prison culture, however, encompasses the totality of prison social relations and practices, including relations between prisoners and between officers, as well as those between prisoners and prison officers. Indeed prisoner—officer relations are central to prison life (Baldry et al. 2011; Halsey and Harris 2011). Curtis (2014), for example, describes the relationship between prisoners and officers as both "intimate" and "mutually constitutive" and one that, at its core, revolves around the 'struggle over what it means to be a "real man"' (p. 123). In this context, violence, whether potential or actual, officially sanctioned or exercised as authoritative control, is vital to the performance of masculinity. This is to recognise the exercise of power and control as achieved through, and embodied in, formal and informal hierarchical structures as well as ordinary and everyday relations between individuals.

A division between prisoners and officers, based on the idea of fundamental differences, is widely recognised as an enduring feature of prison life and central to the "proper" functioning of the prison. As the basis for identity work, the importance of group solidarity for (re)affirming masculinity is especially significant, ensuring clarity regarding the "who's who" of prison and a means of "policing the divide" (Grunseit et al. 2008, p. 236) between "us" and "them". Identity work, in this respect, constitutes the dangerous masculinity of the prisoner and the "protective masculinity" (see Britton 2011) of the officer, both highly compatible with broader masculine ideals. This is to say that, as observed some time ago by Pogrebin and Poole (1997, p. 56), although prisons certainly reinforce, reflect and even magnify gender normativity and related stereotypes, this normativity has already been firmly established in/by wider society. Central to my argument here is the recognition that, whilst there are certainly differences between what might be called "prison masculinities" and broader, societal notions of masculinity, these are not *in essence* different; rather, the distinction lies in their intensity and, perhaps, given the negation of vulnerability that characterises prison life and the targeting of those who show it (see Toch 1998), the associated stakes. Whilst the prison context of confinement, institutional authority and deprivation is, of course, critical, I argue that there is little that is fundamentally different about the masculinities as valued, embodied and performed "inside" and "outside" the prison.

Identity Work

Identities, in general, relate to how we make sense of the world and how we operate in relationship to others; in other words, identities are both symbolic and social, incorporating the material and the discursive. To focus on the politics of identity, then, is to acknowledge complexities by resisting the temptation of generalisations and "easy" categories. Thinking about identity/ies as "shifting performance/s" (Gilchrist et al. 2010, p. 4) directs attention towards the ways in which identities are expressed differently in diverse settings, 'drawing on the most useful, comfortable or least risky dimensions of our identities for a given situation' (p. 8). In the prison, as in society, notions of solidarity and loyalty are fraught, underpinned by the perpetual tension between "fitting in" and risking the isolation of difference. Agency, then, is always bound by structure—both societal and institutional—within the context of the prevailing culture. Thus, the performance of identity can be understood as the embodiment of agency-constrained, this recognising that people perform the identities that 'enable them to lead "liveable lives"' (Gilchrist et al. 2010, p. 8).

"Crims" and "Screws"

It is generally only when things "go wrong" that the public is allowed a glimpse into the, otherwise, closed prison environment, for example, via the written records generated by official inquiries and investigations. Throughout this chapter, I draw upon public records as an "illustrative strategy" (May 2001, p. 196); a means of highlighting the complex interplay between diverse masculinities and violence in this context. Records from five of Australia's seven states and territories are represented here and include: an independent inquiry into the functioning of the Risdon Prison Complex, a medium to maximum facility in Tasmania; an Ombudsman investigation into the circumstances surrounding the murder of a (high-profile) prisoner in a Victorian maximum security prison; a defamation case initiated by one prison officer against another in Adelaide, SA; media reports regarding bullying experienced by two (separate) prison officers in Western Australia (WA); and a survey of employees undertaken by Queensland Corrective Services. My method for selecting these was not complicated, consisting of little more than an online search using the keywords "Australia" + "prisons". Search results, which included media stories and government documents and websites, were subsequently narrowed down by date/recency (restricted to the period 2010–2015) and content, in accordance with my interest in the "internal life", for lack of a better term, of prisons. With the exception of two media reports, one concerning a coronial inquiry, preference was given to formally documented and/or institutionally sponsored inquiries, that is those for which records were publically available. In drawing on these diverse examples, my aim is to highlight the ways in which hierarchies of difference and dominance shape relations within *and* between prisoners and officers.

It is well established that prisons are structured and operate in ways that are fundamentally hierarchical, with a defined chain of command and an emphasis on rules, regulations and compliance (see, e.g., Ehrlich Martin and Jurik 1996; Coyle 2005; Jewkes 2007). Prisons represent a complex amalgam of coercion, abuse and confinement; as observed by Brown (2009, p. 3), they epitomise 'what it is to position people in fundamentally unequal structures'. The structures, processes and practices of imprisonment are, in and of themselves, fundamentally dehumanising; a prerequisite, perhaps, for the emotional and symbolic distance that enables the "us and them" of prison life. Hierarchy, domination and control—the defining features of prisons—can be seen as, both "euphemisms" (Hearn 1996, p. 44) and key justifications for violence, officially sanctioned or otherwise. It is clear that, within this context, officers occupy a position of power in exercising authority over prisoners' lives. Relations of power—in prisons as in society—are nonetheless complex and 'mediated by constructs of social difference' (Walton 2011, p. 140). Paying attention to these complexities highlights the significant diversity that exists within and across groups (of officers, of prisoners, of males and so on) that we might otherwise think of distinct and homogenous. For example, a key finding of the Risdon Prison Complex (RPC) inquiry in Tasmania was the "marked division" that existed within groups of officers as well as between officers and other (non-custodial) prison workers (Palmer 2011, p. 61). "Many" of the staff interviewed for the inquiry referred to the "destructive effect" of "factions"—or "long-standing self-interest groups"—on the "careers and aspirations" of individual officers (Palmer 2011, p. 61). Extensive "bullying and ostracisation" was also observed by Palmer (2011, p. 169), with officers recounting their experiences of being 'openly criticised and/or ridiculed by other officers' (p. 169).

The existence of an "inmate code" emphasising solidarity and an oppositional relationship with officers was first identified by Clemmer (1948) and Sykes (1958) over 60 years ago. More recent research suggests that, whilst elements of this continue to exist, the social relations of prisons are considerably more complex—and contradictory—than has often been assumed. In their study of NSW prisons, for example, Grunseit et al. (2008) found that prisoners did 'define themselves as being in opposition to correctional officers' (p. 232) but that ideas about solidarity between prisoners were generally "overstated" (p. 234). Indeed, they noted that the divide between prisoners and officers was policed, perhaps, even more intensely by prison officers, with strong emphasis placed on an "officer's loyalty to his [sic] peers" (p. 236). Grunseit et al. (2008, p. 243) further observed, however, that although this division was "informally but intensively monitored" (p. 243) by both groups, its enactment through everyday practices and interactions was complex and unstable, this reflecting the 'matrix of gender, race, class and sexuality' (Britton 2003, p. 216) that shapes relations between, and within, officer and prisoner groups.

Whilst bullying is widely recognised as a significant issue within prisoner populations, prisoners in the RPC inquiry placed more emphasis on the behaviour of (some) officers than that of fellow prisoners. Prisoners acknowledged the existence of a "general pecking order" amongst themselves but felt that, once this had been established, relations were generally smooth and prisoners tended 'to be more accepting of each other' (Palmer 2011, p. 151). Although some prisoners did express "fears for their own safety" in relation to other prisoners, it was clear to Palmer that prisoners, in general, feared certain officers who 'appeared to dominate and use excessive force' (Palmer 2011, p. 157). Combative tactics used to reassert the division between officers ("screws") and prisoners ("crims") included goading prisoners "into a response" that would then impact on their security classification, sentence plan and placement, privileges and so on (p. 151). Thus, while it is possible that the concept of an inmate code is becoming less relevant, the significance of a distinct officer "culture" characterised by division and bullying features strongly across the public records that I have examined. Evidenced here, as discussed next, are the ways in which cultural ideals of masculinity shape hierarchical relationships *across* the prison, 'with status allocated differentially to those who most effectively display or embody those ideals' (Michalski 2015, p. 9).

Masculinities Divided

Prisons, like all social institutions, are social hierarchies, shaped by 'larger patterns of social exclusion and dominance' (Curtis 2014, p. 139). Gendered/classed/raced relations of power provide the context for the everyday "business as usual" of prison life and, to this extent, transcend the officer/prisoner role. Moreover, broadly, the relations between officers and between prisoners are both highly compatible and mutually reinforcing, underpinned by shared understandings about the way things are (or should be). The "masculinity" of the prison, of which so much has been written (see, e.g., Toch 1998; Lutze and Murphy 1999; Sabo et al. 2001; Evans and Wallace 2008) is very much "front and centre" in the public accounts I have examined. Rather than taking this at face value though, here I offer a slightly different reading that reflects a broader vision of the politics of identity which encompasses, but is not reducible to, men and masculinity. Thus, the presence of identities of "difference", within the context of the "relational, structural and individual configurations" of normative masculinity (Ricciardelli et al. 2015, p. 507), both complicate *and* solidify the overall cultural dynamics of the prison.

An investigation into the circumstances surrounding a prisoner's murder in a Victorian prison highlights key aspects of an officer culture characterised by homophobia, sexism, racist abuse and harassment. In concluding that the prison had 'failed in its statutory duty to ensure [prisoner's] safety', the Victorian Ombudsman (2012, p. 6) referred to extensive "unacceptable [and] unprofessional" conduct and was highly critical of prison officers' routine 'use of offensive and derogatory language' and their 'distribution of sexually explicit and/or inappropriate material' and "violent images" (p. 115). He further noted the lack of a clear distinction between the cultures of prison staff—both officers and managers—and prisoners, referring in particular to parallels between these groups in terms of the 'acceptability of firearms, male dominance and an inference of violence' (Victorian Ombudsman 2012, p. 130). In other words, the Victorian Ombudsman emphasises a certain type of violent masculinity—"deviant" or criminal masculinity—implicitly linked to prisoner culture but notable here due to its adoption by prison officers. The RPC inquiry in Tasmania similarly identified the prison's "male dominated environment" and the 'inappropriate attitude of some male prison officers towards female staff' (Palmer 2011, p. 153) as key elements contributing to its "volatile environment of distrust" (p. 21) and bullying.

The entrenched nature of a "bullying culture" (Adshead 2013) amongst officers is highlighted in another example—a media report—from regional WA. The article describes the bullying experienced by a female prison officer, perpetrated by fellow officers and including hate mail delivered to her home address, which culminated in her decision to leave the prison service. Epitomising the hierarchy and precariousness of identity and belonging in this context, the former officer is quoted as saying that, 'they [other officers] break you down. You either stay and become a nut-case or leave' (cited in Adshead 2013). Around the same time, also in WA, a Coroner investigating the death, by suicide, of a male prison officer suggested that the bullying and racial vilification perpetrated by his fellow workers was a key contributing factor (Orr 2013). Similar concerns have been raised elsewhere; in Queensland, for example, high rates of work-related bullying and harassment have led to calls for an independent investigation into the "entrenched culture" of bullying within Queensland Corrective Services (Together Union 2015). Indicating that these are not isolated instances, prison officers, according to Safe Work Australia (2015, p. 2), represent the third highest occupational category for workers' compensation claims in relation to work-related harassment and/or workplace bullying.

The court records of a South Australian defamation case vividly illustrate the ways in which culturally dominant ideas of masculinity shape officer/peer relations and drive social exclusion and division. The case involved the circulation of a group email—purportedly written and sent by Officer A but actually authored by Officer B using Officer A's employee email address—announcing his (Officer A's) homosexuality. In the subsequent legal action, initiated by Officer A, the court found that the email conveyed "defamatory imputations" including that Officer A was 'promiscuous, was of loose moral character, [and] was seeking to solicit sexual relationships with persons he did not otherwise know' (Tassone v Kirkham 2014) via his employment. That this was not simply the action of a "rogue" individual was made clear in Officer B's explanation, confirmed by other officers, that the email was "just a joke" and common practice in this work setting. Reference was also made to the "blue code", that is, the expectation amongst officers that they support each other in a crisis and never "dob each other in". It is of course no coincidence that the "joke" hinged on the association of homosexuality with deviance and predatory promiscuity (see Herek 1991; Simon 1998); in this context, (inaccurately) aligning Officer A with non-heterosexuality functioned to disqualify him from the dominant masculinity of officer solidarity.

The public records examined here highlight the profound implications of identity (and identifications). The defamatory claims regarding Officer A's sexuality and "moral character" (Tassone v Kirkham 2014) and the targeting of the WA officer at her home address, for example, exemplify the ways in which the distinction between work and home, public and private are undermined. That is, the abuse directed at these individuals is all encompassing; it is not just their "work" self that is maligned but their very identity. It is notable that what is perhaps more self-evidently the case for prisoners—that imprisonment is an intentional incursion of their privacy and autonomy—is also relevant to officers. Assessed against the backdrop of a dominant, shared masculinity that is normative across officer and prisoner groups, the targeted officers represent (feminised) difference and are, thus, seen as worthy of contempt (see Toch 1998). Illustrating the everyday politics of identity, hierarchical relations of difference and dominance thus bridge the personal and the professional. The practices and processes of violence, as explored next, play a critical role, expressing and reinstating the hierarchies that shape life inside *and* outside the prison environment.

Violence, Difference and the Politics of Identity

The association between masculinity and violence, while commonly invoked in discussions about crime and punishment, is generally assumed as relevant only to "criminal" violence (or the violence *of* criminals). Violence encompasses more than physical, and criminal, acts though. Shepherd (2007, p. 250), for instance, points to the "ordering function" of violence—the ways in which violence works to (re)produce power relations and gendered/raced/classed subjects. In the prison, for example, violence reflects, expresses and reproduces the hierarchies that structure prison life (Hearn 1996, p. 51). Considered more broadly, however, a focus on "bodies as arenas" (Connell 2000, p. 218) draws attention to the critical link between masculine identity/identification and the bodily *capacity* for violence, confrontation and domination. Regardless of its source and form, violence is closely bound up with—and inseparable from—the power differentials associated with hierarchies of identity and difference. Patterns of violence thus mirror and (re)produce existing hierarchies of privilege, dominance and entitlement. Violence, then, is more than specific acts and incidents; rather it represents the relationship *between* bodies.

The ways in which we talk and think about violence emerge from "social knowledge [and] cultural legacies" (Stanko 2003, p. 11) which are institutionally supported. Gender normative beliefs and assumptions, including ideas about femininity and masculinity, are critical dimensions of social knowledge, reflecting 'widely held dominant and persuasive notions about what men are and, by implication, what women are' (Morgan 1987, p. 180). Dominant ideas about risk, dangerousness and fear thus inscribe "subjects with gendered characteristics" (Lee 2001, p. 141), as in the association of masculinity and violence and femininity with victimisation. Here, "femininity" does not only reference women's bodies though; rather it is the experience of victimisation that is feminising—not because it is impacts only on women (which it does not) but because it implicates "feminised others" including, as seen here, men who are "racially, culturally and economically marginalised" (Peterson 2005, p. 508). Evidence of this pervasive devaluation of "feminised bodies, identities and activities" (Peterson 2005, p. 507) can be seen in the public records examined here: in the culture of "bullying and ostracisation" at RPC observed by Palmer (2011, p. 169); the "unacceptable and unprofessional"—or, more accurately, homophobic and sexually aggressive—conduct identified by the Victorian Ombudsman (2012, p. 5); and the explicitly homophobic bullying of Officer A in SA. Thus, whilst violence, in all its forms, is indeed an "effect of domination" (Nayak and Suchland 2006, p. 467), it is not merely this. Rather, as argued by Nayak and Suchland, violence *both* 'constitutes and is constituted by power relationships' (p. 468) which are, in themselves, enabled by—and simultaneously enable—the hierarchies associated with identity and difference.

Mason (2006, p. 175) observes that violence "makes a statement", marking the "bodies of its victims" with "signs of vulnerability". In other words, dangerousness—and vulnerability—are embodied social positionings; gender, age, "race" and ethnicity are 'translated into vulnerability through the body' (Hollander 2001, p. 105). As apparent in the Tasmanian RPC inquiry, however, perceptions of danger (who represents danger) and fear (who should be feared) do not map easily onto particular bodies. Rather the relations of fear are complex and shifting, reflecting the dynamic manifestations and performances of masculinity as well as the negative connotations of vulnerability within the prison context (see Toch 1998). While violence encompasses individual and collective masculinities, individual men and masculinised institutions—within *and* beyond the prison—violence is not inherently male nor is it caused by, or a consequence of, "maleness". Instead, violence is embedded within "hierarchical, competitive, and oppressive" (Carver 1996, p. 681) relations of (intersectional) identity and difference. The gender/violence nexus—in prisons as in broader society—is considerably complex and goes beyond "men" and "women", masculinity and femininity to encompass the differential positionings of (different) men and women: the hierarchies of masculinit*ies* and femininit*ies*. Violence, then, is not simply "caused" by, or an effect of, gendered norms and beliefs but rather functions to (re)produce dominant discourses of (gendered, raced and classed) identity and difference (see Shepherd 2009).

Violence Talk as Identity Work

Violence—whether potential, threatened or actual—is omnipresent in men's prisons as it is, although perhaps less overtly so, in broader society. Based on a dichotomized understanding of strength and weakness/passivity, dominance and control are implicated in both "normal" masculinity and, paradoxically, in the practices of violence associated with "abnormal" or criminal masculinity. Whilst prisons are inherently violent (see, for example, Cowburn 1998; Toch 1998), I have argued in this chapter that violence cannot be reduced to sex (as something that men do) nor gender (as unique to "prison masculinity" for example); rather the relations of violence, of diverse masculinities and hierarchies of identity and difference are interconnected. Although not inherently "male" then, violence is closely intertwined with relations of power including those of gender, "race", ethnicity, social class, sexuality and so on. In this, the final, part of this chapter, I expand upon this argument by exploring a fascinating paradox inherent within the ways in which violence is commonly talked about. I focus here on violence talk *as* identity work; how talking about violence accomplishes identity through the performance of dominant masculinity.

"Talking tough", when it comes to violence against women, is increasingly the "Australian way". Violence prevention campaigns, in Australia but also internationally, are characterised by condemnatory messages based on "declarations of manliness" (Salter 2016): that "real men don't hit women" (see, e.g., Kenny 2016); that men need to "take a stand" against other men's violence against women; and exhortations to "man up", "be the hero" and so on. Such messages have broader currency though; as Salter (2016) observes, '[e]very boy in Australia grows up being told not to hit women. The reasoning is simple: women are, allegedly, too weak to make it a fair fight'. Violence against women and children (VAWC) is, in this context, "unmanly" and deeply shameful[1]—not something that many men would willingly admit to. The vehement public condemnation of violence against women is especially strong in prisons, shared across prisoner and officer groups; it is on this basis that convicted child sex offenders, seen as the "lowest of the low" (see, e.g., McMah and Palin 2016), are isolated from the mainstream prison population. In this context, the denunciation of violence perpetrated against the smaller and weaker is puzzling, both given that VAWC is, for some prisoners, why they are there, and because it seems to contradict the normalised—and oft-cited—predation and victimisation of those who are vulnerable. It is in this sense that, I argue, the "never hit a woman" mantra represents an important means of (prison) identity work.

Violence talk rests upon a (gendered) logic that evokes the schoolyard refrain of 'pick on someone your own size'. The "wrongfulness" of violence, then, is relative to the victim: reflecting the potency of ideas regarding what constitutes an appropriate victim and a "fair fight", men should not hit women *because* women are weak(er). Men who *do* hit women are thus fundamentally suspect—the "deviant minority" (Salter 2016). The denouncing of violence against women, along with silence regarding other forms and uses of violence, can be seen as a key gendered/gendering strategy, one that embodies, enables and reproduces masculine identity(ies) and hierarchies of difference. Framing VAWC as a problem of "atypical men" (Hearn and McKie 2010, p. 149) performs two important functions: firstly, it isolates and stigmatises some men as the "problem"; and secondly, it bonds those other "right-thinking" men, including prisoners and officers, 'who see themselves as unlike the targeted group'

(Bacchi 2009, p. 115). A study by Ray et al. (2003), focusing on a Probation Service in the UK, illustrates this point. In their exploration of probation responses to racist violence, Ray et al. (2003) observed that targeting—and demonising—"racist offenders" allowed the "ordinary" racism of others to go unchallenged. Indeed, they argued, the very 'category of the "racist violent offender"' makes it possible to "establish a moral pariah" who can then be held up against the "ideal subject of anti-racist discourses" (p. 225). Applied to the prison environment, the making of a "moral pariah"—here, the violent man—via the conceptualisation of VAWC as atypical—diverts attention from the everyday, unmarked, violences that constitute relations within and between groups of, both, prisoners and officers. As identity work, focusing on the "unmanly" violence of others represents a critical point of connection, a reassertion of "normal" masculinity.

Curtis (2014, p. 137) discusses the ways in which ideas about "dangerous masculinity" are mobilised in the drawing of divisions between prisoners, officers and "outsiders". The twin assumptions, that all male offenders/prisoners are "dangerously masculine" (p. 124) and that dangerous masculinity is an "inherent identity" (p. 123), represent the default position of many inside and outside of the prison. In this context, "male prisoners threaten" (Curtis 2014, p. 132) and prison officers protect. Crucially, however, the invocation of protective masculinity in this context "confers material and social benefits", not the least of which is the ability to distance oneself from 'the negative associations (of weakness and inferiority)' (Mehta and Bondi 1999, p. 79). Associating VAWC with a certain kind of masculinity, an "aggressive, less self-controlled, subordinate masculinity" (Coleman 2007, p. 210), embodied by certain kinds of men (whether prisoners or "bad apple" officers), provides prisoners and officers with access to a solidarity of sorts. This recognises that the assertion of identity is, at heart, a way of distancing "oneself or one's group from others" (Stokes 1997, p. 5). Because certain masculinities—in Australia, Indigenous masculinities and migrant masculinities—are "highly visible and pathologised" (Bilge 2009, p. 17), we lose sight of—or can choose not to see—the intricate interconnections of gender, violence, risk and vulnerability within and beyond the prison.

Official statistics confirm men as the primary perpetrators of criminal violence and we are surrounded by examples of the socially sanctioned, largely male, violences of sport, corporate competition, war and combat. Violence is not, however, inherently masculine, nor does masculinity "belong" to men. Rather, as I have argued here, concentrating on violence as, solely, *physical* violence—both within prisons and otherwise—"misses too much harm" (Scott 2015, p. 58) while overlooking the importance of "violence talk" for the accomplishment of identity. Violence talk is thus a critical means for performing masculinity, albeit a dominant masculinity, and of differentiating oneself by claiming a certain—culturally valued—identity. In other words, violence—and talking about violence—works to fix "particular meanings and practices" (Nayak and Suchland 2006, p. 470). Thus, it is crucial to acknowledge the "ordering function" (Shepherd 2007, p. 250) of violence; the interconnections between hierarchies of difference and diversity—the intersectionality of identity/ies—and the ways in which we talk about, understand and experience violence.

Conclusion

Silko (1996, cited in Meiners 2007, p. 25) argues that 'there is no better way to uncover the deepest values of a culture than to observe the operation of that culture's system of justice'. There are many stories about prisons and what apparently goes on inside them; in this chapter, I have highlighted just a few that have attracted official responses and, hence, are on public record. It has not been my intention to suggest that these are representative of the overall state of prisons in Australia. Rather, in striving to broaden the focus on prison "culture", I hope to have highlighted both its complexity and the ways in which it transcends particular groupings, subcultures and/or roles. Indeed, if it is possible to draw any conclusion from these public stories, it is that relations between officers, like prisoners, are profoundly marked by hierarchies of identity and difference. Prisons are not, however, "isolated from the outside world" (Curtis 2014, p. 139); rather they exist within the societal context of a harsh, competitive and hierarchical culture, a culture that goes beyond individual men and women. This is to recognise the "shared social fabric" (Fitzroy 2001, p. 283) of our lives, structured by hierarchical power relations and shaped by the normalised positioning of certain others as "different" and lesser. The hierarchies of the prison mirror those of society; constructs of identity and difference intersect—across both realms—in ways that both shape and transcend the actions and motivations of individuals. Recognising the contingency and contestability of masculinities (Connell 2000) is, I argue, a critical prerequisite for disrupting both the "natural(ised)" association of men, masculinities and violence, and the conceptualisation of violence as, merely, the actions of individuals (prisoners, "rogue" officers) or the product of particular environments (such as prisons). The prison "way of life" is, to a large extent, "*our*" way of life.

Notes

1. Arguably, this may account for the routine "misnaming" (as, for example, self-defence or an expression of "passion") and misattribution (framed as mental illness, intoxication and so on) of violence against women.

References

Adshead, G. (2013, July 1). Bullying culture 'rife' in jails. The West Australian. Retrieved from https://au.news.yahoo.com/thewest/regional/south-west/a/17817322/bullying-culture-rife-in-jails/. Accessed 12 Aug 2015.

Australian Bureau of Statistics. (2015). Cat. No. 4517.0 – Prisoners in Australia, 2015. Retrieved from http://www.abs.gov.au/ausstats/abs@.nsf/mf/4517.0. Accessed 10 Oct 2016.

Australian Prisons Project. (n.d.). APP research documents: Indigenous imprisonment: Statistics and charts. Retrieved from http://cypp.unsw.edu.au/sites/ypp.unsw.edu.au/files/APP-%20Indigenous%20Imprisonment%20Statistics%20and%20Charts.pdf. Accessed 10 Oct 2016.

Australian Productivity Commission. (2016). Report on government services 2016 Volume C: Justice, Chapter 8. Canberra ACT, Australian Government.

Retrieved from http://www.pc.gov.au/research/ongoing/report-on-government-services/2016/justice/corrective-services/rogs-2016-volumec-chapter8.pdf. Accessed 10 Oct 2016.

Bacchi, C. L. (2009). *Analysing policy: What's the problem represented to be?* Frenchs Forest: Pearson.

Baldry, E., Brown, D., Brown, M., Cunneen, C., Schwartz, M., & Steel, A. (2011a). Imprisoning rationalities. *Australian & New Zealand Journal of Criminology, 44*(1), 24–40.

Baldry, E., Brown, M., & Cunneen, C. (2011b). Guest editors' introduction. *Australian & New Zealand Journal of Criminology, 44*(1), 4–6.

Bilge, S. (2009, February). Smuggling intersectionality into the study of masculinity: Some methodological challenges. Paper presented at *Feminist research methods: An international conference*, University of Stockholm, 4–9.

Britton, D. (2003). *At work in the iron cage: The prison as gendered organization*. New York: New York University Press.

Britton, D. (2011). *The gender of crime*. Lanham: Maryland, Rowman & Littlefield.

Brown, M. (2009). *The culture of punishment: Prison, society, and spectacle*. New York: New York University Press.

Carver, T. (1996). 'Public Man' and the critique of masculinities. *Political Theory, 24*(4), 676–686.

Clemmer, D. (1948). *The prison community*. New York: Reinhart and Winston.

Coleman, L. (2007). The gendered violence of development: Imaginative geographies of exclusion in the imposition of neo-liberal capitalism. *The British Journal of Politics & International Relations, 9*(2), 204–219.

Connell, R. W. (2000). *The men and the boys*. St Leonards: Allen & Unwin.

Cowburn, M. (1998). A man's world: Gender issues in working with male sex offenders in prison. *The Howard Journal of Criminal Justice, 37*(3), 234–251.

Coyle, A. (2005). *Understanding prisons: Key issues in policy and practice*. Berkshire: Open University Press.

Crewe, B., Warr, J., Bennett, P., & Smith, A. (2014). The emotional geography of prison life. *Theoretical Criminology, 18*(1), 56–74.

Cunneen, C., Baldry, E., Brown, D., Schwartz, M., Steel, A., & Brown, M. (2013). *Penal culture and hyperincarceration: The revival of the prison*. Aldershot: Ashgate.

Curtis, A. (2014). "You have to cut it off at the knee": Dangerous masculinity and security inside a men's prison. *Men and Masculinities, 17*(2), 120–146.

Ehrlich Martin, S., & Jurik, N. (1996). *Doing justice, doing gender: Women in law and criminal justice occupations*. California: Sage Publications.

Evans, T., & Wallace, P. (2008). A prison within a prison? The masculinity narratives of male prisoners. *Men and Masculinities, 10*(4), 484–507.

Fitzroy, L. (2001). Violent women: Questions for feminist theory, practice and policy. *Critical Social Policy, 21*(1), 7–34.

Foucault, M. (1977). In A. Sheridan (Ed.), *Discipline & Punish: The birth of the prison*. New York: Vintage Books.

Gilchrist, A., Bowles, M., & Wetherell, M. (2010). *Identities and social action: Connecting communities for a change. ESRC identities and social action Programme*. Milton Keynes: The Open University.

Grunseit, A., Forell, S., & McCarron, E. (2008). *Taking justice into custody: The legal needs of prisoners*. Sydney: Law and Justice Foundation of NSW.

Halsey, M., & Harris, V. (2011). Prisoner futures: Sensing the signs of generativity. *Australian & New Zealand Journal of Criminology, 44*(1), 74–93.

Hearn, J. (1996). Men's violence to known women: Historical, everyday and theoretical constructions by men. In B. Fawcett, B. Featherstone, J. Hearn, & C. Toft (Eds.), *Violence and gender relations: Theories and interventions*. London: Sage Publications.

Hearn, J., & McKie, L. (2010). Gendered and social hierarchies in problem representation and policy processes: "Domestic violence" in Finland and Scotland. *Violence Against Women, 16*(2), 136–158.

Herek, G. M. (1991). Stigma, prejudice, and violence against lesbians and gay men. In J. C. Gonsiorek & J. D. Weinrich (Eds.), *Homosexuality: Research implications for public policy* (pp. 60–80). Newbury Park: Sage Publications.

Hollander, J. A. (2001). Vulnerability and dangerousness: The construction of gender through conversation about violence. *Gender and Society, 15*(1), 83–109.

Jewkes, Y. (Ed.). (2007). *Handbook on prisons*. Oxon: Routledge.

Karp, D. R. (2010). Unlocking men, unmasking masculinities: Doing men's work in prison. *Journal of Men's Studies, 18*(1), 63–83.

Kenny, M. (2016, September 24). Prime Minister Malcolm Turnbull to go hard against domestic violence. *The Sydney Morning Herald*. Retrieved from http://www.smh.com.au/federal-politics/political-news/malcolm-turnbull-to-go-hard-against-domestic-violence-20150923-gjtcui.html. Accessed 26 Oct 2016.

Lee, M. (2001). *The "fear of crime" and governance: A genealogy of the concept of "fear of crime" and its imagined subjects*. Doctor of Philosophy Thesis, University of Western Sydney, Hawkesbury.

Lutze, F. E., & Murphy, D. W. (1999). Ultramasculine prison environments and inmates' adjustment: It's time to move beyond the "boys will be boys" paradigm. *Justice Quarterly, 16*(4), 709–733.

Mason, G. (2006). Symposium. The spectacle of violence: Homophobia, gender and knowledge. The book at a glance. *Hypatia, 21*(2), 174–177.

May, T. (2001). *Social research: Issues, methods and process* (3rd ed.). Berkshire: Open University Press.

McMah, L., & Palin, M. (2016). Jailhouse justice: A look at inmate society in Australian jails. Retrieved from http://www.news.com.au/lifestyle/real-life/news-life/jailhouse-justice-a-look-at-inmate-society-in-australian-jails/news-story/f14a395233ea83b6967c010b71102123. Accessed 26 Oct 2016.

Mehta, A., & Bondi, L. (1999). Embodied discourse: On gender and fear of violence. *Gender, Place & Culture: A Journal of Feminist Geography, 6*(1), 67–84.

Meiners, E. (2007). *Right to be hostile: Schools, prisons, and the making of public enemies*. New York: Routledge.

Michalski, J. H. (2015, September 14). Status hierarchies and hegemonic masculinity: A general theory of prison violence. *British Journal of Criminology*. doi:https://doi.org/10.1093/bjc/azv098. Advance Access published.

Morgan, D. (1987). Masculinity and violence. In J. Hanmer & M. Maynard (Eds.), *Women, violence and social control*. London: Macmillan.

Nayak, M., & Suchland, J. (2006). Gender violence and hegemonic projects. *International Feminist Journal of Politics, 8*(4), 467–485.

Orr, A. (2013, July 3). Calls for inquiry over racism, bullying. *WA Today*. Retrieved from http://www.watoday.com.au/wa-news/calls-for-inquiry-over-racism-bullying-20130703-2pb75.html#ixzz3tEV1k0ik. Accessed 12 Aug 2015.

Palmer, M. (2011). Risdon prison complex inquiry. Retrieved from http://www.justice.tas.gov.au/correctiveservices/risdonprisoninquiry. Accessed 7 Jul 2015.

Penal Reform International. (2015). Global prison trends 2015. London: Penal Reform International. Retrieved from http://www.penalreform.org/resource/global-prison-trends-2015/. Accessed 10 Dec 2015.

Peterson, S. V. (2005). How (the meaning of) gender matters in political economy. *New Political Economy, 10*(4), 499–521.

Pogrebin, M. R., & Poole, E. D. (1997). The sexualized work environment: A look at women jail officers. *The Prison Journal, 77*(1), 41–57.

Ray, L., Smith, D., & Wastell, L. (2003). Racist violence from a probation service perspective: Now you see it, now you don't. In R. M. Lee & E. A. Stanko (Eds.), *Researching violence*. London: Routledge.

Ricciardelli, R., Maier, K., & Hannah-Moffat, K. (2015). Strategic masculinities: Vulnerabilities, risk and the production of prison masculinities. *Theoretical Criminology, 19*(4), 491–513.

Roberts, J. V. (2004). *The virtual prison: Community custody and the evolution of imprisonment.* Cambridge: Cambridge University Press.

Sabo, D. F., Kupers, T. A., & London, W. J. (Eds.). (2001). *Prison masculinities.* Philadelphia: Temple University Press.

Safe Work Australia. (2015). Psychosocial health and safety and bullying in Australian workplaces: Indicators from accepted workers' compensation claims. *Annual statement,* 2nd edn., 2015. Canberra, ACT, Safe Work Australia. Retrieved from http://www.safeworkaustralia.gov.au/sites/swa/about/publications/pages/psychosocial-health-and-safety-and-bullying-in-australian-workplaces. Accessed 20 Sept 2016.

Salter, M. (2016). Real men do hit women: The violence at the heart of masculinity. *Meanjin Quarterly,* Autumn, 2016. Retrieved from https://meanjin.com.au/essays/real-men-do-hit-women/. Accessed 12 Aug 2016.

Scott, D. (2015). Eating your insides out: Cultural, physical and institutionally-structured violence in the prison place. *Prison Service Journal, 221,* 58–62.

Shepherd, L. J. (2007). 'Victims, perpetrators and actors' revisited: Exploring the potential for a feminist reconceptualisation of (international) security and (gender) violence. *The British Journal of Politics & International Relations, 9*(2), 239–256.

Shepherd, L. J. (2009). Gender, violence and global politics: Contemporary debates in feminist security studies. *Political Studies Review, 7*(2), 208–219.

Simon, A. (1998). The relationship between stereotypes of and attitudes toward lesbians and gays. In G. M. Herek (Ed.), *Stigma and sexual orientation: Understanding prejudice against lesbians, gay men, and bisexuals* (pp. 62–81). Thousand Oaks: Sage.

Stanko, E. A. (2003). Introduction: Conceptualising the meanings of violence. In E. A. Stanko (Ed.), *The meanings of violence.* London: Routledge.

Stokes, G. (1997). *The politics of identity in Australia.* Cambridge: Cambridge University Press.

Sykes, G. (1958). *Society of captives: A study of a maximum security prison.* Princeton: Princeton University Press.

Tassone v Kirkham. (2014). SADC 134 judgment of her honour judge Cole 7 August 2014. Retrieved from http://www.austlii.edu.au/au/cases/sa/SADC/2014/134.html. Accessed 2 Nov 2015.

Toch, H. (1998). Hypermasculinity and prison violence. In L. H. Bowker (Ed.), *Masculinities and violence* (pp. 168–178). Thousand Oaks: Sage.

Together Union. (2015, September 24). Important update for corrections members. http://www.together.org.au/news/member-emails/important-update-corrections-members/. Accessed 30 Nov 2015.

Victorian Ombudsman. (2012). The death of Mr Carl Williams at HM Barwon Prison – Investigation into corrections Victoria. Available at: https://www.ombudsman.vic.gov.au/Publications/Parliamentary-Reports/The-death-of-Mr-Carl-Williams-at-HM-Barwon-Prison. Accessed 2 Nov 2015.

Walton, G. (2011). Spinning our wheels: Reconceptualizing bullying beyond behaviour-focused approaches. *Discourse: Studies in the Cultural Politics of Education, 32*(1), 131–144.

11

Exploring Masculinity Construction, Subject Positioning and the Relationship with Dad

Tony Evans

This chapter I begin by examining a narrative analysis study exploring the masculinity narratives of male prisoners in the UK. This initial research identified a man's relationship with his father as a key factor in shaping his own sense of maleness. My later research explored men's experience of constructing and performing the masculine self as influenced by the father–son relationship and the 'gap' between the man's masculinity subject positioning and that of his father. The effect of these relative subject positions on the individual's psychology is discussed.

We are often told it's a man's world. However, in the UK men, on average, live for 3.7 years less than women. In school, 90% of children with behavioural difficulties are boys. Men comprise over 95% of prison inmates in the UK (Government Statistics 2015). In 2013, there were 6233 suicides in the UK of which 78% were male (Office for National Statistics 2015). Young men drive more dangerously; more frequently engage in binge drinking and indulge in riskier sexual practices (Courtney

T. Evans (✉)
University of Roehampton, London, UK

1998). Since the 1950s, suicide rates among young white males in the United States have nearly tripled, the homicide perpetrator rate for males is 400% higher than for females, whilst the majority of those killed are also male (Pollack 1995). As Levant (1997) has pointed out, traditional masculinity ideology may offer social power advantages for some men, but men are still hugely overrepresented among substance abusers, the homeless, sex addicts, sex offenders, accident victims and people with stress-related fatal illnesses.

Pollack (1995) argues boys are taught to repress their yearnings for love and connection and build a wall of toughness around them in order to be accepted as men. He feels they:

> don a mask of emotional bravado which leaves them isolated. All their vulnerable, empathic, caring emotions which they show from birth until we push it out of them, get repressed and pushed down as a result of being teased or shamed (1995, p.42).

Qualitative research has focussed on what male experience tells us about the social construction of masculinities. Key factors emerging include masculinity as something 'achieved' (Edley and Wetherell 1997), a set of 'performative acts' (Butler 1990) and as something as much defined through what it is not (female, gay or sensitive) rather than in positive terms. Seidler (1994) has argued this means masculinity is 'ultimately an empty thing'. It is perhaps then no surprise that young men often come to associate being male with the more external aspects of performance; physical size, willingness and ability to fight, power and dominance, what Frosh et al. (2002) characterised as 'hardness'.

In some contexts, performing the type of masculinity that sits atop the pile frequently involves violence or threat (Archer 1994; Bowker 1998). As Bowker put it, violence represents the "dark side of masculine role performance" with 90% of violence being perpetrated by men. Edwards (1989) pointed out "the safest place for men is the home, by contrast home is the least safe place for women". The acceptance and dominance of hegemonic masculinity supports the view that violent behaviour in men is normal and may help to explain men's huge overrepresentation among those involved in crime (Newburn and Stanko 1994).

Kimmel (1994) suggested the overriding emotion of masculinity is fear—of one's sexuality, emotion and, not least, of other men and the fear we will be exposed as less than men. This provides the conditions for the thriving of homophobia and the objectification and abuse of women. Much male complicity in anti-gay or anti-female attitudes stems from a fear of being 'cast out' and declared not a proper man like 'us'.

Defining Hegemonic Masculinity

Over the last two decades, a main focus in understanding masculinities has been the investigation of *'hegemonic masculinity'* (Connell 1995). This is broadly defined by Garde (2003) as having four main features: power, ambivalence towards femininity, domination and objectification of nature and the psyche and the avoidance of emotion. Garde's first feature, power, is the most crucial to understand when conceptualising hegemonic masculinity. The remaining three features can be seen as maintaining the sense of power within oneself but, more importantly, demonstrating constantly to others that you are powerful and not to be controlled, challenged or threatened lightly.

The *hegemon*, over time, comes to be seen as at the top of the pile. Eventually, they (the hegemon) do not 'rule' merely by exercising violence but through some widely shared sense that they occupy powerful positions. The majority within society have sufficiently internalised the idea that this is the 'natural' order of things, even if they suffer terribly within its hierarchical order. This point, that hegemony works most effectively inside people's minds, was originally made by the Italian Marxist Gramsci (1986), who said that eventually naked brute force is no longer needed to enforce hegemony, as those subjugated by it will often come to consent to its rule and even believe it is natural. Danaher et al. (2002) made the point that dominant discourses and their associated control over knowledge, truth claims and power "are the result of power struggles in which they have triumphed over other disciplines and forms of knowledge" (p. 27). This idea has been expanded to examine the historical domination of some nations over others, and to look at how some races, genders, religions or sexualities have been oppressed as less 'deserving' of power than others.

Until relatively recently *hegemonic masculinity* was so widespread as to be almost synonymous with maleness itself. It is still often observed across the planet within single male systems (such as prisons, gangs, military and some schools), where women are still oppressed within patriarchal societies and within impoverished communities where there is much crime or social breakdown. It received the most social approval from those in powerful positions (usually other hegemonic men) and could offer individual men great power.

It is important to distinguish here between *hegemonic masculinity* and *traditional masculinity*. In certain time periods, or specific locations today, the two would be fairly interchangeable. Traditional masculinity would be hegemonic masculinity. However, in the West following the industrial revolution and the rise of waged employment and societies ruled by the force of law, the nature of dominant masculinity, certainly amongst the working classes, began to shift. A poor man working in a mine or a steel foundry could not afford to be too violent or domineering in public space as this would likely lose him his job or see him in trouble with the police. More often the exercise of unrestrained power moved to the home, where he could still be dominant over his relatively powerless wife and children.

As social mores have altered, and particularly since the changing role of women, the last 60 years have seen the increasing dominance of the *good provider traditional masculinity,* described by Pleck 1987 (p. 92) as the 'distant breadwinner' when related to fathering. In subscribing to this 'distant breadwinner' role, a man could still avoid being seen as too emotional, feminine or gay and maintain his sense of himself as being a good financial provider. He would still be perceived by others as masculine or manly, but he would act very differently from the more 'thuggish' man, who may often get drunk, be frequently brawling or involved in criminality, and who enjoys the fact that others are afraid of him.

The traditional good provider may be respectable in ways the hegemonic male is not. In a capitalist society, the traditional good provider is seen as a useful model citizen whereas the outright hegemonic male is more usually seen as a threat. It is worth noting that many of these rules do not apply the further up the socio-economic ladder we move. Big business bosses, sports stars and celebrities get to exercise hegemonic male behaviour and have it celebrated and admired by others. A poor boy from a sink estate acting in the same way will be treated very differently for the same behaviour, outside of his own social group.

Two of Garde's four features tend to be of supreme importance to modern young men in establishing their masculinity in the eyes of their peers: the avoidance of femininity and its associated emotionality. Within *hegemonic masculinity*, this usually expresses itself by hostility towards anything seen as 'gay'. Another way of understanding this would be to recognise that underlying most homophobia is misogyny. Girls generally have greater scope to take on typically male attitudes and behaviours, without being totally stripped of their femininity. Men have far less scope the other way. Teen boys are desperately aware of this fine line and may defend their own masculine credentials by attacking those of somebody else. Having defined hegemonic masculinity, below I use this theory to illuminate aspects of the performance of masculinity in a number of prison-based studies.

First Study: A Prison Within a Prison—Masculinity Narrative of Male Prisoners

In this study (Evans and Wallace 2008), we talked to nine male participants from a Category B London prison, where the researcher (Evans) was on clinical placement. Three distinct groups emerged in the findings, and each of the groups illuminates aspects of hegemonic masculinity in prison:

Group 1: Loving Paternal Relationship: Softer Gentler Men
Experienced a strong and loving paternal relationship where emotional dialogue played a central role. They had never internalised the codes and rules of hegemonic masculinity and defined themselves as men outside of its dictates.
Group 2: Hegemonic Masculinity Internalised and Maintained
Experienced very negative and/or abusive relationships with fathers, or their fathers had often been absent from a young age. They often expressed huge dislike for their fathers, but still lived predominantly from within the same hegemonic masculine codes.

Group 3: Hegemonic Masculinity Transformed
This group also experienced abusive/negative/absent paternal relationships and initially internalised the hegemonic masculine codes. However, through certain turning point experiences they had begun to evaluate the codes and move towards a more balanced view of their own masculinity. I present three examples of these groups below.

Liam (Masculinity Maintained) adopts many extreme aspects of hegemonic masculinity. The key theme emerging was the use of violence to protect oneself and one's masculine image. Liam is 22:

> *Some of the blokes are big, but if they start you just smack em in the face……you might get the shit kicked out of you then, but someone's gonna think twice about starting on you again.*
>
> *If you walk around letting everyone treat you like shit then they will treat you like shit, then you start to feel like shit don't you?*
>
> *(in jail) you can't show no weakness, you can't or they are on you like roaches.*

The law of the jungle is in operation in Liam's mind—one display of weakness and you move to the bottom of the heap. Position in the 'pecking order' is determined or maintained through violence:

> *Just gotta do your bird you know what I mean? .In other institutions they threaten you and that…it's different here, unless you fuck with them then they ain't gonna fuck with you…but I see the bigger men in here, obviously you show them a bit of respect, you know they ain't big men cos they go around bullying everyone, they're big men cos they have done a lot of bird. It's not like it was in the young offenders, where a bloke was a big man, cos he got a lot of his power through fighting, so you don't fuck with him.*

For Liam, personal belief systems are projected out to other men and the world in general:

> *"Men don't cry do they?" Men take it on the chin… you have to hold it in…. where I live its part and parcel of the way you live, you can't really be soft where I live*

> Like I said out there you know how to walk about, if someone fucks with ya I mean, if like a big man who's gonna smash you in a fight, you get a knife. If you know he's got a knife you get a gun, just make sure you win.

Liam has interpreted maleness in the 'classic' way: the concept of male power embodied in physical size, strength and violence. His choice of words demonstrates this clearly: 'big', 'hard', 'bottle', 'shit kicked out of him'. For him, if you show 'weakness', you are 'a pussy' or an 'idiot'.

Matt (Masculinity Transformed) typifies the male struggle in prison. He steps outside a key rule of hegemonic masculinity—the avoidance of emotion and vulnerability.

> It's nothing to ashamed of, for a man to cry. You are more of a man if you show your emotions. A lot of people in here,… they are here for drugs, but there is so much more that has happened to people than… **they are in a prison within a prison with themselves.**

Matt shows awareness of how masculine codes can function to keep the man locked away within his own mind, unable to find any emotional release or support.

James (Softer Gentler Men) is the only middle-class and relatively well-educated participant in this study. Objectively, James is a man for whom the patriarchal system delivers power and authority:

> I am unfortunately the stereotype definition of the alpha male.
>   My size, physicality, communication, leadership…And yet I am not.

In that 'yet I am not', he refers to an internal world unafraid of emotion. He feels other men cannot take away his sense of position or self-esteem. In this way, he feels outside of the system by which other men judge their own masculinity.

> I can look on it and smile, but maybe because
>   I had it naturally…. It's easy when you are the alpha male isn't it?

James' internal locus of evaluation about himself is clear. Because he is capable of 'intellectualising around my confinement' and has a value system that "helps me to develop and grow in here despite the environment", he can find some peace and happiness. He sees the hegemonic masculinity existence as 'tragic.. sad….bravado….artifice'. He feels sorry for these men, but they also annoy him. There is a core self in James, which although displayed cautiously in prison, is unaffected by his surroundings.

Around the 'growing up' theme, the story Matt tells is one of violence and exclusion, where secrets were kept and men were seen as 'arrogant, selfish and naive'. Of his own children he speaks about 'listening', 'bonding' and 'helping'. When he said 'daddy will be home soon' (referring to a telephone conversation with his son from prison), he was clearly very moved. He strives to provide a holding, loving, fathering relationship in complete contrast to his own childhood experiences.

For Liam, the root of his belief system was obvious:

From me old man… If someone hits you then you hit em back. I remember when I was about 6yrs I was having a row with a girl, and this girl pulled me hair, me old man said 'hit her' I said 'but she's a girl' he said just 'hit her'.

He was an idiot, I don't know what's wrong with him. But now it's different, he can't really say anything to me now cos I'm a big man, cos I'll knock him down.

But my son? In today's world, you can't just teach them to be placid and a fucking pacifist. You've got to teach them obviously right from wrong and to keep your wits about ya. If someone hits you you hit em back.

We can see the flow of the idea that "if someone hits you, you hit them back" from his father, through to the idea he would pass on to his son. Liam doesn't respect his father but characterises him as a 'big man'. This idea was consistently evident in this study. Now Liam feels big enough himself to dominate his father, so his masculinity feels secure.

For James, there is no mystery as to the causal relationship between childhood and adult attitudes:

I would say 99% of how you turn out tends to be how much one is loved. I come from an environment of openness, discussion, intellectual, emotional, sexual … I always consider myself as a very balanced happy man.

His father had no problem showing emotion, therefore he doesn't. And in his advice to any future son "follow your heart, follow your soul" and seeing his duty as being one of support, he reveals himself to be a man who was not exposed to hegemonic masculinity as a child. Later in public school and the Royal Marines, he lived within largely all male environments, where he learned to be judicious about revealing his true self: "here (prison) you maintain a certain front, just like the Royal Marines".

Growing older seems to involve moving from an external to an internal locus of evaluation in terms of ones masculinity. I found a range of masculine codes in action: from swallowing the archaic rules of hegemonic maleness to a more traditionally 'female' way of being (emotions, caregiving, not dominating through violence). Men who fit this second pattern formed almost half the group. Within this group, there is a clear divide between those exposed to 'negative' masculinity as children and those exposed to 'good' male role models.

Several key themes emerged: even those not endorsing hegemonic masculinity continue to see the male role as that of provider. Those who show and feel emotions are still careful in judging how, when and to whom these feelings are displayed. All have created an overarching narrative about how one must act in prison. They observe the dominant expressions of maleness, how that may dictate one's position in the hierarchical structure, and then evaluate their personal belief system against these norms. They may disagree with them but feel it prudent to pay them lip service.

Even one positive, loving, respectful relationship with a man in a father figure role is enough for these boys to develop a more balanced view of maleness. From a psychodynamic viewpoint, they have managed to internalise a good, holding male 'object' (Gomez 1997), that is able to express caring, gentle attributes as well as those more traditionally seen as male.

Aside from Liam, Matt and James, of the other six participants in this earlier research study, not one described a positive paternal relationship. Fathers were either portrayed as absent, violent or both. In this group, fathers are described variously as 'idiots', 'he physically abused me', 'not one ounce of respect for him', 'violent', 'beatings', 'thug', 'arrogant', 'selfish', 'aggressive'. Three men were able to transform their original internalisations about maleness into something more balanced, emotional, supportive and 'soft'.

The Bridge to Manhood: How the Masculine Self Is Affected by the Father–Son Relationship

The second research project considered here, explored how the father–son relationship shaped the sense of the masculine self in greater depth.

It employed a mixed methodology using Hollway and Jefferson's Free Association Narrative Interview model, (2000), Farough's Photo-Ethnographic Interviewing technique (2006) and a data analysis informed using Foucauldian concepts (Graham 2005). These methods and analysis facilitated an exploration of father–son dynamics of 20 male participants and the associated adoption of masculinity subject positions. The mixed method design allowed access to the intrapersonal, interpersonal and wider social fields, in which the gendered self is built, performed and negotiated.

There is a long history of work which seeks to illuminate the role of fathering in establishing a man's sense of emotional well-being (O'Neill 1981; Wester et al. 2002). Studies such as Veneziano (2003) show paternal availability as much less significant for emotional well-being in adulthood than paternal warmth, particularly when considering aggression and anti-social behaviour. This suggests fathers have a crucial role in preparing boys for their entry into wider society—acting as a bridge to healthy manhood.

An emotionally close relationship with a father who does not embody toxic or hegemonic masculinity can help boys to realise that a man's private space is more complex, unsure and nuanced than the maleness sold as the norm within mainstream public space. Revealing that he too may have shared such struggles, and offering to talk about them, may be one of the greatest gifts a father can offer his son. In recent generations in the West, it was a gift all too rarely received by sons in the past, with fathers often constrained from opening up by the performances of hegemonic masculinity which were damaging their sons in the first place.

In their meta-analysis of studies looking at parental involvement and child educational outcomes, Pleck and Masciadrelli (2004) found most studies showed significant positive relationships between the level of father participation and both male and female child's development (these studies all controlled for mother involvement and found similar outcomes for both boys and girls). Children with involved fathers were more likely to achieve economic and educational success, manage good careers and display greater emotional and psychological well-being (Amato 1987; Furstenberg and Harris 1993). One crucial base for well-being established in attachment theory is a child becoming securely attached to primary care-givers. Normally, this refers to mothers but studies have shown that, when fathers are involved in caring for infants, the baby is as likely to develop a secure attachment to them. Father involvement had been positively correlated with lower rates of depression (Furstenberg and Harris 1993); lower levels of fear and guilt (Easterbrooks and Goldberg 1990) and greater emotional well-being when the paternal relationship is secure, supportive, sensitive, nurturing and warm (Biller 1993; Radin 1981).

Without a good masculine object to idealise and receive mirroring confirmation from, the boy fills this empty masculine 'vat' with whatever is instantly available; often the posturing, aggressive, unfeeling, strongman imagery to which he is exposed via peer groups, sports and music video scenarios. The '*hardman*' archetype, so prized by hegemonic masculinity, leads many men straight to prison, the morgue, the gang or the unemployment office and others to a life of emotional isolation, violence and conflict.

However, there is a growing body of research suggesting that notions of acceptable masculinity may be expanding, especially around fathering. Johansson and Klinth (2007) found the majority of the new Swedish fathers in their study showed far greater involvement with their children than previous generations. They suggest traditional hegemonic structures may be changing fast. And if that underlying construct of masculinity is expanding, to incorporate a different response to children, then the emotional impact we see in many of today's adult males may start to shift in the next generation. The very nature of hegemonic masculinity may be radically changed, as most hegemonies do over time in response to changing conditions.

This shows that individual men are not making choices and decisions about maleness in a vacuum. Men can sometimes to think of themselves as free agents who decide who they are and how they express ourselves, but most men realise that this process takes place within a much wider series of power structures, political and social discourses about gender and exposure to different ways of 'doing' maleness. Just as we will have operated within such discourses, so will our fathers.

The Importance of Employing Mixed Methodology Research When Analysing the Construction of Gender Identity

Fundamental to my argument in the remainder of the chapter is the notion that gender identity construction and father involvement are influenced at a variety of inter-related levels. Trying to access the lived experience of any of these levels during research without considering the impact of the others will, I believe, leave any research with serious gaps. The first level is the *intrapsychic arena (self)*, where the boy (and later the man) will try to make sense of gender ideas and messages within his own psychological and emotional inner world. Many of these beliefs and instinctive responses will operate at an unconscious level. The second is the *interpersonal arena (me and dad)* of the father–son relationship and its emotional dialogue, modelling and transmission of desirable and non-desirable male characteristics.

Finally, both are located within, and affected by, the *broader political and social gender discourses (other men and women, media, society)* that both father and son are exposed to. How the boy digests gender messages, images, judgements and discourses within the *intrapsychic arena* will be shaped, to a large extent, by what occurs in the other two fields. Indeed, from the Object Relational viewpoint we see an internalisation of a particular masculine object. The boy takes in masculinity material from outside of the self, pre-loaded with the beliefs, attitudes, fears and fantasies of others around maleness, and wrestles with it inside of himself—holding onto some aspects and rejecting others. The way he then presents his maleness in the other two fields will be affected by what has taken place in this first, internal, field: there is a continuous loop of creation, feedback and expression which runs across all three fields. This is true even for the wider social and political discourses, for although the individual man has a limited effect on shaping wider social narratives around gender, he has much greater control over his own response to these discourses, whether he accepts, resists, challenges or promotes them as a version of 'truth' on masculinity.

This approach also bears comparison to Foucault's idea of '*technologies of the self*' set out in 'The Archaeology of Knowledge' (1972) which explores the psychological 'processes of construction of selfhood' (Kendall and Wickham 1999). Foucault points out that we are neither completely constrained by the available discourses in which we find ourselves located nor are we completely free to choose. Selecting and expressing certain subject positions and giving voice to particular discourses may win us some power, status or privilege or expose us to exclusion, judgment or attack. The discourse itself will operate certain dividing practices over which we have little control. His argument is that the intersection of power, knowledge and subject must be considered together when considering how an individual subject is produced.

The Masculinity Subject Position Spectrum Drawn from Evans' Doctoral Research Work Conducted in 2010

In the third study included in this chapter, I interviewed 21 men regarding their sense of their own masculinity, their father relationships and how they feel that relationship shaped their own sense of maleness. The main outcome of this study was the construction of the *Masculinity Subject Position Spectrum*. It should be noted that no man will consistently occupy only one position on the spectrum. A man who we could situate at position 3 (Fake show off Empty Masculinity) when drinking with his mates at a football game may well display traits associated with position 8 (New Masculinity, Strong, Emotionally Available) when playing with his small son at home. All men have multiple masculinities which will be heavily influenced by a number of factors including their age, the company they are in and the way they are trying to present themselves. However, the data in this study suggests that one masculinity position will tend to dominate much of the time, particularly within a man's private internal world and in his closest relationships. As has already been mentioned, there may well be tension between the public masculine self and the private one.

A dominant masculinity location for each participant (and his father) was allocated after a further close reading of the interview transcript. For example, Karl is placed at position 7/8 (Emotionally Present New Masculinity). This was based on aspects of his story and descriptions of himself as a father analysed from his transcript (e.g. "I would be very different to my dad, I would be more affectionate, I would strive to have a healthy relationship, I would do more things with him that I didn't do with my dad, definitely. I know what it is like to be a good person, I don't think it's relevant or necessarily because of your sex"). Karl's father was placed at position 5 (Decent Provider, Cold Distant) based on comments such as these ("He was always there, but there wasn't really wasn't any closeness, he was always there if you needed a lift or some money, good provider kind of thing, but no real emotional relationship with him at all. It was a very kind of cold relationship").

In many instances, participants report fathers 'mellowing' as they have grown older. The schematic representation of a 'spectrum' of masculinity (Fig. 11.1) is drawn from the data reporting the participants' experiences of their fathers in childhood and adolescence. It is important again to highlight how such masculine positioning has a strong temporal component—many men report huge changes over time in their positioning (usually, but not exclusively, in a shift rightwards along the spectrum).

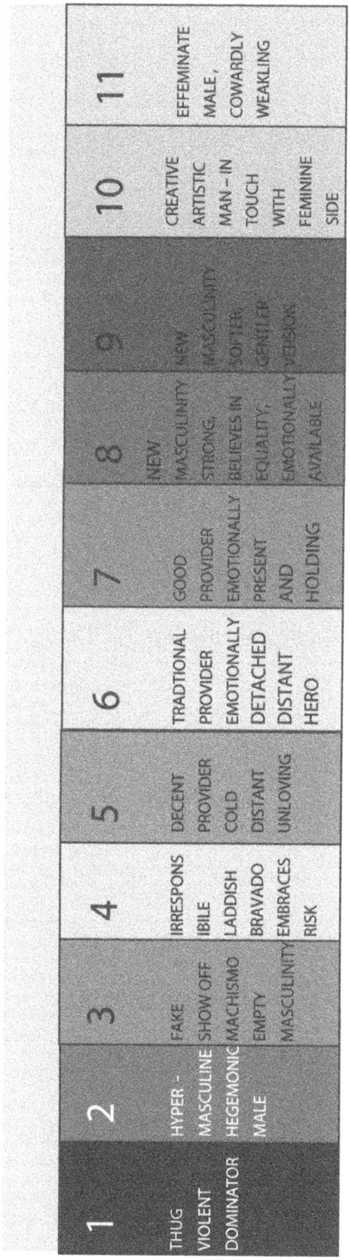

11 Exploring Masculinity Construction, Subject Positioning... 261

1	2	3	4	5	6	7	8	9	10	11
THUG VIOLENT DOMINATOR	HYPER-MASCULINE HEGEMONIC MALE	FAKE SHOW OFF MACHISMO EMPTY MASCULINITY	IRRESPONSIBLE LADDISH BRAVADO EMBRACES RISK	DECENT PROVIDER COLD DISTANT UNLOVING	TRADTIONAL PROVIDER EMOTIONALLY DETACHED DISTANT HERO	GOOD PROVIDER EMOTIONALLY PRESENT AND HOLDING	NEW MASCULINITY STRONG, BELIEVES IN EQUALITY, EMOTIONALLY AVAILABLE	NEW MASCULINITY SOFTER, GENTLER PERSON	CREATIVE ARTISTIC MAN-IN TOUCH WITH FEMININE SIDE	EFFEMINATE MALE, COWARDLY WEAKLING

Fig. 11.1 Evans masculinity spectrum

The table below brings together the data outputs from all three scans of the data.

Example categories	Masculinity positions	Spectrum position
Not at all masculine, he has lost control Disgusts me but that's just how men are Not masculine just a bully	Thug, dominator, violent, loses control	POSITION 1 THUG DOMINATOR
Brave, averse to risk, machismo Masculine, loving machinery Gut instinct says it's girly or gay The soldier as the ultimate man Men and women should have clear and separate roles	Hegemonic male: the hard man	POSITION 2 HYPER MASCULINE HEGEMONIC MALE

Big muscles equals a

real man

Father's direct negative

influence on masculinity

Shallow, fake   Shallow fake empty masculinity

masculinity

POSITION 3

FAKE, SHOW OFF, EMPTY MASCULINITY

Brave, foolish,

dangerous, flamboyant,

Showing off

Doing the more

extreme adrenaline

things

The boys are back in   Laddish, one of the boys

town

Running with the herd

Laddish bravado

One of the boys

discourse

Longing for some attention from dad	Cold distant father – emotion under control at all costs	**POSITION 5** **DECENT PROVIDER COLD DISTANT UNLOVING**
Independent, controlled and emotionally opaque		
Men must stand on their own two feet		
Men should keep their emotions under control and private		
Father as emotionally distant, absent or closed off		
Lost opportunities for connection		
Dads only cry at funerals		
Closed internal world of my father		

Men are getting mixed messages from society	Masculinity is contextual – some emotion yet still distant, still good provider, well respected by son	POSITION 6 TRADITIONAL PROVIDER EMOTIONALLY DETACHED DISTANT HERO
Work kept him apart from me		
Emotionally absent		
Bringing home the bacon		
Context is all		
It's ok to cry when you've been through hell		
Respecting dad		
Dad as good provider: admiring his commitment to family		
Emotionally available	Father as positive emotional presence	POSITION 7 GOOD PROVIDER EMOTIONALLY PRESENT AND HOLDING
Knowing love is there – but never spoken or shown	Tends toward mainstream male position for self; non-judgmental of others	
Showing his pride in me		
Respecting dad		

Dad as good provider: admiring his commitment to family

Men should be the protectors

Balancing good provider role with emotional presence

Seeing masculinity and sexuality as two different ranges	Contains all of attributes of position 7 but with more emotional expression, political awareness and belief in equality issues.	POSITION 8 NEW MASCULINITY STRONG, BELIEVES IN EQUALITY, EMOTIONALLY AVAILABLE
Influence of wider society or culture		
Masculinity is about more than size – it's how you act		
Discourse of editing masculine performance	Defining your own masculinity, softer gentler maleness – rejects all violence	POSITION 9 NEW MASCULINITY SOFTER, GENTLER VERSION
Positive masculinity discourse		
Discourse about		

challenging and moving

beyond hypermasculine

    attitudes

Locating self outside of

    usual masculine

        discourse

Flawed and Fragile Emotionally distraught Devotion through art Seen as gay or feminine Doing girlie things	Defines self through artistic, creative means – often perceived by others as feminine or gay	POSITION 10 CREATIVE ARTISTIC MAN – IN TOUCH WITH FEMININE SIDE
Effeminate, stupid, cowardly Feminine Skinny weakling – no masculinity at all The ultimate insult to man	Effeminate, cowardly, weak, skinny	POSITION 11 EFFEMINATE COWARDLY WEAKLING

It is useful to examine the relative positions on the spectrum above, of each participant and his father. Where there is a very low gap between the father and son position on the masculinity spectrum, this suggests that the participant has developed very similar masculinity beliefs and behaviours as his father. This might suggest that he found something reasonable, attractive or meaningful in the masculinity template offered by his father. Alternatively, it could mean that a man and his father were exposed to similar messages and pressures around maleness and came to very similar conclusions. Those men with higher gaps between their own spectrum position and that of their father may well represent the opposite phenomenon: there was something unpleasant, undesirable or unfathomable in their father's masculine presentation which they chose not to adopt for themselves. In the following section, I explore the implications of high, intermediate and low gaps in the masculinity scale between participants and their fathers.

High Gap

Robbie: the 'gap' between Robbie and his father was 6 places on the schematic masculinity spectrum presented above. Dad was characterised as 2 (Hegemonic Male) and Robbie as 8 (New Masculinity). In terms of dad's impact, Robbie seems to have experienced a doubly negative situation. Dad was absent much of the time through work (Oil Rigs) and because Robbie was sent away to school as a weekly border from age 4. When dad was present, he was 'hard' and 'strict', Robbie and his siblings were often frightened of him and would come to 'dread' his discipline. Robbie's grandfather provided an alternative, warm, engaged, adult male presence throughout Robbie's childhood. Although his relationship with his father has improved in recent years, it is still very unemotional. His father has struggled to come to terms with his son being gay and with his original career choice (Air Steward).

Here, I argue, we have an almost complete set of factors making a distant or broken father relationship more likely: physical absence, emotional absence, violence or strict discipline, a stronger bond with another male role model and intrinsic difference within the boy.

Intermediate Gap

Eric: The gap between Eric and his dad is smaller (dad is classed as 5—Decent Provider, Cold, Distant, Unloving, Eric as an 8—New Masculinity, Emotionally Available). Eric is 46 and when he was younger may have been closer to a 6 (Traditional Provider, Distant Hero) on the spectrum. There was a real struggle for supremacy with his father in his teen years and as he has grown older and moved towards an 8, his sense of the gap with his dad has grown stronger.

Gustaf: Gustav also has a gap of 3 places on the spectrum between himself and his father (dad is 6—Traditional Provider, Distant Hero, he is 9—New Masculinity, Softer, Gentler). Gustaf's account appears to illustrate a case where the emotional absence of a traditional provider dad, who tended to be away often in the military or isolate himself from the family in his shed even when at home, had a fairly powerful impact on a sensitive and intelligent little boy. For other participants, somewhat older than Gustaf, who also had a Traditional Provider Emotionally Detached dad, it proved much less of a problem. They developed a very similar masculinity performance style themselves (their father–son spectrum gaps are zero) and portray themselves as able to bond with dad around sport, humour and practical activities which are commonly an arena for father–son bonding. There was a difference in Gustaf; not sexuality in this case but rather gentleness, a quiet intelligence to which the father struggled to attune himself.

The different experience of this group of men with their fathers raises a vital question. Is the father sufficiently aware of his own masculinity style and wider masculinity issues to be alert to and explore with his son, own growing struggles with what it means to be a man, even if that maleness may be different from his father? If the son is starting to model a style of maleness very different from his own, how does the father react? By accepting the difference or by showing shock, disappointment, confusion or withdrawal? If the latter is the case, then the effect on the son seems powerfully negative. Whereas if dad and son are very similar in how they do maleness, an immediate platform for bonding is created: where I feel like dad and dad feels like me.

Low Gap

The men that I have characterised as 'low gap' men are all highly represented in the categories which typify a warm, positive and respectful father relationship: *Father as positive emotional presence* and *Father as respected provider and role model.* These correspond with positions 6, 7 and 8 on the Masculinity spectrum outlined in Fig. 11.1. These men all have fathers I have located either at 6 or 7 on the spectrum. Only two men break this pattern: Yousef was a political prisoner in Iran from nine years of age and then became a refugee; his contact with his father in childhood was very limited. Peter is something of an outlier within this group. Although both he and his father were classified as 6 on the scale, they are both alcoholics and struggle with relationship and intimacy issues.

Men positioned in categories further to the right of the spectrum are likely to face very different life issues to their counterparts on the left. Whilst those representing positions 1–4 may sometimes come into conflict with others and the law, they are likely still to be seen as 'properly' male in the eyes of many. Men classified at positions 10 and 11 may experience exclusion, mockery, negative judgment and shame outside of particular artistic or sexual sub-cultures, particularly during adolescence and young adulthood. Even within the gay world, such men are often seen as less desirable and not as 'proper men' whilst many are seeking to emphasise their muscularity and strength (Taywaditep 2001).

What Do the Relative Positions Tell Us About the Effect of Father Relationship

I would argue that this particular way of classifying men from their accounts, and or characterising father–son relationships offers strong support for Veneziano (2003), who argued that paternal warmth was more important in determining emotional well-being in adulthood than paternal presence per se. Much writing on masculinity and fathering makes the clear distinction between good, loving, emotionally present fathers and those fathers who leave the family, often typified by media discourses about 'broken homes' 'single mothers' and 'deadbeat dads'. These participant accounts tend to ignore two key positions: the father who separates from mum but manages to retain a strong, positive ongoing relationship with his children and the father who, whilst physically present in the family home, is completely remote from his children and feels cold, removed and unknowable.

The masculinity spectrum I have outlined does not focus on the physical presence of the father or the survival of the parental relationship; rather it privileges the quality of the emotional and psychological relationship as remembered and recounted by the son. The physically present/emotionally distant father is represented on the spectrum by positions 5/6. A full 12 out of 20 participants have fathers located here. We could make a tentative assumption that these masculinity positions were among the most common adopted by men raising sons over the past 50 years. The fathers would all have grown up before the rise of the second wave women's movement, gay rights movement or the gradual softening of gender roles particularly evident over the past 20 years. These fathers, it may be presumed, worked hard to meet what they saw as their main masculine obligation: 'bringing home the bacon' and providing a protective roof over the heads of their wife and children. They were decent, solid providers, often unwilling, or unable, to reveal their internal emotional world to their children. Softer, more sociable, attributes were witnessed from afar (as in the distant hero paradigm), with much of dad's emotional energy and real self directed outside of the family (e.g. Gustaf's father in the military, Frank's father fighting the British Union of Fascists or Simon's with his boxing and the Territorial Army). Or his energy seemed to be more internally directed, as in Peter's father struggling with alcoholism, Karl's shut away in his computer room or Eric's struggling with depression.

None of the 12 men with a father in category 5/6 adopted a masculinity position to the left of their fathers on the spectrum moved to the left on the spectrum (the more hypermasculine, violent side). Four were characterised as being at the same position as that ascribed to their fathers; the remaining eight were classified in categories further to the right of the masculinity spectrum outlined in Fig. 11.1. If a boy has a father with the attributes characterising position 5/6, with whom he senses some underlying love and affection or admires from a distance, he may tend to adopt much of the same masculine style. Some rightwards movement (towards the softer, more include side) on the spectrum could be accounted for by changing social and cultural contexts. One example is Lou, who grew up in socially conservative rural Ireland with a 'god-fearing' father. However, he has travelled widely in adulthood, including living in San Francisco for 10 years, has been exposed to other ways of being male and has grown comfortable with them. Alternatively, if the predominant sense within the psychodynamic space created between father and son is one of coldness, distance, conflict or fear, there may be little to admire or emulate in sons who feel different or sensitive, and the rightwards shift is more pronounced.

The model of 'ideal' masculinity spoken of by most participants, has space for opening up one's emotional world and sharing it with others. That the majority of men in this study now describe this as a desirable trait, which adds to one's masculinity, appears to be a shift from the past. It is vital to add here that this move towards a more 'new man' orientation has limitations. Any suggestion of effeminacy, preening, weakness or cowardice is sometimes condemned and mocked. Any sense of not protecting and providing for his family is still anathema to these men. Also worth noting is that most of the straight men interviewed (17 out of the 21 men interviewed identified as heterosexual) would not automatically place gay men in this undesirable group. This may also suggest change in social attitudes is occurring (or merely that it is now thought less socially acceptable to express such views).

Masculinity Policing and the 'Boy Code'

The gendered self is woven into the subjective lived experience of the wider self and may, in actuality, go some way to explaining how that wider self was and is shaped and constrained. The way a young man experiences the 'boy code' policing of later childhood and adolescence, and the choices and performances it imposes upon him, will leave a deep psychological mark. This is just as true for the laddish or the emotionally cold, as for boys who express alternative ways of being male. As argued earlier, homophobia and the avoidance of femininity do not only affect gay young men; straight young men are often hurt by it too. One may have swallowed many of the hegemonic rules and tried to live by them, whilst the other may have been forced to question aspects of the code and striven to find new ways to do maleness outside of its confines. Both have been shaped by the '*dividing practices*' they were exposed to in youth.

A key price paid for maintaining this 'in' position is the suppression of emotionality. Boys who do not initially fit the 'in group' template may well come into their own as they grow older, whereas the more rigid hegemonic positioning becomes increasingly problematic as the man ages. The hypermasculine positions characterised as 1–4 on the masculinity spectrum presented offer social status and power among male peers (and to a lesser extent in the eyes of some women) during adolescence and young adulthood. This is far less true as we age; a man expressing these subject positions at 40, 50 or 60 may come across as somewhat pathetic, immature or pitiable.

Such men may struggle to become productive, law abiding members of society; we are likely to find them in large numbers in gang and prison cultures, where physical size, threat of violence and avoidance of feeling is the swiftest guarantee of top dog status. For the therapist encountering such men in their older years, it will be important to understand that the man may have become stuck in a male identity which worked for him in youth, but has increasingly imprisoned him as he ages.

Alternatively working with young men at positions 9–11 may mean helping them to value their own unique way of being male. They may have been mocked, abused, excluded or shamed in childhood and the therapist will need to be sensitive to this. Much of the wounded child self may have been split-off, repressed or denied so the child could survive psychologically in very hostile environments. He may have learned to hate and fear parts of the self. Ultimately, a therapist will need to provide good mirroring for these discarded, lost or hated aspects of self to assist the client in reintegrating them.

References

Amato, P. R. (1987). *Children in Australian families: The growth of competence.* New York: Prentice-Hall.

Archer, J. (1994). *Male violence.* London: Routledge.

Bowker, L. (1998). *Masculinities and violence.* Thousand Oaks: Sage.

Butler, J. (1990). *Gender trouble: Feminism and the subversion of identity.* London: Routledge.

Connell, R. W. (1995). *Masculinities.* Cambridge: Polity.

Courtney, W. (1998). College men's health: An overview and call to action. *Journal of American College Health, 46,* 279–290.

Danaher, G., Schirato, T., et al. (2002). *Understanding Foucault.* London: Sage Publications.

Easterbrooks, M. A., & Goldberg, W. A. (1990). Security of toddler-parent attachment: Relation to childrens sociopersonality functioning during kindergarten. In M. T. Greenberg, D. Cicchetti, & E. M. Cummings (Eds.), *Attachment in the preschool years: Theory, research and intervention* (pp. 221–244). Chicago: University of Chicago Press.

Edley, N., & Wetherell, M. (1997). Jockeying for position: The construction of masculine identities. *Journal of Discourse and Society, 8,* 203–217.

Edwards, S. (1989). *Policing domestic violence.* London: Sage.

Evans, T., & Wallace, P. (2008). A prison within a prison? The masculinity narratives of male prisoners. *Men and Masculinities, 10*(4), 484–507.

Farough, S. (2006). Believing is seeing. The matrix of vision and white masculinities. *Journal of Contemporary Ethnography, 35*(1), 51–83.

Frosh, S., Phoenix, A., & Pattman, R. (2002). *Young masculinities.* Basingstoke: Palgrave.

Furstenberg, F. F., & Harris, K. M. (1993). When and why fathers matter: Impacts of father involvement on the children of adolescent mothers. In R. I. Lerman & T. J. Ooms (Eds.), *Young unwed fathers: Changing roles and emerging policies* (pp. 117–138). Philadelphia: Temple University Press.

Garde, J. (2003). Masculinity and madness. *Counselling and Psychotherapy Research, 3*(1), 6–16.

Gomez, L. (1997). *An introduction to object relations.* London: Free Association Books.

Graham, L. J. (2005). Discourse analysis and the critical use of Foucault *Queensland university of technology: Paper presented at Australian association for research in education 2005 Annual Conference, Sydney 27th November – 1st December.*

Gramsci, A. (1986). *Selections from prison notebooks* (Eds., & trans: Quinton Hoare and Geoffrey Smith). London: Lawrence and Wishart.

Hollway, W., & Jefferson, T. (2000). *Doing qualitative research differently.* London: Sage.

http://www.ons.gov.uk/ons/rel/subnational-health4/suicides-in-the-united-kingdom/2013-registrations/suicides-in-the-united-kingdom--2013-registrations.html

https://www.gov.uk/government/statistics/prison-population-figures-2015

Johansson, T., & Klinth, R. (2007). Caring fathers: The ideology of gender equality and masculine positions. *Men and Masculinities.* OnlineFirst, published on March 9, 2007 as https://doi.org/10.1177/1097184X06291899.

Kendall, K., & Wickham, G. (1999). *Using Foucault's methods.* London: Sage Publications.

Kimmel, M. (1994). Masculinity as homophobia. In H. Brod & M. Kaufman (Eds.), *Theorising masculinities.* Thousand Oaks: Sage.

Levant, R. (1997). The new psychology of men. *Professional Psychology, Research and Practice, 27*(3), 259–265.

Newburn, T., & Stanko, E. (1994). *Just boys doing business?: Men, masculinities and crime.* New York: Routledge.

O' Neill, J. (1981). Male sex role conflicts, sexism, and masculinity: Psychological implications for men, women, and the counselling psychologist. *The Counselling Psychologist, 9*(2), 61–80.

Pleck, J. H. (1987). American fathering in historical perspective. In M. Kimmel (Ed.), *Changing men: New directions in research on men and masculinity* (pp. 83–97). Beverley Hills: Sage.

Pleck, J. H., & Masciadrelli, B. P. (2004). Paternal involvement by US residential fathers: Levels, sources and consequences. In M. E. Lamb (Ed.), *The role of the father in child development.* Hoboken: Wiley.

Pollack, W. (1995). Deconstructing dis-identification: Rethinking psychoanalytic concepts of male development. *Psychoanalysis and Psychotherapy, 12*(1), 30–45.

Radin, N. (1981). The role of the father in cognitive, academic and intellectual development. In M. E. Lamb (Ed.), *The role of the father in child development* (3rd ed., pp. 379–428). New York: Wiley.

Seidler, V. J. (1994). *Unreasonable men: Masculinity and social theory*. London: Routledge.

Taywaditep, K. (2001). Marginalisation among the marginalised: Gay men's anti-effeminacy attitudes. *Journal of Homosexuality, 42*(1), 1–28.

Veneziano, R. (2003). The importance of paternal warmth. *Cross-Cultural Research, 37*(3), 265–281.

Wester, S; Vogel, D., & Archer, J. (2002). Male restrictive emotionality and counseling supervision. *Journal of Counselling and Development, 82*(1), 91–98. Winter 2004.

12

Inside the Prison Parenting Classroom: Caring, Sharing and the Softer Side of Masculinity

Katie Buston

Introduction

The Scottish Prison Service (SPS) believes that the role of the prison is not simply to keep its participants locked away from the rest of society (Scottish Prison Service 2013). A great deal of intervention work takes place in the prison setting, providing its residents with opportunities to tackle addiction problems, gain academic qualifications and learn to manage their anger, amongst other things. Much of this work is delivered one to one, sometimes with a strong therapeutic element, such as supportive intervention for survivors of childhood abuse within the prison (e.g. work by Open Secret www.opensecret.org). Other interventions, however, are delivered in groups, with the potentially supportive element of the group context likely to be one of the ways in which more socially based interventions are theorised to work. But delivering such group-based interventions in the male prison setting potentially raises important questions about performances of masculinity. Might the widely portrayed hyper-masculine environment of the prison

---

K. Buston (✉)
MRC/CSO Social and Public Health Sciences Unit, University of Glasgow, Glasgow, UK

© The Author(s) 2018
M. Maycock, K. Hunt (eds.), *New Perspectives on Prison Masculinities*,
Palgrave Studies in Prisons and Penology, https://doi.org/10.1007/978-3-319-65654-0_12

(Sabo et al. 2001b) compromise attempts by staff to undertake intervention work which seeks to encourage exploration of potentially difficult emotions and experiences? Sharing, caring and publicly offering support to one another might not be the characteristics one immediately associates with groups of young male prisoners. This chapter focuses on deliveries of the same parenting programme to two different groups of fathers incarcerated in a Scottish Young Offender Institution (YOI), exploring the extent to which the discourses and performances of the participating young men supported, and compromised, facilitator attempts to create a caring and sharing space in which to deliver the programme within the prison parenting classroom.

Background Literature

Young Masculinities

The setting for this study was a YOI, its 16–21-year-old residents somewhere on the transitional line from boys to men. Few studies in criminology have explicitly focused on performances of masculinity; even fewer focus on young masculinities (Earle 2011; Bengtsson 2015). Although the young men in this study were fathers, a few of them had never had a job. Most appeared to relate more to their relatively recent school-day experience—even if that tended to involve truanting and lack of engagement with schools rather than actual school attendance—than they did to any traditionally conceptualised adult world of work and responsibility (see also Katz 2002; Earle 2011).

Willis's (1977) seminal study of white working class young men making the transition from school to employment found masculine culture amongst the group he studied to be violent, misogynistic and anti-school. Work on young masculinities that has followed has emphasised the complexity of the performativity of 'doing boy/young man' in specific contexts, taking account of not only the everyday, perceived as 'approved' by peers, practices associated with hegemonic masculinity (Connell 1995), but also the commonalities and differences in such gendered identities and performances created by factors such as social class and race (Frosh et al. 2003). Frosh et al. (2003), for example, found that there was widespread acceptance that 'doing boy' in London involved avoiding anything perceived as being what girls do and so in order to achieve popular (hegemonic) masculine status 'hardness', 'sporting prowess', 'coolness', casual treatment of schoolwork and 'cussing' were required. Frosh et al. (2003) also identified homophobia as a key and prevalent way in which the boys in their study policed each other's masculine identities across races and social class.

More recently, work by Anderson (2009) and others (e.g. McCormack 2012) has focused on concepts and themes such as 'inclusive masculinity', 'the declining significance/erosion of homophobia' and 'the softening of masculinity' amongst young men. This focus on newer acceptable masculine practices sits alongside the earlier literature which recognises the distinction between outward displays of masculinity, as manifested in these actual day to day practices, and what might lie beneath this in the more anxious and insecure psyches of the young men (Mac an Ghaill 1994; Hyde et al. 2009; Sewell 1997; Measor et al. 2000; Frosh et al. 2002). As such, the concept of vulnerability amongst young men comes to the forefront. The 'boy code' (Pollack 1999) which may require a macho performance when with peers, or, indeed, more widely, may not always co-exist easily with what is going on inside the heads of these young men, including with regard to their hopes, fears and aspirations for the future (McDowell 2002).

[Young] Prison Masculinities

Messerschmidt (1993) argues that hegemonic constructions of masculinity predispose males to criminality and violence; it is certainly easy to conceptualise an association between the two. Stereotypes of 'criminal youth' involve conceptualisations of hyper-masculine men who thrive on violence, risk, aggression and danger, and who are callous and unemotional (Mosher 1998; Collier 1998). The 'prison code', uncovered primarily in studies of adult institutions (Toch 1998; Sabo et al. 2001a) but also recognisable in the relatively few studies of YOIs which have masculinity as a focus (see Bengtsson 2015; Earle 2011), involves maintaining this hyper-masculine persona by acting as if you do not mind hurting, or even killing, someone, and not revealing any details about your personal life, or, indeed, any weaknesses at all (Sabo et al. 2001a):

> Suffer in silence. Never admit you are afraid… Do not snitch… do not do anything that will make other prisoners think you are gay, effeminate, or a sissy. Act hard…. Do not help the authorities in any way. Do not trust anyone. Always be ready to fight, especially when your manhood is challenged…. As a result, prisoners lift weights compulsively, adopt the meanest stare they can muster, and keep their fears and their pain carefully hidden beneath a well-rehearsed tough-guy posture. (pp. 10–11)

Carceral has made similar observations about what is required and what may render masculinities vulnerable in such contexts: "There are certain actions and moods one has to project….To save face, and thus your future existence in prison, you have to fight. Kindness is weakness, gentleness is weakness. Care is weakness, sadness is weakness, and love is weakness" (Carceral 2004, pp. 28, 35–36).

Those who best manage to hide their vulnerabilities in these ways (see also Jewkes 2005 and her concept of 'masculine front-management') are, it is asserted, uppermost in prison hierarchies (Karp 2010) and thus least likely to be exploited or dominated during their prison time. Furthermore, Curtis claims, though again based on work undertaken in adult prisons, such 'dangerous masculinity' (Curtis 2014) is embedded in the structure of the prison, through its rules and policies, with the prisoners seen as a force to be controlled, and any vulnerabilities they may have denied.

Alternative accounts have, however, emerged more recently, though again focusing on adult institutions. These accounts explore softer performances of masculinity amongst male prisoners which allow for: "humour and playfulness, friendship and camaraderie, educational enlightenment, successful therapeutic intervention and transformative achievement" (Jewkes 2015, p. xi), all of which draw on emotional expression. Crewe (2014) highlights the importance of homosocial relationships where friendships are formed/developed within the prison, often based on coming from the same neighbourhoods on the outside, whether or not people knew each other well before entering the jail.

Fathers in Prison

There is a growing body of work focusing specifically on imprisoned fathers (Arditti and Parkman 2011; Boswell and Wedge 2002; Clarke et al. 2005; Day et al. 2005; Meek 2011), including young imprisoned and/or offending fathers (Buston 2010; Nurse 2003, 2005; Meek 2007; Wilkinson et al. 2009; Parra-Cardona et al. 2008). There has been discussion about whether young men who identify themselves as fathers may find it easier to show warmer and softer sides within the prison context. That is, does the hyper-masculine prison code permit exceptions to the general rules for dads? Certainly, a performance of hyper-masculine maleness appears to be incompatible with being the caring father that young men (including those who are incarcerated) appear to aspire to (Buston 2010). Being such a father includes being warm, sensitive, attentive, protecting one's child and being there to spend time with and support him/her. It is, however, unclear whether, when, to whom, and how young incarcerated men advertise their status as fathers within the prison, and thus it is opaque as to whether and how the overall prison culture shapes this, and whether and how this might in turn shape the overall prison culture.

The Research Context

The Prison

Polmont Young Offender Institution is Scotland's only YOI. Situated in the relatively heavily populated Central Belt, between Scotland two largest cities Glasgow and Edinburgh, its capacity is just over 800 prisoners, aged 16–21 years. Run by the SPS, strategic decisions around the institution, as is the case for all the SPS establishments, are made in conjunction with the Scottish Government. Contributing to the new vision for the prison service, which is increasingly expanding beyond protecting the public and reducing reoffending (Scottish Prison Service 2013), the strategy for young offenders is to develop the institution as a Learning

Environment, with a key development area within this being parenting and families. A purpose built education wing opened in 2014 in order to facilitate the increasing numbers of prisoners involved in educational and other interventions. Also during this year, two dedicated Parenting Officers were recruited and SPS tendered for a third sector organisation to develop parenting services, including a parenting intervention to be co-delivered with the Parenting Officers. Barnardo's Scotland, a well-established and highly regarded children's charity providing services across the country, won the tender in early 2014, with programme delivery commencing in the second half of the year.

The Parenting Programme

Barnardo's 'Parenting Matters' is an established parenting course, delivered for over 20 years largely in Northern Ireland. For delivery within HMP YOI Polmont, the programme was adapted by incorporating materials focusing specifically on young fathering. "Being a Young Dad Parenting Programme" runs for a full day a week over ten consecutive weeks, although a condensed version (six weeks) is available for those who will be released sooner. It includes information-based, skill-based and more reflectively based sessions which include: 'What children need from parents', 'Attachment', 'Self-esteem', 'Baking', 'The importance of play', 'Dangers of second hand smoke', 'Positive disciplining', 'Behaviour management' and 'Budgeting'.

The programme is voluntary and open to fathers who, in theory if not always in practice, have access to their children, or who have the prospect of such access (in cases where there are ongoing issues). In the full ten-week version of the programme three extra (to those available routinely), and enhanced, family visits are incorporated, including a final celebratory one which marks the end of the programme.

The programme's primary aim is to help young fathers understand the positive role they can play in their child's life, if they choose to do so. Key to the programme theory is the development of a positive relationship between participants and facilitators, and amongst the participants themselves. It is posited that if this can be achieved, the young men will feel more relaxed and supported and will therefore be more likely to engage, and actively participate, in the programme, setting the context for behavioural change. Through the process of sharing and reflecting on their experiences, it is theorised that they will realise the importance of the role of father, and this will motivate them to change, drawing on other skills taught during the course. As well as working through the formal content of sessions, the atmosphere created within the classroom session is key; informal discussion, playing board games and generally relaxing together are essential components of the course alongside the traditional worksheet, materials on DVD and directed discussions. Barnardo's Scotland requested a kettle and fridge for the classroom, and the facilitator provided milk and biscuits at each session in order that the young men could help themselves to refreshments. Money was also spent on resources for the programme, including games such as Monopoly and Chatter Matters (a question-based game where one moves around the board based on answering conversation inducing questions such as "What person from the past or present would you like to invite for dinner?" and "What was one of your first childhood memories"), a stock of occasion cards they could send to loved ones, a radio for background music and bean bags for relaxation.

Whilst one of the greatest challenges identified by Barnardo's staff involved in implementing the parenting intervention with young men in general (i.e. outside of the prison context) is that they may feel uncomfortable talking about their lives, feelings and concerns. This may be even more the case for young men in prison as they try to divert their classmates' and facilitators' attention away from difficult issues in their lives such as poor literacy and dysfunctional family backgrounds. A flaunting of hyper-masculine aspects of their identities may be one such diversionary tactic, as they initially disrupt and refuse to engage with the programme. In this context, a key goal for the programme facilitators is to enable the young men to understand that they can display their softer sides and embrace more inclusive masculine performances within the parenting classroom.

Incarcerated Fathers

It is estimated that around one in four incarcerated young men in the UK are fathers or expectant fathers (Macmillan 2005), although earlier work the author was involved with found that, at that time at least, around one in three of the prisoners reported being fathers or expectant fathers. During this study, the Parenting Officers maintained that the figure was considerably less within this institution (around 40 of the 500 inmates). In Scotland, it will soon be a legal requirement that all prisoners will be asked for details of any dependent children they have, but thus far these data have not been available.

The Study

Background and Data Collection

This study grew out of collaboration with Barnardo's Scotland. The staff who led the tender to develop and co-deliver parenting services within HMP YOI Polmont were keen that the implementation of the parenting programme within Polmont was evaluated, in order that it could be further developed for future iterations. After receiving permission from both the SPS Research and Ethics Committee and Glasgow University's Social Science Ethics Committee, I arranged to sit in on all the parenting sessions—a full day a week for ten weeks—of delivery of the intervention to one group, and to attend several sessions of the delivery to another group who were undertaking the condensed version of the programme over six weeks.

On each occasion, I arrived at the prison at around 7.45 am in order to wait for one of the Parenting Officers to escort me to the classroom. The young men participating in the programme usually arrived in the classroom at around 8.30 am. The morning, until around midday when they were escorted back to the halls for lunch, was spent doing the formal coursework as well as passing time on some of the more informal elements such as drinking coffee together and perhaps starting a board game. I brought in my lunch and ate it in the same classroom with the Barnardo's facilitator. One or both of the Parenting Officers usually joined us, though they sometimes also spent time in the adjoining office catching up with administrative work relating to the programme. The men arrived back in the classroom at around 1.30 pm, and the afternoon

12 Inside the Prison Parenting Classroom: Caring, Sharing...

session continued until around 3.45 pm when the men were collected and taken back to their cells. I left with the Parenting Officers and the Barnardo's facilitator at around 4 pm. Between February and April 2015, I spent around 100 hours in the parenting classroom, observing, and participating in (see below), the programme delivery and 'hanging around' between sessions talking to the staff and the young men. I also attended several Family Visits in the visiting room which provided an opportunity to observe some of the young men interacting with their child(ren) and their partners, or ex-partners, during the two-hour-visit period.

Before I commenced the observation of this programme, I had visualised my role as primarily an observer, sitting quietly at the back of the classroom, perhaps helping staff out with small tasks such as handing out worksheets, if required. From the earliest session, however, it very soon became apparent that this expectation was unrealistic. As soon as they arrived, the young men wanted to know who I was and were keen to engage me in conversation. As delivery of the programme commenced, both they and the facilitators would regularly turn to me and try to get me involved by asking my opinion or inviting me to share my own parenting, and other, experiences. In the context of a small classroom, it would have looked out of place for me to sit unobtrusively and do nothing—there were cups of coffee to make, dishes to be done, IT problems to be solved, art work to be helped with as well as many chats to be had. Whilst it was clear to me early on that I had had very different life experiences to the young men and the three core staff, I quickly found that I liked nearly all of them a lot. An important aspect of my own life, and a common bonding currency whilst sitting in on this parenting programme, was that I was a parent myself. This was something I often talked about during my time in the prison, both with the young fathers and the staff (two of the three were parents themselves, and the third spent a lot of time around small children). I was nearly always the oldest in the classroom, excluding times when particular visitors came to deliver elements of the programme. With the young men being around 18/19 years old, and me being in my mid-40s, I quickly calculated that I was probably round about the age of many of their mothers, which also drew me into performing in a maternal nurturing way when interacting with them. Whether this was how they regarded me, I am unsure. There seemed to be a general perplexity as to what I was doing there every week, with most understanding I was not one of the facilitators, but not really grasping what my declared role as a researcher from the university involved and why I needed to spend so much time there. The young men, however, seemed to welcome my presence and were happy for me to engage them in conversation and, indeed, often went out of their way to include me in any informal discussions they were having, as well as accepting I was taking part in the class alongside them. The staff also welcomed me into every aspect of their interactions and at no point made me feel like my presence was threatening in any way.

I returned to the prison around six weeks after I had completed the programme observation, and conducted in-depth interviews with the young men who were still in the prison (6 of the 16 who had attended the two courses). The topic guide for these interviews focused on: whether and how they thought the programme had increased their knowledge, changed their attitudes and had changed or might change their behaviour with regard to aspects of parenting their child; and their lives as sons themselves, now fathers, and their identities both within and out with the prison. The gap between observing the course delivery and returning to conduct interviews with the young men allowed me to consolidate my thoughts and follow-up particular issues I wished to know more about in a much more systematic way than had been possible in the daily, sometimes chaotic, hub-bub of the classroom, where I might have conversations with some young men about a particular issue one day, and others another day, and where I would overhear conversations between various combinations of them, focusing on various things, in an ad hoc way.

I did not conduct formal interviews with the facilitators whom I had observed, feeling I had taken up enough of their time by asking them to organise the interviews with the young men, and requesting documentation and materials around the course, as well as having engaged them in numerous informal conversations about their work during the three months I spent in the YOI. Prior to the prison field work, I did, however, interview one of the Barnardo's staff who had led on introducing the programme into the prison.

Analysis

My aim in undertaking the fieldwork was to evaluate the parenting programme in a formative way, gaining an in-depth understanding what the programme involved, how it was delivered by the Barnardo's facilitator and the Parenting Officers, and how it was received by the men. It was agreed in advance that my conclusions would be fed back to senior staff responsible for the implementation of the programme within Barnardo's Scotland, and used to further refine the programme and aspects of its delivery.

After each visit, I wrote detailed ethnographic fieldnotes on leaving the prison, aided by the notes I had scribbled during the day, often in code, to remind me of the day's structure. These included notes on: who was there, who said what—formally and in conversations I had and had overheard—and other key things that interested me at the time. As Curtis (2014, pp. 28, 35–36) found in her, similar, prison work attending a fatherhood group, I found 'thick description' to be very important in my endeavour to understand the happenings in the parenting classroom. The one-to-one post-programme interviews were recorded and transcribed with participants' permission, I also had access to copies of the end of programme reports written by the facilitators for each man. These commented on attendance, the sessions covered and the individual men's engagement with the course and with particular aspects of it.

All of these sources—ethnographic notes, transcripts, reports and course materials—have been analysed for this chapter. After considering the materials as a whole, a coding framework was drawn up and the data were coded to the following themes: the atmosphere within the parenting classroom; the atmosphere within the prison more widely; the visit room; prison identities; the outside world; the programme; conceptualisations of fatherhood; themselves as fathers; and their own childhoods. The central theme of interest for this chapter is the atmosphere in the parenting classroom—which encompasses data around caring, sharing, supporting, showing emotions, racism, misogyny, homophobia, violence, banter, hierarchies, the role of the facilitators and group dynamics—in the context of the broader data collected.

Where quotes from young men are presented, below, a pseudonym is used, alongside his age and how many children he had at various stages (baby, toddler and pre-schooler). Pseudonyms have also been used for their children if mentioned, and the Parenting Officers and Barnardo's staff.

The Participants

The young people who took part in this study should be viewed as young men first, and 'young offenders' second (see Katz 2002). However, they are, technically, 'criminal youth'. They were in the YOI for a variety of crimes, some dangerous and violent. Eight men participated in the full length Tuesday course, which I observed in its totality, and another eight participated in the truncated Wednesday course of which I attended half of the sessions. All but one of the participants were white Scottish, the other being English and of Black Caribbean origin. They were between 18 and 21 years old. Most had only one child, but several had two children, and one had three (though he was not the biological father of one of them). Around half said they were still with the mother of their child(ren). All had been assessed, within the prison, as dyslexic *and* as having Attention Deficit Hyperactivity Disorder. In the findings below, I generally refer to the young men as 'boys', as this was how they referred to themselves, and how they were referred to by all staff associated with the prison. It was also how I came to think of them as I watched them engage with the programme and talked with them about their lives.

The Facilitators

The two Parenting Officers, appointed during 2014 to deliver this course and to develop other parenting services, were both longstanding Prison Officers who had worked in HMP YOI Polmont for several years and had applied for these posts. Their different personalities and styles of delivery allowed me to contrast different ways of implementing the same programme. Whilst this is not the focus of this chapter, I do reflect on this where relevant to the men's engagement with the course and their performances of masculinity. The Barnardo's facilitator co-delivered the programme with the Parenting Officers. She had extensive experience of delivering parenting interventions to vulnerable mothers—including young mothers—but had only been working in the prison for a short time, and had relatively little previous experience in delivering parenting work to fathers.

Findings

Being in the Jail

As I was only able to spend time with the young men in the parenting classroom (plus some visit room time), I was interested in learning about their overall experience of 'being in the jail'. Most of the boys presented this as being relatively unproblematic, just something they had to sit out until their sentences ended, eating the awful food and putting up with 'the fannies' (annoying fellow prisoners) and 'the steamers' ('daft wee people') who messed around, and who were overly boisterous. All of those who had previously spent time in an adult prison said they preferred the adult prison, as they did not have these irritating hall-mates who appeared to be annoying by dint of their immature manner, but were instead looked after by older prisoners with whom they might have some family or territorial connection and who "just want to get their head down and get on with their time" (Saul, 20, toddler). Some of the men described their initial arrival in the jail as frightening: "first time in I was crapping myself" (Christian, 19, baby). None, however, described the actual (in contrast to the anticipated) experience in this way. As Dino (19, toddler) explained to me:

> a lot of boys hear stories from outside and they've not been in the jail before and they come in going, 'oh shit, am I going to get dusted [beaten up], am I going to get stabbed', stuff like that, and it's not like that. It's… You get the odd fight but you've got five hundred under twenty-one year olds from hundreds of different schemes [housing estates], obviously you're going to get fights, but it's not as bad as everybody makes it out to be. Boys come in

and they're, like they're quite upset about going to jail, so you just reassure them that they're going to be all right and nothing's going to happen to them. (Dino, 20, toddler)

Dino also advised that so long as you: "stick up for yourself' and don't let anybody step on your toes you would be fine".

'Banter' was regarded as an everyday part of life on the prison hall, which passed the time rather than being threatening or sinister. The banter described did not just take the form of joking and conversations between the prisoners, and between the Prison Officers and the prisoners, but also included practical jokes. Tyson (19, baby), for example, described to me and others in the classroom how he had arrived back in his cell the previous night to find his shoes filled with hair gel. He believed one of the Prison Officers had done it, and although slightly annoyed at the waste of his precious hair gel, he appeared to regard the incident as humorous, and as just one of the occurrences that happens in the largely very boring prison environment, in which 'getting a laugh' was important.

Fighting, which seemed to be largely based on territorial issues associated with where the prisoners came from, was also seen, by some of the young men at least, as an everyday part of prison life, whether or not they chose to get directly involved. Saul told me:

> It's all young boys in here, know what I mean? We are all basically fighting, trying to make a name for ourselves. The Glasgow boys and the North Lanarkshire boys, we all stick together. That's like all the Aberdeen and Dundee boys, they all stick together. But Glasgow and that boys, we run this jail, definitely. [Saul, 20, toddler]

I did observe first-hand the fascination of nearly all the young men when a fight occurred in the vicinity (a couple of times the alarm sounded, on the belt of the Parenting Officer who was not delivering the programme that day, and s/he ran to provide assistance). Each time, there was much speculation on the part of the boys, then and afterwards, as they sought detailed information from the Parenting Officer on his/her return, as to what had gone on, who was involved and what elements of violence had occurred. The incidents were referred to frequently in subsequent weeks and they seemed to glean some vicarious excitement from these happenings, which comprised a fight between prisoners in the bike sheds with some tools which had been left lying around, and an incident in the prison gym where no one was hurt but which involved machinery being dropped on one prisoner by others. Several years earlier, a multi-part documentary had been filmed within the prison, containing footage of one or two violent scenes. This was also referred to often by the boys, some of whom took pride in knowing some of the protagonists, who were from their area.

I explored with the boys, in the interviews and in informal conversations, whether they felt they could 'be themselves' in the prison. They all asserted that 'of course' they could and, what is more, that 'self' was tough:

> try and put this fucking front on and you're just going to get walked all over. Cunts are just going to be like that 'you fucking mongo [unintelligent person], man'. [Timmy, 20, baby]

None of the boys acknowledged that bullying went on either. Fights between the boys were portrayed by them as a meeting of equals, rather than any kind of bullying behaviour. When I asked Timmy about whether any of the prisoners perceived that staff bullied them, he replied:

> there's a couple that's just dogs. But most of them are all right, know what I mean… they couldn't even try and bully any cunt in the fucking hall, man. [Timmy, 20, baby]

Whilst then, none of the young men 'admitted' that the jail itself was a frightening place to be once they had settled in, they did describe fighting and banter as integral parts of daily prison life, occurrences which did not dent their 'natural' toughness and ability to deal with such an everyday context.

The Parenting Classroom

In contrast with boys' second-hand accounts of life in the institution more broadly, I had much time to observe first-hand what it was like within the parenting classroom. I (quickly) formulated a picture in my own head, as I listened to the young men talking about life in the halls, of the parenting classroom being a bit of a sanctuary from all of this (not that the boys presented any need for such sanctuary). When they arrived in the morning, the kettle would be put on and we would all chat about various things—perhaps a programme that had been on television the night before that several of us had watched or an upcoming family visit or a fight that had taken place in the halls the previous day—before beginning the formal session of the morning. In this section, I begin by discussing the facilitators' attempts to create an atmosphere within the parenting classroom which permitted and encouraged the boys to show their softer side, demonstrate caring attitudes and share emotional experiences with one another. I then consider how successful these attempts were by discussing the extent of hyper-masculine manifestations, as well as much softer demonstrations of alternative masculinities.

Creating a Softer Sharing and Caring Ethos

Against the backdrop of the overall prison culture where it seemed that being tough was required, though apparently effortless, one of the primary aims of the Barnardo's worker (known here as Maria), who delivered the first iteration of the course alongside the Parenting Officers, was to create an atmosphere in the classroom that reflected the programme's objectives of changing attitudes and behaviour around parenting to emphasise nurture and caring, and strong supportive relationships. As she said:

> you could have the best programme in the world, but if you don't have the subtle relationship, unconditional, positive regard type skills you're not going to get anywhere. [Maria]

During my interview with Maria, as well as during the numerous conversations we shared, she outlined the explicit ways in which this sort of classroom climate could be created by the facilitators including through: the facilitators sharing personal details about themselves, in a limited and appropriate way; sending birthday cards to the boys; providing a kettle in the classroom and making tea, coffee, juice and biscuits available; challenging homophobic, misogynistic, racist and other negative comments; calling participants by their first names; and introducing themselves by their first names. Maria had not worked in a prison setting before introducing the parenting programme to Polmont, but was aware that all of these things were at odds with the conventional prison ethos. For example, on the concept of giving something of yourself in order to foster a sharing ethos, she observed that:

> perhaps, maybe, in the hall mentalities, you don't tell them [prisoners] anything, but I think you have to [in the parenting classroom]. If you are going to be part of somebody's life and meeting their child and their partner and they're letting you in, you need to give something. [Maria]

She explained the underlying rationale further:

> if we can help someone to know how it feels to have somebody else thinking about you, then they can open up something for their little one. We're really good at telling people all the ways to change a nappy, to feed them, to do all of these things. But we're not good at challenging the emotional connection.

The female Parenting Officer also fully subscribed to this idea of the creation of a conducive atmosphere for delivery of the programme, describing it as needing to be 'relaxed, comfortable and, above all, equal'.

Hyper-Masculine Presentations of Self

I turn now to consider how successful these attempts were and whether there were examples of hyper-masculine presentations of self in this friendly and nurturing classroom environment? Unsurprisingly, perhaps, yes, there were many such examples. Homophobic comments were common, and misogynistic and racist ones less so but still not infrequent. Jokes with underlying hints of violence were also often made. All of these would almost certainly have been referred to, and were, as 'banter' by the boys. Indeed, the ground rules that one of the groups put together during Session 1 made the distinction between 'fun banter' which was seen as acceptable, and other banter, which was recognised as potentially damaging as it was directed towards, and against, a particular individual in the group.

There were also examples of more insidious comments, probably seen even by the boys as crossing the line of 'fun banter' and having more harmful intent. Violence against someone who had wronged them, for example, appeared to be seen as legitimate. In one such instance, Saul talks of what he would do if he discovered that his ex-partner, the mother of his child, had a new partner:

> I know for a fact when I get out there [on liberation] and I know she's with somebody else, I'm just going to attack him on sight. I'm jealous like that, know what I mean? Especially if he's anywhere near my child then I'll take him out. [Saul, 20, toddler]

In another instance, Dylan was adamant during a session which focused on self-esteem and bullying, that he would bully someone if they were gay, stating:

> I fucking despise gay people. [Dylan, 20, baby, toddler plus pre-schooler step daughter]

During the same session, the facilitator asked the boys to think about the difference between hitting your mother, something the boys were outraged by the thought of, and hitting your partner, a common reason for conviction amongst the HMP YOI Polmont prisoners. This was something they appeared to find difficult to reflect on. The former was taken as self-evidently unacceptable and there was something wrong with you if you hit your mothers, whilst the latter was, if not condoned by all the boys, was treated as a common fact of life and just the way things were.

On occasions when contraception was being discussed as part of the programme, there were also portrayals of apparently hyper-masculine attitudes to sex and sexual behaviour. Whilst the boys did not appear to feel the need to be boastful about any aspect of their sexual career (perhaps they had felt they proved themselves as sexual beings by having a child?), they were apparently proud of being apathetic around contraceptive use. Timmy (19, baby), for example, said he had never worn a condom in his life, and never would, adding that he would not be interested to find out whether his partner was on the pill or not.

During the session on bullying the immorality (and illegal nature) of forwarding on nude pictures or videos of girls/young women in their social networks was discussed. This was something the boys appeared to find difficult to understand: why would you not pass on a nude picture? Was it not natural, normal and an obvious thing to do? I found this session extremely uncomfortable as I watched the apparent complete lack of understanding on their part as to how the girl in question would feel about naked pictures of herself being circulated. There was even discussion of the girl being 'frigid' if she refused to have such pictures taken in the first place, or objected too loudly to a wider audience seeing them. Dylan (20, baby, toddler and pre-school step-daughter) asserted at this point that 'most girls are slags nowadays', a comment that went unchallenged by the other boys (or by the Prison Officer). There was no 'fun banter', designed to be witty and to fulfil the masculine code, during this discussion of passing on nude pictures and videos. The boys, as a group, appeared to feel entirely comfortable in de-personalising the girls and young women they had known from their own schools and neighbourhoods who had been victims of 'revenge porn', and appeared to be finding it very difficult to see the situation from the point of view of these young women.

Interestingly, this session, which was facilitated by a male visitor, included a discussion about 'the problem' of never backing down. Although it was introduced as a problem, the visitor gave indications that he felt this was an admirable trait: it is sometimes good and necessary to big yourself up, to show authority at all times, and never, ever, back down. Saul and Dylan indicated their agreement that this behaviour engendered respect and made you look 'better' than you actually were. The visitor joined in with the boys' banter and did not challenge several blatantly misogynistic comments made during the session. He referred to girls who dress in a certain way being partly to blame for sexual assaults, and also made a number of 'jokes' around homosexual behaviour in adult prisons. His interactional style was very different from the Parenting Officers and

Barnardo's facilitators, and the resulting atmosphere in the classroom and the way the boys behaved and spoke during this session seemed to reflect this.

As well as being reactive to specific styles of facilitators, as demonstrated above, the extent of the boys' hyper-masculine behaviour appeared to depend on the dynamics of the particular group at any given session. Although attendance was very good, there were inevitably weeks (or mornings/afternoons) where individual boys were not able to attend because of a court appearance, a visit or a doctor's appointment, for example. Whilst for some sessions there was a full house, mostly one or two boys would be missing. Saul, for example, portrayed himself in a very masculine way some weeks, when Dino and Dylan were both in attendance, which he moderated when they were not, and in our one-to-one interview, I saw a completely different, softer, side to him that he had not revealed during the classes. Dino, a long-term prisoner, had been given the role of peer mentor, attending all of the courses and supporting the facilitators. He commented on the difference between the groups:

> that group we just done, there was a lot of my pals or boys, a few of pals in it. So, a wee bit more rowdier, but like the first group I was just getting to know the boys and that, first group was all right. They just got down into it. (Dino, 20, toddler)

Softer Sharing and Caring Presentations of Self

The parenting classroom was, however, also a place where most of the boys seemed to have little difficulty in expressing a softer side. Much of the work conducted within the parenting classroom potentially touched on deep emotions. For example, there were times when the boys were encouraged to talk about aspects of their childhood, or how they felt when they discovered their partners were pregnant, or when their baby was born. There were also a lot of activities which centred around expression of feelings, in one form or another. Artwork was done regularly; the boys had the opportunity to make Mother's Day cards, for example, and were strongly encouraged to put together a story book for their child using their own artwork and words. Nearly all of them engaged in these activities whole-heartedly, and there was never any ridicule expressed, or even any sense of self-consciousness that these self-proclaimed 'big tough' guys were sitting together sticking hearts onto Valentine's or Mother's Day cards and writing sentimental messages inside these and their books for their children. Harry, for example, dedicated his story book to his son Benjamin 'blessed angel'.

At some time or another, most of the boys expressed their appreciation to the facilitators for their positive experiences of doing the programme. For example, towards the end of the programme, Lorcan repeatedly asked whether he could come down to the classroom on days when the programme was not being delivered so that he could continue to work on his story book. He said he felt really relaxed when he was there. Harry, whilst dismissing the notion that the parenting classroom was any sort of respite from the negative experience of being imprisoned and all that that involved, did tell me that he appreciated the respect shown to him by the facilitators "everyone that was part of the course was good people" [Harry, 18, baby]. One of the boys asked me several times, and I heard him ask the facilitators too, whether we thought of him as an 'ordinary father' or a 'young offender'. He seemed very pleased to hear that, of course, we saw him as the former. A couple of the other boys asked me over the weeks whether I had ever felt scared or intimidated by them, and appeared delighted when I said I had not.

Especially in the early weeks of the programme, some of the boys also attempted to look after me. I was frequently asked whether I wanted a cup of tea, and when they had made cakes and other snacks on the occasions when a visitor came in to do nutrition sessions with them, I was offered samples by a number of them. They seemed happy to engage me in conversation, when I was not instigating a conversation with them, and seemed interested in anything I talked about. Only one of the boys, across the two groups, was hostile. He repeatedly asked me over the first few weeks what my job was, and why I did that, telling me several times that it sounded like a waste of time. Although on the first occasion or two I treated this as a joke (responding to it as 'fun banter'), as did the other boys, when he repeated it in later weeks some of the other boys got quite defensive on my behalf. A few brought photos of their children to show me as the course went on, and they seemed happy to share with me at least some aspects of their family and personal lives. Not once did I feel threatened during my time in the prison and, in fact, with a couple of exceptions including during the bullying session, I felt I was a part of the more sharing and caring atmosphere that the facilitators had striven to create. Maria also described how she had felt the nurturance shown to the boys in the classroom led to them wanting to reciprocate:

> Davey turned up… he turned up one week and he had brought me a teabag on a string 'cause he knows I drink green tea and he's found it for me, which is really sweet. [Maria]

There were many examples of the boys revealing personal insights into their lives. A game we all played on a number of occasions was 'Chatter Matters' where questions were asked about the life of the person who landed on particular squares. Christian, for example, talked in quite an emotional way about a friend he had lost through suicide, and also talked about how he felt about his family including his gran who suffered from chronic back pain, saying he wished he could take her pain away. Harry opened up about his feelings of guilt for a crime he committed, and Lorcan talked about the distress he felt growing up when his parents argued all the time, as well as movingly talking about his cousin who had killed herself a few years previously, and how he wished more than anything that he could speak to her again to understand why. Other 'revelations' were also made as part of other discussions in the group also; group members were all sensitive to disclosures and it was always universally recognised when something being talked about needed to be taken seriously, listened to, and respected.

In the final classroom session, the boys talked about what they had got out of the programme, and this was something I focused on during the one-to-one interviews. Whereas in the class context, the boys tended to point to the more information based and less emotional topics (e.g. fire safety, budgeting) as being highlights for them, in the one-to-one interviews they opened up more and reflected in more depth about what they had found useful. Christian, for example, said the most useful aspect for him had been learning:

how to build a good bond with your child in the first few years of their live, and I need to do that just when I get out.… I always knew you had to speak to them and that to get them but I learnt it encourages them and stuff like that. And just to get them laughing and stuff. (Christian, 19, baby)

Similarly, in the one-to-one interview, Harry said:

Communicating. To me this is what I got back, what I learnt in the lesson was communicating. I find it hard to communicate – like you're lucky I'm even talking to you now. I don't know what it is, I don't know… before I never used to communicate. It's just why waste my time, what's the point?… So I'm just looking forward to get out and spending time with Benjamin. [Harry, 18, baby]

Nearly all of the boys mentioned that they had enjoyed being with the other boys in the parenting group, during the post-programme interviews, as exemplified by Christian and Dylan:

you can relate and that. They can say how they do stuff and you can tell them how you do stuff… they're actually like a group. [Christian, 19, baby]

It was totally different up here [in the parenting classroom], yeah. Down in the halls anything can happen. Up here it was just great to come up and not have to look behind you and that. [Dylan, baby and school age plus step father to pre-schooler]

Similar sentiments were also expressed in the group context. At the final session, before the award ceremony, the boys were asked to write a comment about each of the others in the group. A piece of paper was passed round for each of the boys, on which every other participant wrote a comment, so although the comments were not publicly made, they were not completely private either. These were amalgamated and added to the boys' final reports, which they were handed at the ceremony. All were positive, to varying degrees, about others in the group; indeed, I learned that, in this context, calling someone 'a good cunt' or 'a sound cunt' is intended to be a compliment. Comments made included:

really good cunt, brilliant peer mentor and is inspirational and essential to this group

makes a good contribution to the group and he is sound

a sensitive big guy who just needs to be himself

good guy, gets on with everyone, good laugh..

The boys were able to talk about their idea of being a 'good father', both in the classroom during the programme and in the one-to-one interviews. These conceptualisations reflected conventionally accepted positively framed ideas of the caring and present father:

loving affection for your child and you're like giving them obviously the time of day, playing with them and helping out as much as you can with the mum and that.… Just being there as much as you can kind of thing.… he should be first, not making other things priority like drink or drugs or something like that. [Christian, 19, baby]

You be there for your child, always considerate, consistent, loving and caring, and like not aggressive obviously. Discipline them but not to an extreme. [Dino, 19, toddler]

They also talked about their intentions/aspirations on release, specifically in relation to their children:

I want to go out [be released] and, well, yes, live with my mum but stay up at Maggie's now and again so I'm there in the morning and I'm there at night, putting him to his bed and waking up with him. Just get a better bond, and get a good bond with him at this age because I've missed a lot. [Christian, 19, baby]

I've always been a caring person, like to be honest I care too much so now I've got a son, it's just the same 'cause he's my son, isn't he, so I've just got to know how I want to treat him, like if that was me how would I want to be treated.… So I'm just going talk to him more [and find out]. [Harry, 18, baby]

The Visit Room

I attended three visit sessions where some of the boys had their partners/ex-partners and child(ren) visit them for a two-hour session. Although for two of the sessions only those boys who were scheduled to have a visitor attended, for the third and final session (which was also the award ceremony at the end of the programme) all of the boys came along. During this time, the boys hugged and kissed their children—and interacted with other people's children—getting down on the floor and playing with them, and even sang along to nursery rhymes with them in a whole group format led by one of the Parenting Officers. I was not privy to the many private conversations the boys had with their visitors, but I observed no obvious manifestations of the more extreme masculine discourses and behaviours that had sometimes been apparent in the parenting classroom. Intimacy, in this context at least, appeared to be accepted and valued by all.

Discussion

Whilst I saw and heard hyper-masculine performances and comments from most of the young men during my time in the parenting classroom, I also witnessed a softer side exhibited by all of them as they participated in the parenting programme. The classroom climate (Buston et al. 2002) created by the facilitators appeared to have enabled them to show this softness: to share personal and emotional aspects of their lives and to listen respectfully to others doing the same and to talk about how they cared for their children and wanted to be good fathers and do their best for them.

This has implications for social interventions delivered within YOIs, many of which will theorise change around sharing, talking, nurturing and reflecting on attitudes and emotions in the group context in order to facilitate behavioural change. The prison is a prime setting for intervention such as the parenting programme described here. A key attraction is that participants are, literally, a captive audience, often with time on their hands to attend! But, as with most interventions, if participants are reluctant to engage there is little point in implementing them. The young men who participated in the programmes observed here were certainly not reluctant to engage. They shared and demonstrably cared, and supported one another. There were, certainly, limits to this but overall they opened up and showed themselves to be amenable to changes in their parenting attitudes and behaviour in line with more emotional and intimate conceptualisations of fatherhood. It is notable that the only time I felt uncomfortable was during the bullying session, where a sea change seemed to sweep across the classroom as the very masculine visitor arrived to take charge of the session, and the boys appeared to find it acceptable and desirable to talk about young women in very denigrating ways. Skilled facilitation—being able to lead, manage discipline and boundaries, build good relationships, and engage the group—in line with the programme aims is key.

It could be argued that an intervention around parenting, for any parents, may be more amenable to the exhibiting of 'sharing and caring' than interventions around other behavioural aspects, such as addiction work or weight loss programmes. Magaletta and Herbst (2001) note that fathering is one of the rare domains in which prisoners display an intrinsic motivation to learn and a voluntary willingness to change (p. 89). I have not observed other types of interventions within a prison setting so I cannot make direct comparisons with how young incarcerated men respond to other types of group-based intervention. However, through my observations and interviews, the power of skilled facilitation to create a climate in which the young men feel able to open up about aspects of their lives, not just their experiences of parenting per se, should not be underestimated. Skilled facilitation can permit, and encourage, young incarcerated men to go beyond the traditionally expected prison performances of hyper-masculinity, performances which were probably very familiar in pre-prison days, and which possibly contributed to these young men ending up in jail in the first place. My view, following this ethnographic work, was that there appeared to be considerable attitude change amongst the young men in relation to parenting. Of course, what happens beyond the parenting classroom and, particularly post-liberation as these young men return to their communities, their families, their peers and their children and (ex) partners is another question.

Karp (2010) writes about prison intervention, asserting that the men should be able to 'take off their mask' in trusted circles within the classroom. He identifies the importance of a space within the prison where self-protection is not necessary, and where the prison code can be challenged and emotional self-expression made possible. This resonates with what was observed in this ethnographic study. However, the analogy of taking of a mask to reveal the 'real' young man begs the question of what is more 'real'; it seems to me that these young men are complex, multifaceted young people who have many sides and who can perform in a number of ways and express a number of different discourses. To assert that the softer side which these young men exhibited during the parenting programme is a more 'real' demonstration of how they see themselves (or wish to be seen) as men, than the more stereotypically hegemonic performances of masculinity may be more wishful thinking than actuality. De Visser and Smith's (2007) exposition of alternative masculinities, whereby young men can use one distinctive and positively evaluated masculine behaviour (e.g. being a good father) to compensate for another (e.g. being a hardened criminal) might be a more useful way of considering varying facets of the imprisoned men, as might Meek's (2011) 'possible selves'. Nevertheless, it is an important and heartening finding that these young man, who have been convicted of a variety of crimes including violent ones, do have the capacity to engage with emotional reflection around their lives, and to offer support to one another around fathering and relationships, and other aspects of their lives.

References

Anderson, E. (2009). *Inclusive masculinity: The changing nature of masculinities*. New York: Routledge.

Arditti, J., & Parkman, T. (2011). Young men's reentry after incarceration: A developmental paradox. *Family Relations, 60*(2), 205–220.

Bengtsson, T. T. (2015, July). Performing hypermasculinity: Experiences with confined young offenders. *Men and Masculinities, 19*(4), 410–428.

Boswell, G., & Wedge, P. (2002). *Imprisoned fathers and their children*. London: Jessica Kingsley.

Buston, K. (2010). Experiences of, and attitudes towards, pregnancy and fatherhood amongst incarcerated young male offenders: Findings from a qualitative study. *Social Science and Medicine, 71*, 2211–2218.

Buston, K., Wight, D., & Hart, G. (2002). Inside the sex education classroom: The importance of context in engaging pupils. *Culture, Health & Sexuality, 4*, 317–335.

Carceral, K. C. (2004). *Behind a convict's eye: Doing time in a modern prison*. Belmont: Wadsworth Publishing Company.

Clarke, L., O'brien, M., Day, R. D., Goodwin, H., Connolly, J., Hemmings, J., & van Leeson, T. (2005). Fathering behind bars in English prisons: Imprisoned fathers' identity and contact with their children. *Fathering, 3*, 221–241.

Collier, R. (1998). *Masculinities, crime and criminology: Men, heterosexuality and the criminal(ised) other*. London: Sage Publications.

Connell, R. W. (1995). *Masculinities*. Cambridge: Polity Press.

Crewe, B. (2014). Not looking hard enough: Masculinity, emotion and prison research. *Qualitative Inquiry, 20*, 392–403.

Curtis, A. (2014). "You have to cut it off at the knee". Dangerous masculinities and security inside a men's prison. *Men and Masculinities, 17*, 120–146.

Day, R. D., Acock, A. C., Bahr, S. J., & Arditti, J. (2005). Incarcerated fathers returning home to children and families: Introduction to the special issue and a primer on doing research with men in prison. *Fathering, 3*, 183–200.

De Visser, R., & Smith, J. (2007). Alcohol consumption and masculine identity amongst young men. *Psychology & Health, 22*, 595.

Earle, R. (2011). Boys' zone stories: Perspectives from a young men's prison. *Criminology and Criminal Justice, 11*, 129–143.

Frosh, S., Phoenix, A., & Pattman, R. (2002). *Young masculinities: Understanding boys in contemporary society*. Basingstoke: Palgrave Macmillan.

Frosh, S., Phoenix, A., & Pattman, R. (2003). Taking a stand: Using psychoanalysis to explore the positioning of subjects in discourse. *British Journal of Social Psychology, 42*, 39–53.

Hyde, A., Drennan, J., Howlett, E., & Brady, D. (2009). Young Men's vulnerability in constituting hegemonic masculinity in sexual relations. *American Journal of Mens Health, 3*, 238–251.

Jewkes, Y. (2005). Men behind bars: "Doing" masculinity as an adaptation to imprisonment. *Men and Masculinities, 8*, 44–63.

Jewkes, Y. (2015). Foreword. In D. H. Drake, R. Earle, & J. Sloan (Eds.), *The Palgrave handbook of prison ethnography*. Basingstoke: Palgrave Macmillan.

Karp, D. R. (2010). Unlocking men, unmasking masculinities: Doing men's work in prisons. *The journal of Men's Studies, 18*, 63–83.

Katz, A. (Ed.). (2002). *Parenting under pressure: Prison*. London: Young Voice.

Mac an Ghaill, M. (1994). *The making of men: Sexualities and schooling*. Buckingham: Open University Press.

Macmillan, C. (2005). Public health initiative at a young offenders institute. *Community Practitioner, 78*, 397–399.

Magaletta, P. R., & Herbst, D. P. (2001). Fathering from prison: Common struggles and successful solutions. *Psychotherapy, 38*, 88–96.

Mccormack, M. (2012). *The declining significance of homophobia: How teenage boys are redefining masculinity and heterosexuality*. New York: Oxford University Press.

Mcdowell, L. (2002). Masculine discourses and dissonances: Strutting 'lads', protest masculinity and domestic respectability. *Environment and Planning: Society and Space, 20*, 97–119.

Measor, L., Tiffin, C., & Miller, K. (2000). *Young people's views on sex education*. London: Routledge Falmer.

Meek, R. (2007). The parenting possible selves of young fathers in prison. *Psychology, Crime & Law, 13*, 371–382.

Meek, R. (2011). The possible selves of young fathers in prison. *Journal of Adolescence, 34*, 941–949.

Messerschmidt, J. W. (1993). *Masculinities and crime: Critique and reconceptualisation of theory*. Maryland: Rowan and Littlefield Publishers.

Mosher, C. J. (1998). *Discrimination and denial: Systematic racism in Ontario's legal and criminal justice system, 1892–1961*. Toronto: University of Toronto Press.

Nurse, A. (2003). Fatherhood arrested: Parenting from within the juvenile justice system. *Social Forces, 82*, 437–439.

Nurse, A. (2005). The impact of the juvenile prison on fathers. In K. H. Barrett & W. G. George (Eds.), *Race, culture, psychology, and law*. Thousand Oaks: Sage Publications.

Parra-Cardona, J. R., Sharp, E. A., & Wampler, R. S. (2008). 'Changing for my kid': Fatherhood experiences of Mexican-origin teen fathers involved in the justice system. *Journal of Marital & Family Therapy, 34*, 369–387.

Pollack, W. S. (1999). *Real boys: Rescuing our sons from the myths of boyhood*. New York: Henry Holt & Company.

Sabo, D., Kupers, T. A., & London, W. (2001a). Gender and the politics of punishment. In D. Sabo, T. A. Kupers, & W. London (Eds.), *Prison masculinities*. Philadelphia: Temple University Press.

Sabo, D., Kupers, T. A., & London, W. (Eds.). (2001b). *Prison masculinities.* Philadelphia: Temple University Press.

Scottish Prison Service. (2013). *Unlocking potential: Report of the Scottish prison service organisational review.* Edinburgh: Scottish Prison Service.

Sewell, T. (1997). *Black masculinities and schooling: How black boys survive modern schooling.* Stoke-on-Trent: Trentham Books.

Toch, H. (1998). Hypermasculinity and prison violence. In L. H. Bowker (Ed.), *Masculinities and prison violence.* Thousand Oaks: Sage Publications.

Wilkinson, D. L., Magara, A., Garcia, M., & Khurana, A. (2009). Fathering at the margins of society: Reflections from young, minority, crime-involved fathers. *Journal of Family Issues, 30,* 945–967.

Willis, P. (1977). *Learning to labour: How working class kids get working class jobs.* New York: Columbia University Press.

13

Paternity and the Paradigms of Possibility: Comparing Two Fatherhood Programs in American Prisons

Anna Curtis

Traditional gender roles have created a longstanding expectation that men in America should provide financial stability and discipline within their families (Coltrane 1996; Kann 2005). More recently, there is an increasing belief that men should also nurture their children (Coltrane 1996; Kaufman 2013). Balancing these expectations can be challenging, even for men who have not been separated from their children through imprisonment (Coltrane and Adams 2008; Cooper 2000). While in prison, prisoners are largely excluded from both the provider and nurturer role and are often defined—by actors in the criminal justice and the larger public—as "bad" men who have little to offer their children. Furthermore, the structure of prison demands masculine practices that confirm incarcerated men's parental unfitness: namely, the will and capacity to hurt, emotional coldness, and physical isolation from children (Sabo et al. 2001).

A. Curtis (✉)
State University of New York at Cortland (SUNY Cortland), Cortland, NY, USA

Drawing on two-and-a-half years of participant observation of fatherhood programs inside prison—one at a youth facility and one at an adult facility—as well as content analysis of the programs' materials, this chapter considers the challenges of running fatherhood programs for incarcerated fathers. One of the most important findings of this fieldwork was that group facilitators struggled to manage and blend contradictory expectations about masculinity and fatherhood within prison. Part of the struggle reflected participants' varying expectations for fathers and men outside of prison. Group facilitators of the fatherhood programs sought to carve out space for incarcerated men to nurture their children; however, this was mainly done by relying on more traditional understandings of masculinity, such as using self-control to improve co-parenting relationships and offering advice on how to protect children from harm despite the physical separation.

Group facilitators also had to manage the enormous pressure—from prison staff, their employers, and the wider culture—to define the difficulties prisoners face as personal struggles rather than structural failings. This hurdle reflects the large-scale shift toward neoliberal governance, particularly as it relates to the criminal justice system (Garland 2001; Wacquant 2009). The emphasis that prison staff place on personal responsibility over structural inequality has been well documented in women's prisons (e.g. Haney 2010; Hannah-Moffat 2000; McKim 2008) and, to a lesser extent, among young male juvenile offenders (Abrams et al. 2008). This chapter extends that analysis to include fatherhood programs in men's prisons. Before describing the research that I undertook in two American prisons, I first discuss fatherhood and masculinity in America. I then briefly discuss the rise of neoliberal thought and the centrality of individual responsibility in the American legal system.

Perspectives on American Fatherhood

Even outside of prison, the question of what makes a man a good father is rife with anxiety and uncertainty. Historically, the answer, in theory at least, was clear for American men: fathers provided material resources and enacted discipline in the family unit (Coltrane 1996; Kann 2005).

Indeed, the philosophical thought embedded in the social structures that emerged in early America relied on men who were "sociable, industrious family men predisposed to comply with political authority" (Kann 2005, p. 39). Men who refused or were unable to enact masculine familial responsibilities in early America became legitimate targets for incarceration and correction at the hands of the (fatherly) state.

Though this ideal has been disrupted over the last 50 years, due in large part to changing gender norms and shifting economic pressures on the family, no clear set of answers has arisen to take its place. For many men in the United States, parenting is still a "package deal" that reflects the expectation that being a good father means providing financially and marrying the mother of your children (Townsend 2002). When marriages end, many men have significantly less involvement with their children (Juby et al. 2007). Much of the literature, however, has focused on married couples rather than fractured families. Recently, Tach et al. (2010), using data from the Fragile Families survey, examined nonresidential paternal involvement in children's lives when the couple was unmarried at the time of their child's birth. They found that it was a mother's repartnering that had the biggest negative impact on men's continued involvement with their children. However, their data did not allow them to assess whether fathers withdrew or mothers pushed them out in order to "swap daddies" (pp. 200–201).

For poor men outside of prison, parenting programs in the 1990s in America proliferated under the banner of "Responsible Fatherhood" (Curran and Abrams 2000; Roy and Dyson 2010). From a state-level perspective, the goal of "responsible" fatherhood was to increase men's financial involvement in their children's lives and to decrease the burden of welfare on state coffers (Roy 1999). Despite this emphasis on finances, Roy and Dyson (2010) found that both staff and participants in Responsible Fatherhood programs emphasized the value of social connections (especially those that emerged from the program itself) and the ways that caregiving was as important as breadwinning. A number of fatherhood programs in prison also emerged under the banner of "Responsible Fatherhood," though by necessity such programs cannot focus on encouraging incarcerated men to financially support their children (Jeffries et al. 2001).

Despite impermeable walls, prisons are nonetheless a "template or vector of broader social forces, political nexi, and cultural processes that traverse its walls" (Wacquant 2002, p. 386). Ideas flow freely into and out of prisons, carried by correctional officers (COs), staff, social workers, prisoners, visitors, and media outlets (Jewkes 2002). The average prison churns with barely suppressed contestations over identity, security, social value, masculinity, and, in the case of incarcerated fathers, the meanings of paternity.

Incarceration is highly stressful and many romantic and familial relationships dissolve as men serve their sentences (Maldonado 2006; Tewksbury and DeMichele 2005; Waller and Swisher 2006). Some of the erosion of relationships reflect institutional barriers such as expensive phone calls home, the costs of materials for letters, the stigma of receiving letters stamped with prison return addresses, and the distance from home for visitors (Hairston 1998; Hoffman et al. 2010; Tewksbury and DeMichele 2005). The relationships between men and their families prior to incarceration, however, also impact long-term connections. For example, Waller and Swisher (2006) found that risky behaviors (drug, alcohol, or physical abuse) decreased the likelihood that mothers were willing to remain in communication with the incarcerated fathers of their children. Mothers' perception that the prison environment could negatively impact children also decreased the frequency of visits to prison. Finally, multiple incarcerations decreased women's perceptions of men's trustworthiness and impacted incarcerated fathers' ability to remain connected with their children while in prison (Waller and Swisher 2006).

Fatherhood programs in prison offer incarcerated fathers the opportunity to re-imagine more positive possibilities for their futures. Without question, the possibilities of a fatherhood identity are tangled up in promises of rehabilitation and reintegration as a valued member of society (Earle 2012; Meek 2007). Many incarcerated men engage in "jail talk" (Yocum and Nath 2011), or the tendency of incarcerated people to imagine the world outside of prison as better than it really was, is, or will be when they get out. The materials and facilitators of fatherhood programs cannot ignore the rich and fertile ground of the imaginary wonderful world outside, and yet, assuming they are committed to helping men achieve realistic goals, they must also resist the temptation to paint an overly positive picture of the future.

Neoliberal Governance and Individual Responsibility

Though it has existed as a school of economic thought since the 1940s, neoliberalism did not become the dominant ideological regime until the 1970s (Harvey 2005). Neoliberal practices focus on creating a good business environment, often by creating laws that ensure a flexible labor market, state-supported infrastructure such as tax breaks for businesses, easy access by business owners to political power players, and protecting financial institutions at the expensive of individuals. The ripple effect of neoliberal laws, policies, and practices extends beyond the marketplace, including into prison systems. For example, Garland (2001) considers the transition in the United States and the UK to a more punitive, less-rehabilitative system as a response to anxieties about the threat of the expanding underclass in an increasingly neoliberal world.

Despite the commitment of neoliberal policy makers to protecting the institution over the individual, a major tenet of neoliberal theory is the importance of "individual responsibility." Indeed, it is personal responsibility that provides the logic for decreasing governmental interference in the free market. The combination of the "free market" and "individual responsibility" has had a profound impact on social welfare programs (Wacquant 2009), including laws that increasingly link social welfare with the criminal justice system (Gustafson 2009) and laws that criminalize debt (Coco 2012). Over the course of the 1980s and 1990s, as social welfare in the United States was scaled back, programs emphasizing individual men's financial obligations to the family proliferated, and criminal laws expanded and became more punitive.

Macro-level changes connect to create and define micro-level experiences. The ideal neoliberal subject is one who governs him or herself in ways that most effectively serve the state with little direct coercion from state actors or agencies. A deserving citizen under a neoliberal regime is one who does not rely on the state unless absolutely necessary, who is individually responsible for their success or failure, and who ultimately understands and supports the importance of the "free market." Thus, the strategies for dealing with "undeserving" members of society hinge on teaching, demanding, and coercing individual responsibility (Soss et al.

2011). In her analysis of two motherhood programs in women's prisons, Lynne Haney argues that the refusal of the staff to consider the outside social forces that frame poor women's lives accomplished two things. First, focusing on individual responsibility made these programs appealing to public and private actors who controlled funding decisions. Second, "there are very real dangers to bracketing the social from these women's lives—not only does it psychologize their troubles and distort their lives, but it denies them a potential source of alliance" (p. 224). Though male prisoners have very different experiences to female prisoners, the neoliberal ideal of self-governance also impacts on paternal parenting programs.

Methods

In February 2007, I began attending fatherhood groups at two prison facilities—one for adults (over 18) and one for youth offenders (ages 14–21)—in a Northeastern state.[1] The adult facility, North Correctional Institution (NCI), and the youth facility, Southeast Youth Correctional Institution (SY), were both high security (level four out of five). A nonprofit agency, Healthy Connections, ran fatherhood groups and other programs for prisoners and their families throughout the state.[2] I was technically a volunteer for Healthy Connections during my time in both facilities, though I was rarely asked to do much more than observe.

I observed and participated in the fatherhood programs, the special family visits that served as a reward for successful participation in the fatherhood program, and interacted with COs and staff. I conducted roughly 280 hours of participant observation.[3] I introduced myself to participants of the fatherhood group as someone conducting research on fathers in prison, and explained that I was an observer and not an employee of Healthy Connections. I had fewer opportunities to introduce myself as a researcher to COs, but did my best to be open and clear with them about who I was and why I was in the prison facilities. As an observer, I did not run groups or put together materials, lectures, or activities; I limited how much I spoke unless the men in the group indicated that it was important to them that I participate. Usually, this meant I took part in "icebreaker" activities at the start of group and I usually only spoke when someone in the group directly addressed me.

I took notes during the groups, invited men to look through what I had written, and made it clear that I would erase anything they did not want included in my field notes. While my note taking initially elicited suspicion, the men's ability to examine my field notes and to question what I had written provided an opportunity to establish rapport with men outside of the confines of a program facilitator/prisoner relationship. In some groups, my note taking became a source of amusement, with men instructing me to "write that down" whenever someone, especially a group facilitator, said something potentially embarrassing. Attending the meetings of the fatherhood program gave me a chance to observe how different groups of incarcerated fathers interacted with one another, with the group facilitator(s), with me, and, often times, with COs. I took as my guiding principle the importance of "thick description" (Gertz 1973). This approach served as the bedrock for my analysis as I developed analytic memos and coding schemes (Emerson et al. 1995).

Setting

At SY, a thin black man named Jasper ran the program. He had grown up in a small town in the south and had his first child out-of-wedlock when he was 17. Jasper regularly drew on this life experience, particularly negotiating parenting with the mother of his oldest child, in order to connect with the young men in the group. Jasper often referred to the inspirations that he felt had helped him be a good father despite not living with his child. Jasper directly controlled who was allowed into the fatherhood group and had run the program for several years by the time I arrived. One of the directors of the program told me that, "We [Healthy Connections] pay him to be a daddy to fifty guys a year." Jasper took this responsibility seriously and was deeply involved with the young men in his program. He regularly visited the homes of the men's children and arranged one-on-one visits between men, their children, and their children's mothers. It was also common for Jasper to remain in contact with men after they left the program.

At NCI, the group facilitators changed several times over the two-and-a-half years I was there. The fatherhood groups at NCI were run in 12-week cycles and I observed 5 cycles. A woman named Alice ran the first two cycles; Alice had been running the fatherhood programs at NCI for a couple of years when I started my project. One of the managers, Mariana, ran the third cycle along with a new employee, Katelyn. For the fourth cycle, Katelyn ran the program by herself. A woman named Star ran the fifth cycle. I didn't attend the fatherhood cycle where Mariana trained Star. While there were differences between the four women who ran NCI's fatherhood group, they shared many qualities. All were in the process of obtaining, or had already attained, a master's degree in either social work or forensic psychology. Three—Alice, Katelyn, and Star—were in their mid-to-late 20s, while Mariana was in her late-50s. Both Alice and Star talked about their identity as black women during the fatherhood groups. Mariana had an accent that indicated she was from a Spanish-speaking country and referenced moving to the United States when she was younger. Katelyn stated that part of her ethnic heritage was West Indian. Mariana was the only one of the four who had children.

I also observed men interacting with their children in the "special visits" that served as a reward for successful participation in the fatherhood programs. These visits were between an hour and two hours long, and men were allowed an unusually high amount of physical contact with their children. In normal visits, prisoners and visitors were allowed to hug briefly at the start of the visit, but then were expected to stay on opposite sides of a table with no physical contact. During the special visits, men could hold their children throughout, sit next to them, hug them at will, and play games that were unavailable during normal visits.

The promise of these visits was the principal reason prisoners reported they sought out the fatherhood programs. However, gaining access to the program was quite difficult. At SY, the most common way young men joined was through a recommendation from someone already in the group. Jasper then requested the man's file from the prison administrators and conducted a one- to two-hour interview. Only the fathers who convinced Jasper they were serious about being connected to their children were allowed into the program. At NCI, the group facilitators had no control over who was allowed into the program. Instead, prisoners

13 Paternity and the Paradigms of Possibility: Comparing Two...

submitted an application to the volunteer coordinator, who undertook a fairly extensive background check. Only men who had no record of misbehavior in the past year (in the form of tickets issued by COs), had received visits from their children in the past year, and who had no history of harming children were allowed onto the waiting list. In theory, men were then allowed into the program in the order in which they applied. Some men, however, were convinced that the volunteer coordinator bumped prisoners he liked up the list.

Table 13.1 summarizes key differences between the programs a SY and NCI. I collected all the handouts group facilitators passed around during group sessions. At SY, Jasper used 17 different handouts between 2007 and 2009 (though one appeared multiple times); these tended to emphasize Jasper's interests in teaching young fathers to become accountable "men of honor." The group facilitators at NCI relied much more heavily on written material and 93 handouts were passed out during my time in the field. Seventeen percent of these (n = 16) appeared in three or more different cycles. The materials at NCI emphasized improving communication (with children and co-parents) and strategies for parenting in prison. I conducted a content analysis of these materials to develop a base understanding of how these groups constructed masculinity and

Table 13.1 Differences between fatherhood groups

	Southeast youth correctional institution (SY)	North correctional institution (NCI)
Time to release for fathers	Majority of men had <5 years left on sentence	Majority of men had 10+ years left on sentence
Group facilitator	Same throughout, older black man who grew up in the south	Four different women, aged between the mid-20s and late 50s, black or Hispanic
Structure of group	Ongoing	12-week cycles
Materials used in group	Whatever struck the group facilitator as relevant	Mostly drawn from the same four or five sources
Orientation recommended towards mothers of children	How to repair or maintain relationship	How to treat co-parent with respect so she'll keep bringing children to visit
Theoretical orientation	Religious/Christian	Social work/psychological
Fatherhood model	Man of honor	Co-parent

fatherhood. I then used these ideas to explore how the facilitators presented the connections between masculinity and fatherhood, as well as how these understandings influenced what the group sought to teach incarcerated fathers they could (and could not) expect from their relationships with their children.

Findings

Though the same social work agency ran the programs at SY and NCI, the messaging regarding fatherhood and masculinity was quite different. At the youth facility, Jasper was in charge the whole time and firmly believed that good men made good fathers. As such, his discussions and program materials focused on helping the young men at SY become "better" and more responsible men. At the adult facility, as the group facilitators changed, the program materials provided the most consistency in messaging from cycle to cycle. Here, the program materials and group facilitators focused on improving communication with children and coparents, usually by emphasizing personal responsibility. In their own ways, the materials and facilitators of both programs resisted the wider cultural assumption that incarcerated men have little to offer their children. As a result, many participants spoke highly of the program. At the same time, both programs ignored the structural barriers created by incarceration and reinforced neoliberal beliefs that individuals are entirely responsible for the conditions of their lives.

SY: Being a Man of Honor

Most of the program participants at SY were 18 or 19 and the majority were due to return home within 5 years. Their children were also young (under five years) and in a few cases, still in the womb. A handful of these young fathers were still involved with their children's mothers, though these relationships were tumultuous and their status varied from week-to-week. Nearly all of the young men believed that they could have real, meaningful relationships with their children. With this in mind, Jasper focused on talking with the young men about the challenges of repairing and maintaining relationships with co-parents.

Of the 17 handouts which Jasper gave the young men in the fatherhood group, six focused on: establishing paternity; strategies for developing nurturing relationships with children, fathers, male friends, and mentors; and having a successful visit with children while incarcerated. The remaining handouts focused on how to become an accountable and responsible man of honor; one handout appeared three times (roughly every six months) and captured an important aspect of Jasper's understanding of masculinity and fatherhood:

> A man is created for challenges. He is equipped to overcome, to run the gauntlet, to stand firm as a well-anchored post. Men are the benchmark in life, society, and family. It is part of the masculine responsibility to demonstrate strength and responsibility, to protect and provide for those within their sphere of influence. This is the hallmark of manhood. (Gillham 1999)

The author of this quote wrote several books aimed at teaching men to be men according to Christian principles. For Jasper, Gillham's message resonated with his own expectation that men are the corner stone of the family and that compassion and service are the hallmarks of good leadership.

My observations from one fatherhood group illustrate how Jasper raised the notion of being a "man of honor." In this group, Jasper brought up the way fathers are portrayed on television, a topic he returned to several times over the course of my fieldwork. Jasper disliked the portrayal of television fathers as bumbling and helpless. Jasper pointed out that outside of the home, television fathers are often more competent and that TV shows make it seem as if "the measure of man comes from his job." Jasper asked the young men whether or not they thought that was true. After some uncomfortable shifting, Tarif said, "what kind of car a man has matters." After a short pause, he added, "how many bitches he got." At 19, Tarif was the oldest father in the group and self-identified as both Latino and black. By his own account, he struggled with attention deficit disorder, drug addiction, and violent tendencies. Sometimes, Tarif talked about these issues as problems he had to conquer, while at other times he seemed proud of being wild and strong. Tarif had a conflicted relationship with Jasper; while Tarif wanted Jasper to help and approve of him, he also questioned everything Jasper said.

Tarif's comment about "bitches" made several guys laugh. Jasper rolled his eyes and Tarif shrugged and smiled. Chris jumped into the conversation. At 18, Chris was another dominant personality in the group and Tarif's opposite in almost every way. Boisterous and charming, Chris exhibited no doubts about his ultimate success as a father and dismissed the illegal and sometimes violent things he had done as "just part of the [drug] game." When Chris said, "I always thought it was how much money you had," Jasper nodded gravely and looked around the group and asked what they thought. He motioned at Chris. "How many of you have experienced that?" Some of the young men looked away and others nodded. Tarif, with a glare aimed at Jasper, said, "women want that [money]." With a short, angry slash of his hand, he added, "this is real life. This ain't no fairy tale." It was unclear whether Tarif was angry about women wanting money, that he struggled to provide it to his daughter's mother, or that it was childish to pretend that money wasn't important.

Jasper ignored Tarif and began to talk about how many people got hung up on the job, on the money, instead of what was important. "An attitude of serving is a good thing to have… A good servant is hard to replace… I'm not saying… being a servant is not the same thing as being a slave. They'll replace managers, CEO's, you'll be gone in a second, but someone with an attitude of serving, they're hard to find." Tarif interrupted Jasper with a frown, "I'm not a servant." Several young men in the group nodded in agreement. Speaking over Jasper, Tarif added, "If I'm getting paid, that's different." Jasper finally looked at Tarif and frowned as he scolded for Tarif for thinking it was only about money. Sweeping his gaze around the room, Jasper continued, "If you want to do well with your children, you need to be a man of honor… address injustices when you see them. You could end up inspiring your children's friends as well. You could be coaching them and serving as an example for more than [just] your children."

The young men in the group immediately assumed that Jasper was telling them to jump in when they see violence. Speaking over one another, most threw out a reference to a potentially violent situation: someone with a gun, bullies in the school yard, an argument at a sporting event, someone drunk and yelling. Almost as soon as they finished listing off potential threatening situations, a chorus of young male voices asked Jasper what he would do. Jasper's gaze dropped to the floor in front of him as he shifted uncomfortably in his seat. "It would depend on the situation," he started. Disappointed groans interrupted the rest of his answer and for a moment, Jasper looked uncertain.

Jasper was silent long enough that I felt like I could jump in and not derail his instruction. Into the murmurs of the young men discussing how they would handle this or that kind of fight, I said, "Injustices don't have to just be violent. What happens if your child's teacher is calling them stupid? Do you believe your child? What do you do?" Most of the young men frowned and muttered; they appeared not to like this example. Tarif, still looking at Jasper, said, "Hit the teacher with a golf club!" Again, even though Tarif used a serious tone of voice, several of the young men laughed while Jasper shook his head in disapproval. Chris, nodding at Tarif, added, "You can't know how you're going to respond to a situation until you're in it. If you're going to lose your temper or hit someone, you never know." It was my turn to roll my eyes as I said, "That's not true. People control their tempers all the time." At this, Tarif looked at me for a moment with a considering look in his face. I added, looking at Chris, "And for future reference, don't hit your children's teachers." This made several of the young men grin and snicker.

Jasper brought the conversation back to the importance of being a good man so you can be a good father. The emphasis on being a man with "an attitude of serving" who prioritizes not just his own children, but also the children of his community assumed that men are capable of a particular kind of nurturing behavior, one that requires sacrificing your own needs for the needs of others, of providing consistency in the face of adversity, and was not about the size on one's paycheck. Jasper was not proselytizing or looking to convert the young men in his program. Instead, he was using the tools that had helped him, decades before, achieve a life that he was happy with. He believed that every young man in his program could be a good father, if they were willing to make the necessary sacrifices. The young men in the program at SY liked this about Jasper and during their interviews, spoke positively about Jasper.

At the same time, many of the young men primarily worried about their ability to financially provide for their children. Very little of Jasper's discussion on how to be a man of honor addressed the negative impact incarceration would have on future employment, and while Jasper had indeed overcome significant challenges in his life, incarceration was not one of them. His job, for example, would be unavailable to the young men in the group since having a prison record makes it next to impossible to gain access to prison facilities. Nor did Jasper's advice address the low likelihood that the young men in the program would marry or remain involved with the mothers of their children. Indeed, Jasper dismissed this challenge as an excuse. While there was some truth to this, it is very difficult to be the leader of a family unit that does not exist or to demonstrate responsibility and accountability to children you rarely see.

NCI: Communicating with Co-parents and Children

It is more difficult to provide a singular analysis of the materials and program at NCI because of the changes in facilitators. Instead, I focus on the materials that were handed out across all five cycles and the different emphasis the various group facilitators placed on certain handouts. When compared with the fatherhood program at the youth facility, all of the NCI group facilitators spent more time discussing strategies for communication and less time focused on how participants could become "better" men.

Of the 93 different handouts provided over five different cycles of the program, some were provided to more than one cycle. Each cycle received an average of 33 handouts. Forty-four of the handouts focused on improving communication with children or co-parents, seven addressed violent or negative relationships with co-parents, and 16 addressed how to improve overall parenting skills, primarily by emphasizing the importance of flexible parenting styles and providing logical consequences for misbehavior. The emphasis on communication was one of the strengths of the NCI fatherhood program. At the same time, the focus on the ways men could change to improve their communication with co-parents and children often meant the facilitators downplayed the structural limitations of incarceration.

Star ran the last cycle I observed. When she introduced herself and the agency to the group, she stated, "We'll be spending a lot of time talking about communication, connecting with their families, and being a father… not what it means to be a man because you know how to do that, but how to be a father inside." She noted that men have a lot of different experiences with family: "Some families are like, deal with your time and others say, we'll be there for you. Some families will bring your children and others won't. We [the agency] help you deal with both ends." The handouts that group facilitators provided coincided with this promise. Only one handout—which four of the five cycles received—directly addressed questions of masculinity and femininity. And even this was primarily focused on getting incarcerated fathers to think about the messages their parents taught them about a variety of topics (including how men and women should behave) and whether they wanted to pass those messages along to their children.

This is not to say that the facilitators and participants did not discuss masculinity, femininity, and gender roles. Indeed, much of the discussion of the responsibilities and obligations of fathers hinged on their understanding of masculinity. However, unlike at SY, discussions of masculinity were rarely addressed explicitly. As men at the adult facility discussed their worries and concerns about their children, their implicit understandings of appropriate masculinity emerged. Similarly, the facilitators' assumptions and beliefs about masculinity in general, and incarcerated men's masculinity in particular, emerged between the lines as they prompted men to consider their roles as fathers.

Three handouts were passed around in all five cycles: a handout about the responsibilities of inmate parents to their children, an outline of the strengths and weaknesses of three different parenting styles (lenient, rigid, and flexible), and a visual image of a wheel that was used to discuss violent and abusive relationships.[4] The handout on parental responsibilities was often the most positively received and outlined specific strategies for remaining connected to your children while incarcerated. It included eight recommendations, most of which involved encouraging incarcerated fathers to think about what the experience of having a parent in prison was like and adapting their behavior accordingly. For example, Alice, the facilitator for the first two cycles, argued persuasively that it was important for children to have a realistic idea about what prison was like. Referencing her experience of having a brother incarcerated when she was younger, Alice said she was "terrified" of prison, both for her brother and as a place to visit. Her brother's willingness to tell her the truth helped her to adjust her expectations. Throughout the cycles she ran, Alice emphasized that clear, consistent communication from prison was an important way that men could nurture their children, and her ability to draw on her own life experiences as evidence appeared persuasive to the men in the group.

This handout advised against making specific plans for the future. As Alice said, "Don't feed yourself pipedreams. Don't feed them to your kids. Don't say specific things like, 'We'll go to Disneyland,' when you don't know… Be real with yourself. Just 'cause you want a job, doesn't mean a list of jobs you want appears." Here, Alice was addressing the problems that "jail talk" can cause when prisoners return home and find it difficult to keep the sometimes grandiose promises they made to family while incarcerated. Though they took slightly different approaches, all the NCI facilitators emphasized that it was possible to nurture your children from prison and that it was incredibly important for children. This was part of the logic for spending so much time focused on communication; having a positive or functioning relationship with co-parents would ensure access to children and consistent communication with children would show them that their father still loved them.

However, even this practical handout ran into the challenge of providing advice for problems that were often structural. In several handouts, including the one discussed above, the program material suggested that men do their best to prepare their families for the procedures and challenges of visiting the prison. Some of this was useful, including advising men to have topics to discuss and encouraging men to consider how stressful the visit might be for family members. Rather than getting angry if kids are cranky and could not sit still, Alice advised the men in one group to ask themselves: "Did they come straight from school? Are they hungry? Is there another day that might work better? Think about the context." Yet, the hardest part of visiting prison lay with navigating the bureaucracy, which prisoners could do little to help family members manage. The prison facility could be closed with little or no warning

13 Paternity and the Paradigms of Possibility: Comparing Two...

(meaning families expend effort to visit and are turned away), paperwork could get lost or misfiled (meaning family members could be turned away on arrival), and COs could refuse visitors' entry for a variety of reasons or refuse to allow a prisoner out of his cell when he was called up for a visit. There is little that a prisoner can do to address these issues, other than ask their family to be patient and come back again despite the challenges of visiting.

However, Alice regularly acknowledged the challenges of navigating the prison bureaucracy. She referenced her own challenges as a child and young woman visiting her brother and she did not hide her frustrations about the ways the inconsistency of prison rules made her job more difficult. Alice left for another job after the second cycle. On the last meeting of the group, the volunteer coordinator, Baxter, caught Alice in the hallway to let her know that the special visit for cycle two would be delayed and combined with the next cycle. Baxter was apologetic but stated that they needed enough people in the special visit to justify shutting down the facility for other prisoners' visits. He was referring to the previous cycle's special visit when only five families were able to come. After group was over, Alice complained all the way from the front door to her car. "I love this program! This is the best. I look forward to this! This is what I'm going to miss the most [at my new job]. I've been running this program for years. And this is how they're going to end it? This is my last memory?" When I suggested that she should consider providing the prison administration with data to support her claim that the visit with five fathers was anomalous, she rolled her eyes and shook her head. "Why should I have to justify my existence? This program?" In the end, Alice did not attend the combined special visit for Cycles 2 and 3; by this time, only two men from Cycle 2 were still in the facility and therefore received their visit.

The two facilitators who followed Alice appeared less sympathetic to the problems that the unpredictability of prison rules could cause, particularly for prisoners. They both spent much less class time on the handout that focused on the responsibilities of inmate parents. In Cycles 3 and 4, the group facilitators, Katelyn and Mariana, discussed the handout for about 20 minutes. In the last cycle, Star simply handed the sheet out and suggested the men read it. Katelyn, Mariana, and Star all spent much more time on the handout that discussed parenting styles (see Table 13.2), which was also handed out to participants in all five cycles. Katelyn spent an entire class focused on this handout in both the cycles she oversaw, and Star devoted two group meetings to it. In comparison, Alice spent half of a group meeting discussing parent styles, pairing this handout with another that focused on things parents should never say to their children. Alice's main focus in that group meeting was the consequences of treating children as if they have no feelings.

There was a clear message within the parenting handout that a flexible parenting style was the best (see Table 13.2). However, there was almost no discussion of the time and energy that flexible parenting requires. Even parents on the outside might not have the ability to be a flexible parent all the time and incarcerated parents often struggle even more, yet both Katelyn and Star wanted to apply this parenting strategy to family visits. Given that visits in the facility were no longer than an hour and that most families could not visit every week, it is difficult to imagine how an incarcerated father could engage in any kind of parenting style beyond not getting in his co-parent's way as she tried to keep their child behaving during the visit. When Alice discussed the parenting styles, she first focused on the men's experiences with their own parents (asking them to identify what kind of household they grew up in) and then dis-

Table 13.2 An overview of parenting styles mentioned in NCI handouts

Rigid style	Lenient	Flexible
Uses strict rules to control child behavior	Provides no structure or boundaries	Allows choices within age-appropriate boundaries
Rewards and punishes	Children are allowed to do what they want	Provides consistent and clear consequences
Practices "double standards" (i.e. do as I say, not as I do)	Passive response to children's behavior	Encourages accountability for actions (for both children and adults)
Children learn to please others, rather than themselves	Children don't develop the ability to delay gratification and have difficulty following through on tasks	Children learn to be independent, solve problems, and delay gratification

cussed approaches to the communication that men had with their children and co-parents outside of the visits: writing letters and phone calls. Her goal was to encourage the men to think about how they could improve on their own parents' approaches to parenting, stating, "Just because of the mistake that landed you here, doesn't mean your kids are headed down the same path." This message resonated with many of the men in the cycles she facilitated.

In the fifth cycle, during the second day, Star and the group member discussed parenting styles, one man interrupted Star to ask, "What if you [are] not in a position to be lenient? To be any kind of parenting style? I'm in here and I can't do much." Although a reasonable question, Star remained committed to the flexible parenting style, replying, "It's limited in here, but that doesn't mean that you can't do anything. It's harder if the co-parent isn't working with you, but you still have to do the best you can." Though the basic sentiment, do the best you can, was a good one, Star and Katelyn spent less time discussing strategies than Alice. Star finished that day's discussion of the material by handing out a quote from a spiritual teacher and new age author:

> The secret of making something work in your lives is, first of all, the deep desire to make it work: then the faith and belief that it can work: then to hold that clear definite vision in your consciousness and see it working out step by step, without one thought of doubt or disbelief. (Caddy 1976)

The men in the group nodded thoughtfully after she read this out and a couple indicated that they liked the quote. Immediately thereafter, Star told the men that their special visit would be delayed four to six months as the prison administration now intended to do two special visits a year: one in the fall and one in spring.

The disjuncture between the messages of that group meeting was stark. Throughout the meeting, Star emphasized doing "the best you can" and the importance of "desire" in achieving your goals and then presented an insurmountable institutional barrier. In the end, the men attending Cycle 5 did receive their special visit soon after the end of their program. But the timing had nothing to do with their desires to achieve a goal or any of the agitation on the part of the men in the group. Instead, Healthy

Connections' funding situation changed. The state government's priorities shifted from providing fatherhood programs in prison generally to providing mentoring programs for incarcerated children and expanding re-entry programs for parents about to return to their communities. As a result, the fatherhood program at NCI came to an abrupt end and, because there would be no further groups, the social work agency staff and prison administrators decided that the special visit should be scheduled as soon as possible.

Paradigms of Possibility

Running a fatherhood program in prison is challenging for many reasons. Group facilitators must negotiate what it means—to themselves, the prison staff, and the prisoners—to be a man and a father. These expectations reflect the tensions in the wider culture about men's family roles. Should fathers nurture? If so, how does a man nurture without undermining his masculinity? Is it possible for men to do right by their co-parents and children if they cannot provide financially? What if men cannot provide or nurture because they are restrained from doing so? The answers to these questions make some fathering strategies appear more logical than others and shape not only how group facilitators run prison-based fatherhood groups, but also how prisoners perceive these programs.

For most men in prison, financially providing for their families is impossible. This is part of the reason that all of the group facilitators placed a heavy emphasis on consistent and respectful communication with co-parents and children. This messaging, however, resonated more with older than the younger fathers. The fathers at the adult prison, especially those serving long sentences, had mostly accepted that they could not be financial providers and had instead turned their attention to creating or maintaining emotional ties with their children. As a result, the programming that emphasized successfully communicating with family on the outside fulfilled an important need.

For the younger fathers, the belief that they needed to be good providers was still central to their hopes of being good fathers. Their experiences pre-incarceration, however, meant they were well aware that they might be unable to meet their co-parent's financial expectations through legal means. Jasper's emphasis on becoming "men of honor" did not really address the anxiety these young men experienced regarding their future employment prospects and related anxieties in fulfilling the breadwinner role. Instead, Jasper offered unwavering support, alongside a clear and consistent belief that the young men in his program could be good men and fathers. It was this belief that seemed to have the most value to the young men he interacted with. The success of his program mostly hinged on his personality, commitment, and willingness to take on a fathering role, rather than the materials he provided at group meetings.

Concluding Comments

The United States incarcerates more people than any other country in the world; furthermore, mass incarceration primarily occurred because of a punitive shift in laws and enforcement practices (Alexander 2010) rather than a significant increase in offending. Despite this context, the pervasive impact of neoliberalism means that all incarcerated persons are regarded, first and foremost, as failed citizens. It is therefore no surprise, from a self-governance perspective, that they are also failed men (or women) and failed fathers (or mothers). Understanding how social work agencies, prison staff, and incarcerated fathers think about familial connections has important implications for parenting programs, especially because family connections are important components of successful reintegration after incarceration ends (Visher and Travis 2003).

The facilitators in both fatherhood programs discussed here struggled to balance the unwieldy combination of providing fatherhood programs in prison—an inflexible, highly bureaucratic, and restrictive setting—with the neoliberal emphasis on personal responsibility. Research on programming in women's prisons and juvenile facilities (Haney 2010; Hannah-Moffat 2000; Abrams et al. 2008; McKim 2008) suggests this is a widespread challenge. The neoliberal discourse serves to make invisible very real structural barriers that prisoners face in seeking to improve their relationships with their children.

Notes

1. The names and location of the prison facilities and the agency that ran the fatherhood facilities have been changed (or left out) to protect confidentiality. All of the names (staff, volunteers, and prisoners) have been changed to protect anonymity. The prisoners chose their pseudonyms and I chose the pseudonyms for the staff and COs.
2. Healthy Connections was primarily funded by the state government. However, they also applied for grants from both the federal government and private organizations as well as accepting private donations.
3. I used NVivo software to analyze the first six months of my field notes and to develop the first set of key terms for coding. I then coded the remainder of my field notes and interviews by hand.
4. There isn't enough space in this chapter to discuss the third handout. The discussion around violence in relationships did reveal interesting assumptions about masculinity and femininity, but was much less focused on parenting from prison.

References

Abrams, L., Anderson-Nathe, B., & Aguilar, J. (2008). Constructing masculinities in juvenile corrections. *Men and Masculinities, 11*(1), 22–41.

Alexander, M. (2010). *The new Jim crow: Mass incarceration in the age of colorblindness*. New York: New Press. Distributed by Perseus Distribution.

Caddy, E. (1976). *Footprints on the path*. Scotland: Findhorn Press.

Coco, L. (2012). Debtor's prison in the neoliberal state: "Debtfare" and the cultural logics of the bankruptcy abuse and prevention and consumer protection act of 2005. *California Western Law Review, 49*(1), 1–49.

Coltrane, S. (1996). *Family man: Fatherhood, housework, and gender equality*. Oxford: Oxford University Press.

Coltrane, S., & Adams, M. (2008). *Gender and families: 2nd edition*. Maryland: Rowman and Littlefield Publishers.

Cooper, M. (2000). Being the "go-to guy": Fatherhood, masculinity, and the organization of work in Silicon Valley. *Qualitative Sociology, 23*(4), 379–405.

Curran, L., & Abrams, L. (2000). Making men into dads: Fatherhood, the state, and welfare. *Gender & Society, 14*(5), 662–678.

Earle, R. (2012). Who's the daddy? 'Ideas about fathers from a young Men's prison'. *The Howard Journal of Criminal Justice, 51*(4), 387–399.

Emerson, R., Fretz, R., & Shaw, L. (1995). *Writing ethnographic field notes*. Chicago: The University of Chicago Press.

Garland, D. (2001). *The culture of control: Crime and social order in contemporary society*. Chicago: The University of Chicago Press.

Gertz, C. (1973). *The interpretation of culture*. New York: Basic Books.

Gillham, P. (1999). *Things only men know: What matters most in the life of a man*. Eugene: Harvest House.

Gustafson, K. (2009). Criminal law: The criminalization of poverty. *Journal of Criminal Law & Criminology, 99*(3), 643–716.

Hairston, C. F. (1998). The forgotten parent: Understanding the forces that influence incarcerated fathers' relationships with their children. *Child Welfare, 77*(5), 617–640.

Haney, L. (2010). *Offending women: Power, punishment, and the regulation of desire*. Berkeley: University of California Press.

Hannah-Moffat, K. (2000). Prisons that empower: Neo-liberal governance in Canadian women's prisons. *British Journal of Criminology, 40*, 510–531.

Harvey, D. (2005). *A brief history of neoliberalism*. Oxford: Oxford University Press.

Hoffman, H., Byrd, A., & Kightlinger, A. (2010). Prison programs and services for incarcerated parents and their underage children: Results from a national survey of correctional facilities. *The Prison Journal, 90*(4), 397–416.

Jeffries, J., Menghraj, S., & Hairston, C. F. (2001). *Serving incarcerated and ex-offender fathers and their families: A review of the field*. New York: Vera Institute of Justice.

Jewkes, Y. (2002). The use of media in constructing identities in the masculine environment of men's prisons. *European Journal of Communication, 17*(2), 205–225.

Juby, H., Billette, J. M., Laplante, B., & Le Bourdais, C. (2007). Nonresident fathers and children: Parents' new unions and frequency of contact. *Journal of Family Issues, 28*, 1220–1245.

Kann, M. (2005). *Punishment, prisons, and patriarchy: Liberty and power in the early American republic*. New York: New York University Press.

Kaufman, G. (2013). *Superdads: How fathers balance work and family in the 21st century*. New York: New York University Press.

Maldonado, S. (2006). Recidivism and paternal engagement. *Family Law Quarterly, 40*(2), 191–211.

McKim, A. (2008). "Getting gut-level": Punishment, gender, and therapeutic governance. *Gender & Society, 22*(3), 303–323.

Meek, R. (2007). The parenting possible selves of young fathers in prison. *Psychology, Crime and Law, 13*(4), 371–382.

Roy, K. (1999). Low-income fathers in an African–American community and the requirements of welfare reform. *Journal of Family Issues, 20*(4), 432–457.

Roy, K., & Dyson, O. (2010). Making daddies into fathers: Community-based fatherhood programs and the construction of masculinities for low-income African-American men. *American Journal of Community Psychology, 45*, 139–154.

Sabo, D., Kupers, T. A., & London, W. J. (2001). *Prison masculinities*. Philadelphia: Temple University Press.

Soss, J., Fording, R., & Schram, S. (2011). *Disciplining the poor: Neoliberal paternalism and the persistent power of race*. Chicago: The University of Chicago Press.

Tach, L., Mincy, R., & Edin, K. (2010). Parenting as a 'package deal': Relationships, fertility, and nonresident father involvement among unmarried parents. *Demography, 47*(1), 181–204.

Tewksbury, R., & DeMichele, M. (2005). Going to prison: A prison visitation program. *The Prison Journal, 85*(3), 292–310.

Townsend, N. W. (2002). *The package deal: Marriage, work, and fatherhood in men's lives*. Philadelphia: Temple University Press.

Visher, C., & Travis, J. (2003). Transitions from prison to community: Understanding individual pathways. *Annual Review of Sociology, 29*, 89–113.

Wacquant, L. (2002). The curious eclipse of prison ethnography in the age of mass incarceration. *Ethnography, 3*(4), 371–397.

Wacquant, L. (2009). *Punishing the poor: The neoliberal government of social insecurity*. Durham: Duke University Press.

Waller, M., & Swisher, R. (2006). Fathers' risk factors in fragile families: Implications for "healthy" relationships and father involvement. *Social Problems, 53*(3), 392–420.

Yocum, A., & Nath, S. (2011). Anticipating father reentry: A qualitative study of Children's and mothers' experiences. *Journal of Offender Rehabilitation, 50*, 286–304.

Index[1]

Aboriginal and Torres Strait Islander (AATSI), 224, 225
  female prisoners, 225
Active learning techniques, 137
African heritage, 148
Agency, 78–80, 84
Alienative modes, 96, 116
All-Party Parliamentary Group for Boxing, 200
American Dream, 27, 29, 170, 171
American fatherhood, 308–310
American masculinity, 49
Anderson, E., 7, 38, 81, 84, 217, 279
Armoured bodies in HMYOI Rochester, 51
Ashfield prison, 199

Attention Deficit Hyperactivity Disorder, 288
Australia, imprisonment in, 224–225
Australian prison
  "crims" and "screws", 229–231
  identity work, 228
  inhabiting prison, 225–226
  masculinities, 231–234
  performing masculinity, 226–228
  population of, 225
  violence talk as identity work, 236
  violence, difference and politics of identity, 234–236
Australian Prisons Project (APP), 224, 225
Australian Research Council, 224
Autoethnographic approach, 8, 45

---

[1] Note: Page numbers followed by "n" refer to notes.

Index

B
Bandyopadhyay, M., 20, 68, 199, 203, 205
Baraka, A., 171
Barnardo's Scotland, 282, 289–291
 analysis of, 287–288
 background and data collection, 284–286
 facilitators, 288–289
 incarcerated fathers, 283
 parenting classroom, 291–300
 parenting programme, 282
 participants, 288
 visit room, 301
Beckett, S., 59
Behan, B., 47
Behavioural change, 283, 301
Beier, A.L., 50
"Being a Young Dad Parenting Programme", 282
Black criminology, 170
Black hyper-masculinities, 146
 representation and portrayal of, 172
Black masculinities, 11, 154, 161, 170, 172
 complexities of, 171
 as extension of US criminal justice policy, 171
 framework model of, 172–182
 Ibrahim's story case study, 182
 liminality, 178
 on road, 178
 racialised/spiritual conversion, 180–181
 reincorporation, 181
 representation of, 171
 socialisation, 177–178
 study of, 173–174

Black men, 153
 in prisons, 145–147, 157–162
Black-led Christian organisation, 147
Bodies, 65–69, 72, 75–77, 80, 81, 83, 85
Bodywork, 66, 76, 80–85
 within prison, 76–83
Bordo, S., 52
Borstal Boy, 45–49
Borstal Institution, 49
Borstal training regime, 52
Bosworth, M., 20
Bowker, L., 248
Bowling, B., 170
Boxing, 199
Boy code, 279
 policing, 272
Boyle, J., 53, 126
Broader framework of idealized masculinity, 94
Broader masculinities literature, 22
Brown, G., 10
Brown, M., 225, 229
Brownmiller, S., 139
Bullying, 231, 232, 235
 culture, 232
 session, 302
Bushbay, S., 182

C
Carceral, K. C., 280
Caribbean heritage, 148
Carrabine, E., 20
Carrington, 165
Cash, J., 44, 49

Charitable organisations, 137
Chatter Matters' game, 298
Chesney-Lind, M., 94
Clark, K., 171
Classroom climate, 292, 301
Clemmer, D., 95, 230
Clennon, O. D., 165
Cobbs, P., 171
Code of the streets, 178
Cohen, C., 126, 127
Cohen, S., 94, 96
Colonialism, 170
Combat sports, 199
Communist Party, 57
Community liabilities, 190
Competitive sports, 210
Con and screw, prison regime, 104–106
Condry, R., 56
Connell, R. W., 5–7, 53, 67, 92–94, 172, 202, 203, 205, 210
Consumer masculinity, 131
Contemporary masculinities, 7, 21, 22
 research, 22
Content analysis, 308, 315
Convict criminology, 43, 56, 58
Correll, S.J., 93
Corston Report for men, 125
Corston, B., 124, 125
Crenshaw, K., 174
Crewe, B., 20, 280
Crime, in Portland YOI, 212
Criminal Justice Act 2013, 211
Criminal justice settings, 96
Criminal justice system (CJS), 2, 11, 117, 124, 132, 136, 166, 170–173, 182, 189, 191, 210, 212, 217, 224, 308
Criminal masculinity, 236
Criminal violence, 234
 perpetrators of, 239
Criminal youth, 288
 stereotypes of, 279
Criminality
 of young offenders, 198
 social capital and engagement in, 171
Criminology, 172
 discipline of, 173
Crisis masculinities, 48
Critical race criminology (CRC), 170
Cross, W. E., 180
C training prisons, 118n1
Cultures of masculinity, 96, 278
Curtis, A., 13, 227, 231, 238, 239, 280, 287

Damascus Road Second Chance Programme (DRSCP), 145–148, 150, 153, 154, 157, 158, 161, 163, 165
Danaher, G., 249
Dangerous masculinity, 238
De Boise, S., 7
De Visser, R., 303
Derrida, J., 57
Desistance, 169, 181, 182
 framework model of, 172
 Ibrahim's story case study, 182
 liminality, 178–180
 on road, 178

Desistance (*cont.*)
  racialised/spiritual conversion, 180
  reincorporation, 181
  socialisation, 177
  study of, 173
de Viggiani, N., 9
Discipline and Punish, 68
Divide and rule, prison regime, 101–103
Dominant masculinity, 93, 211, 233, 236, 239, 250, 260
  nature of, 250
Double-consciousness, 170
Du Bois, W. E. B., 170
Duke of Edinburgh Award, 212, 218n4

Edwards, S., 248
Elliott, K.W., 96
Embodied masculinities, 65–70, 82–85
Embodied prison masculinities, 68–70
Embodiment within prisons, 75
Emergent masculinities, 65
Emotional vulnerability, 36, 151
  of prisoners, 201
Empowerment, in prison, 218n2
  body as social capital, 201–202
  gyms and empowerment, 203–204
  negotiating risk, 202–203
Engels, F., 58
English public school system, 47

Entrenched culture, 233
Entrepreneur masculinity type, 27
Entrepreneurs, 26–30
  in prison settings, 30
Ethnic minorities, 10, 123, 124
Ethnographic momentum, 46
Ethnography, 287
European masculinities, 50
Evans, T., 12, 69, 259–268
Exercise, 205–207, 214, 215, 218

Fader, J., 177
Faith, 169, 188
Faith-based activities, 180
Faith-based conversion, 183
Faith-based prison intervention (FBPI), 10, 145, 154
  participation in, 148
Fanon, F., 170
Fatherhood groups, 317
  differences between, 315
  masculinity and, 316, 317
  at NCI, 314
Fatherhood programs, 308, 314, 320
  facilitators in, 327
  group facilitators of, 308
  in prison, 309, 310
  at NCI, 326
  paradigms of possibility, 326–327
  strengths of, 320
Fathers
  father–son relationship, 256–258
  hegemonic masculinity in prison, 251
  in prison, 281

Father–son relationship, 256, 270–272
  high gap men, 268
  intermediate gap men, 269
  low gap men, 270
Feminine, 6, 21, 23, 54, 205
Feminine rehabilitative identities, 54
Femininity, 18, 132, 197, 235, 236, 249, 251, 273, 321
Feminism, 124, 126, 127, 138
  and masculinity, 211
  exploration of, 198
Feminist agenda, 126–130
Feminist criminological scholars, 129
Fenstermaker, S., 93
Figurative castration, 95
Fit for LIFE programme, 71, 72, 83
Fit for Release research project, 213
Flavin, J., 127
Flexible labor market, 311
Flexible parenting style, 324
Football Fans in Training (FFIT), 70
Foucault, M., 68, 94, 97, 115, 198, 226, 259
Fragile Families survey, 309
Frazier, E., 170
Free Association Narrative Interview model, 256
Free market, 311
Free-market capitalism in Britain, 21
Friendship, 33–37, 50, 96
Frosh, S., 248, 279

Gadd, D., 66
Garde, J., 249, 251
Garland, D., 308, 311
Gay, P., 60
Gender, 43, 44, 49, 60
Gender identity, 258–259
Gilroy, P., 173
Glynn, M., 11, 170, 172, 175
Goffman, E., 91, 96
Gold Coast state, 47
The Golden Fleece, 180
Good order and discipline, prison regime, 99–101
Gramsci, A., 249
Greer, G., 127
Grier, W., 171
Group facilitators, 308, 316, 320, 323, 326
  of fatherhood programs, 308
  program materials and, 316
Group-based interventions, 302
  in male prison, 277
Group-based physical activity, 70
Group-based programme, 71
Grunseit, A., 227, 230
Gym orderlies, 209, 215
Gyms, 203
  See also Prison gyms

Hallsworth, S., 51
Halsey, M., 226, 227
Hammersley, M., 98
Haney, L., 312
Hannah-Moffat, K., 131
Harassment rates, 68, 216, 232, 233
Hard prison body, 69
Hardness–softness dichotomy, 205
Harris, V., 226, 227
Healing reasoning, 162–164

Healthy connections, 312, 325, 326, 328n2
Healthy lifestyle programme, 70, 71
Healy, D., 181, 182
Hegemonic masculine culture, 9, 96
Hegemonic masculinities, 4–7, 12, 20, 53, 59, 92, 132, 203, 204, 248–251
  gym orderlies, 209–210
  hardness–softness dichotomy, 205–206
  is heterosexual, 199
  non-competitive sporting activities, 210–212
  in prison, 205, 251
  prison management and masculinities, 206–209
  young offenders, sporting academies, 212–214
Heidensohn, F., 132
Her Majesty's (HM) Prison Service, 129
Her Majesty's Prison (HMP), 213
Her Majesty's Prison (HMP) Doncaster, 199
Her Majesty's Young Offender Institution (HMYOI) Rochester, 46
Herbst, D. P., 302
Heroic masculinity, 53
Heterosexist generalisations, 96
Heterosexuality, 199
HMYOI Rochester, 47–49
  armoured bodies, penal masculinities in, 51–53
Hollway, W., 256
Homohysteria, 81, 84
Homosocial prison culture, 226
Homosocial relation, 24

Homosociality, 43
Hooks, B., 164
Huss, L., 127
Hutchinson, E., 171
Hypermasculinities, 8, 12, 18–20, 131, 204
  attitudes, 294
  behaviour, 296
  black masculinities, mask of, 164–166
  black men, 151
  expectations of male prisons, 128
  hypothesis, 18
  presentations, of self, 293
  traits, 18

Ideal masculinity model, 272
Identity, 151
  violence, difference and politics of, 234
Identity work, 227, 228
  violence talk as, 236
Illustrative strategy, 229
Imaginary masculinities, 49–51
Immobile human commune, 59
Imprisonment, 2, 8, 18–20, 34, 43, 44
  assessment of, 44
  in Australia, 224–225
Incarcerated fathers, 283–284
Incarceration, 2, 5, 11, 46, 52, 124, 135, 155, 209, 217, 310
Incentive-based system, 116
Incentives and Earned Privileges (IEP) scheme, 101, 118n2, 204, 218n3

Inclusive masculinity theory, 7, 217, 279
Independent Monitoring Board (IMB) Report, 147
Indeterminate Sentence for Public Protection (IPP), 160
Indigenous masculinities, 238
Individual responsibility, 311
Industrial revolution, 250
Inherent identity, 238
Inmate culture, 18
International Conference on Masculinities: *Engaging Men and Boys for Gender Equality*, 3
Interpersonal arena, gender identity, 258
Intersectionality, 149, 174
Interventions
  for childhood abuse survivors, 277
  group-based interventions, 277
Intimacy, 18, 34
Intrapsychic arena, gender identity, 258

James, E., 54
Jefferson, T., 60, 256
Jewkes, Y., 20, 97
Johansson, T., 257
Johnsen, B., 197–203, 207, 209, 215
Juvenile Justice Act, 47
Juveniles, 124

Karp, D. R., 164, 226, 280, 303
Karras, R., 50

Kimmel, M., 249
Kinetic masculinities, 49
King, R.D., 96
Klinth, R., 257
Knifing off, 190
Kupers, T., 4, 5

Liebow, E., 171
Liminal masculinity, 216
London, W., 4, 5
Loss of individuality in prisons, 130–132

Magaletta, P. R., 302
Mainstream criminology, 11, 170, 173
Male offender, 13, 127, 135, 137, 197, 238
Male prisoners, 197
  masculinities, 8
Male prisons
  hypermasculine expectations of, 128
  'normality' of, 132–133
Male-dominated institutions, 94
Man Up, 137, 237
Mannerbund, 51
Marcus, 32
Martos-García, D., 69, 70
Marx, K., 58
Masciadrelli, B. P., 257
Masculine domesticity, 55
Masculine individualism, 52

Index

Masculinities, 3–6, 9, 21, 34–38, 43, 45, 48, 49, 51, 53, 60, 66, 92–94, 117, 130, 198, 248
and fatherhood, 308, 315–317
and femininity, 321
Australian prison, 226, 231
fatherhood and, 308, 316
Ibrahim's story case study, 182–189
imaginary, 49
in prison (*see* Prisons)
narrative of male prisoners, 251–256
normative performances of, 114
on the wing, performing, 150–154
outside prison, performing, 155–157
performances of, 2
policing and boy code, 272–273
spectrum, 260, 261, 271, 273
traditional understandings of, 308
work and prison, 22
young prison masculinities, 279
Masculinity Subject Position Spectrum, 259
Mason, G., 235
Mathiesen, T., 95, 117
Mauer, M., 171
Maycock, M., 9
McCormack, M., 7
McDowell, L., 21
McNay, L., 198
McVicar, J., 53
Medieval masculinities, 50
Meek, R., 199, 207, 208, 212–216, 303

Men, 123–125, 127–129
in prison, 129, 130, 134, 135
Mertova, P., 182
Messerschmidt, J. W., 19, 66, 93, 136, 172, 177, 205, 210, 279
Metrosexuality, 83
Mexican prison, 205
Migrant masculinities, 238
Miller, T.A., 83, 95, 96
Mind/body dualism, 53
Moore, H., 66
Multi Agency Public Protection Arrangements (MAPPAs), 211
"Multi-investigator" project, 224
Musclepharm, 77
Muscularity, 52, 199, 270
and 'hard' prison body, 69–72
shape and size, 73

National Alliance of Sport for the Desistance from Crime, 212
National Offender Management application, 149
National Offender Management Service (NOMS), 199, 211
Nayak, M., 235, 239
Neoliberal governance, 311–312
New group-work programme, 137
Newton, C., 3, 95
Nonce, 113, 114, 118n3
Non-competitive sporting activities, 210
Non-gendered offender, 197
Non-hegemonic masculinities, 212
Non-Indigenous female prisoners, 225

Non-muscular bodies, 83
Non-violent offenders, 200
  rehabilitation programme for, 199
Normativity, 9, 12, 70, 77, 91–94, 96, 111, 114, 116, 117, 227, 228, 232, 234, 235
Normative masculinity, 12, 94, 117, 227, 232
North Correctional Institution (NCI), 312, 314
  communicating with co-parents and children, 320–326
  group facilitators at, 314, 315
Norwegian male prisoners, 209
Norwegian prison, 197
  prisoners in, 202
Norwegian prisoners, 203
  Norwegian prisoner discourses, 198
NVivo10, 72, 149

Offenders, 11, 13, 39, 117, 124, 125, 130, 135–137, 191, 192, 198, 200, 225
Ostracisation, 230, 235

Palmer, M., 230–232, 235
Papillon, 53
Papua New Guinea's Last Place: Experiences of Constraint in a Postcolonial Prison (Reed), 44
Parent-child approach, 105

Parenting, 309
  classroom (*see* Parenting classroom)
  programme, 282–284, 287, 301
  styles, 324
Parenting classroom, 291
  hyper-masculine presentations, of self, 293–296
  softer sharing and caring ethos creation, 292–293
  softer sharing and caring presentations of self, 296–300
Pasko, L., 94
Paternalistic authoritarianism
  masculinist ideology of, 117
  regime of, 116
Paternoster, R., 182
Paterson, A., 46, 60
Penal masculinities in HMYOI Rochester, 51
Penal uncertainties, 203
Performativity, 278
Personal and social development (PSD) programme, 145
Personal masculinity, 216
Personal social development programme, 164
Phillips, C., 170
Photo-Ethnographic Interviewing technique, 256
Physical activity, 200, 204
  in correctional settings, 207
  programmes/equipment, 200
Physical education instructors (PEIs), 71
Physical hegemonic masculinity, 209
Physical labour, 198

Pleck, J. H., 250, 257
Pogrebin, M. R., 228
Pollack, W., 248
Polmont Young Offender Institution, Scotland, 281–282
Poole, E. D., 228
Portland YOI, 212, 213
Positive masculine identities, 172, 183
Postcolonial perspectives, 8
Post-war welfare state, 55
Power relations, 12, 93, 139, 172, 197, 198, 203, 205, 210, 226, 234, 235, 240
PRISON B-P1, 73, 74
Prison gyms, 12, 52, 70, 75, 79, 80, 110, 200, 202–205, 208, 209, 214–216, 218, 291
    diversity in, 214
Prison industrial complex (PIC), 127
Prison management, 202
    need for, 218
Prison masculinities, 2, 5, 9, 22–33, 65, 94–99, 116, 223, 227, 228
    discourse on, 172
Prison settings, 2, 30–33, 199, 203
Prison system, 1, 2, 10, 46, 70, 78, 85, 123–140
    in England and Wales, 204
Prison world, 2, 60
    existential staging of, 58–59
Prison, looking inside, 44–45
Prison-based fatherhood groups, 326
Prison-based group interventions, 13
Prisoner body, hegemonic images of, 73–76

Prisoner social relations, 106
    gendered pecking order, 111–115
    prison talk, 107–109
    projecting toughness and machismo, 109–111
Prisoner's Education Trust (PET), 213
Prisoner—officer relations, 227
Prisoners
    emotional vulnerability of, 201
    in high-security prisons, 211
    hypermasculinity, 18–21
    masculinities, 17, 19, 68
Prisonisation, 95
Prisons, 44, 45, 52–60, 281
    abandoning, 59–60
    black men in, 146
    camps, 46
    code, 179, 279, 303
    complexities and contradictions of, 223
    confronts, 54
    culture, 12, 132, 227
    empowerment in, 201–204
    fatherhood programs in, 309, 310
    fathers in, 281
    group-based interventions, 277
    gymnasium facilities, 70
    health, 97–98
    hegemonic masculinity in, 204–214, 251
    hierarchical dynamics of, 226
    hyper-masculine environment of, 277
    labour, 32
    loss of individuality in, 130
    management system, 206

masculinities research, 3, 5, 12
men in, 57, 134
regimes, 99–106, 138
sentence, 52, 54–57
services, 189
sports initiatives in, 216
weightlifting in, 198
wings of, 206
work, 31, 32
Protective masculinity, 227, 228, 238
Protein supplements, 77
Protest masculinity, 202
Public space, 53, 250, 256
Punishment, 10, 46, 47, 56, 123, 204, 225

Queensland Corrective Services, 229, 233

Racialisation
 of crime, 173
 of criminal justice system, 170, 191
 critical perspectives on, 170
 of prison environment, 180
Racialized identities, 172
 importance of, 170–171
Rafter, N., 34
Ray, L., 238
Recidivism, 136–138
Reed, A., 44
Reflexive ethnographic approach, 71
Reflexivity, 174
Rehabilitation programme, 173, 199
Release on Temporary Licence (ROTL), 211
Resistance, 66, 70, 72, 78, 82, 84, 85
Responsible Fatherhood programs, 309
Reviere, R., 126
Riciardelli, R., 19, 20, 68, 199, 201–203, 206, 211
Ridgeway, C.L., 93
Risdon Prison Complex (RPC), 229, 230, 232
 prisoners in, 231
Roberts, J. V., 225
Rose, G., 50, 51
Rumgay, J., 136

Sabo, D. F., 4, 5, 69, 83, 197, 199, 201, 202, 205, 206, 213, 215
Sale, M., 171
Sampson, R., 177
Saracens Sport Foundation, 212
Scottish Prison Service (SPS), 277
Scottish Young Offender Institution (YOI), 278
Seidler, V. J., 248
Self-harm in prison, 125
Self-improvement programmes, 158
Self-sufficiency, 128
Semi-structured one-to-one interviews, 72
Sex offenders, 124, 219n6
Sexual offences, 113
Sharkey, P., 177
The Shawshank Redemption, 53
Shepherd, L. J., 234, 236, 239
Shilling, C., 65, 67, 202
Short, sharp shock approach, 99
Silko, L. M., 239
Silverstone, D., 51

Sim, J., 17, 59, 94, 117
Single-sex imprisonment, 95
Situational accomplishment, 93
Skilled facilitation, 302
Sloan, J., 10
Smith, J., 303
Social group, 91
Social networks, 190
Social proximity, 116
Softer masculinity, 24
South Australian defamation case, 233
Southeast Youth Correctional Institution (SY), 312
    man of honor, 316–320
Spectrum, 259, 268–270
    of masculinity, 13, 260, 261
Sport, 197
    hegemonic masculinities in prison, 204
    masculinity and participation in, 214–218
Sporting academies, 212
Sporting masculinities, 210
Starred Up, 53
Steroids and supplements, 76–77
Stiegler, B., 54, 56–59
Structural context, 181, 190
Structural racism, 173
Suchland, J., 235, 239
Suicides, 115, 137, 217
    in UK prison, 247
Swain, J., 202, 203, 215, 216
Sykes, G.M., 59, 95, 96, 230

T

Tasmanian RPC inquiry, 235
Taylor, L., 94, 96
Team sports, 212

Theoretical criminology, 4, 6, 11, 68
Theories of masculinity, 6–8
Thick description, 287, 313
Toch, H., 57
Tradesmen, 23–26, 29
    in prison settings, 30–33
Tradesmen, 23
Traditional gender, 307
Traditional masculinity, 250
Transitions, masculine, 170
Traylor, L., 177
Troopaid, 218n5

U

Unhealthy prison masculinities, 97–98
Urban, 51
US criminal justice policy, 171

V

Veneziano, R., 256, 270
Victorian Ombudsman, 232
Violence, 234
    patterns of, 234
    rates of, 208
Violence against women (VAW), 237
Violence prevention campaigns, 237
Violence talk, 236–239
Violent behaviour, 248
Violent masculinity, 232
Visit room, Barnardo's Scotland, 301

W

Wacquant, L., 51
Waiting for Godot (Beckett), 59
Wallace, P., 69

Waquant, L., 51, 67, 308, 310, 311
Warfare, decline of, 198
Warwick-Edinburgh Mental Wellbeing Scale (WEMWBS), 148
Webster, L., 182
Weight management, 71
Weightlifting, in prison, 198–201
Wellard, I., 215, 217
Well-being, 201, 205, 218
West, C., 93
Western contemporary culture, 197
White masculinities, 49
Whitehead, S. M., 67
Willis, P., 21, 24, 278
Wilson, D., 20
Wilson, J., 177
Women
  imprisonment for, 124, 225
  in prison, perceptions of, 135
Woodward, K., 199
Work masculinities, 22
Work-related bullying, 233

Young black men, 20, 150
Young masculinities, 278–279
Young men, 2, 39, 46–52, 137, 198, 200, 247, 248, 251, 273, 313, 318, 319, 327
Young offender institution (YOI), 199, 200, 301
  in England and Wales, 204, 207, 208
Young offenders, 124, 198, 211
  criminal justice system for, 217
  criminality of, 198
  Duke of Edinburgh Award on, 212
  sporting academies for, 212
Young prison masculinities, 279–280
Young, V. D., 126

Zizek, S., 51